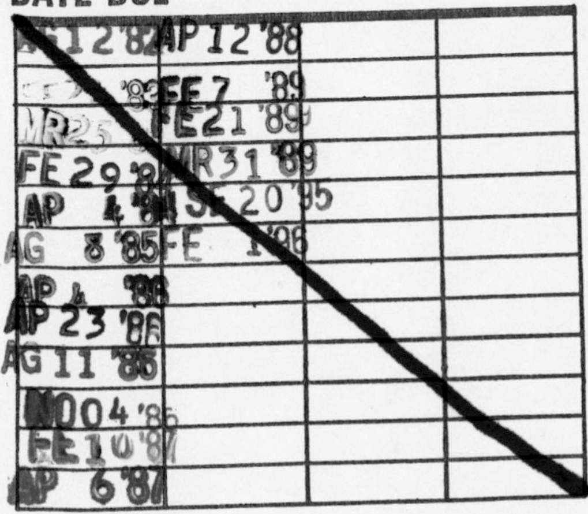

BUREAUCRATIC GOVERNMENT **USA**

BUREAUCRATIC

GOVERNMENT **USA**

David Nachmias and David H. Rosenbloom

St. Martin's Press

New York

Library of Congress Catalog Card Number: 79–55955

Manufactured in the United States of America.
3210
fedcba
For information, write St. Martin's Press, Inc.,
175 Fifth Avenue, New York, N. Y. 10010

cover design: Mies Hora
typography: Jack Meserole

cloth ISBN: 0–312–10805–2
paper ISBN: 0–312–10806–0

To C. N., R. Z. R., and J. R.

Preface

Nearly forty years ago Leonard D. White, the foremost historian of the United States federal bureaucracy, predicted that while the formal seat of power would remain in representative bodies, the determination of the ways in which power is used and of the purposes it is intended to achieve would "continue to shift from directly elected representative bodies to authorities chiefly characterized by expertness and official responsibility rather than by representative qualities." He concluded, "The administration, in short, will wield more power over the citizen."*

This book systematically examines the extent to which White's prediction has come true. Standard, comprehensive texts in American government commonly devote a chapter to the subject of the federal bureaucracy. However, the consequences of the bureaucratization of American government and American politics have become so pervasive, so important to a true understanding of our political life at the threshold of the 1980s, that they cannot be treated adequately in a chapter. We have written this book in an effort to redress this imbalance. Undoubtedly instructors can find a variety of uses for a text on bureaucracy, but the primary purpose of this book is to offer the student of American government and politics a reasonably comprehensive analysis of bureaucracy's impact on the federal government. The book analyzes both the causes and the consequences of the bureaucratization of the American polity. It shows that throughout the federal government, whether in the executive branch, the legislature, or the judiciary, bureaucracy has become a predominant form of organization and that the power of those who exercise bureaucratic roles has expanded considerably. At the same time political parties and interest groups, the traditional links between the citizenry and the government, have had to adjust to the bureaucratization of society. In the process these political organizations have themselves come to rely less upon participatory governance and more upon bureaucratic expertise. Hence the locus of power in American government is now heavily concentrated in bureaucratic structures and nonelected administrative officials. The book's approach to government introduces a new framework

* Leonard D. White, "The Public Service of the Future," in White, ed., *The Future of Government in the United States* (Chicago: University of Chicago Press, 1942), p. 209.

for understanding the contemporary distribution of political power in American society.

Specifically, the book explores several themes. Chapter 1 examines the nature and origins of bureaucratic power. Chapter 2 discusses bureaucratic structure and behavior—its foundations and its relationship to democracy. The next four chapters analyze and document the bureaucratization of the federal government's administrative, presidential, legislative, and judicial components. These chapters indicate the extent to which the locus of political power has shifted toward bureaucratic organizations and bureaucratic functionaries, and they examine the political consequences of these developments. Chapters 7 and 8 deal with the declining role of political parties in the bureaucratized polity and the pervasiveness of bureaucracy within voluntary organizations. The final chapter discusses the evolution of democratic citizenship into bureaucratic citizenship.

We deeply appreciate the assistance of colleagues and reviewers who read and commented on one or more chapters of this book: Ronald J. Bussch, David H. Davis, Kenneth Dolbeare, John Donovan, Brett W. Hawkins, Daniel Hoffman, Ralph Hummel, Fred Lane, Pritam T. Merani, William Morrow, Garison Nelson, Pietro Nivola, Robert Simmons, Michael Sutton, Mark E. Tompkins, and Peter Woll. Of course, the responsibility for the final text is entirely ours.

David Nachmias
David H. Rosenbloom

Contents

Part I

BUREAUCRATIC POWER

1

Political Power and Bureaucracy

For many years American politics could have been studied with little or no attention to bureaucracy. A long intellectual tradition in political science separated politics from bureaucracy (administration). Politicians were supposed to make public policies and decisions about the structure of government and the allocation of scarce resources; administrators were supposed to implement those policies and decisions. Although this tradition had its roots in the efforts of reformers in the 1870s and 1880s to depoliticize the federal bureaucracy, it may also have described public administration in an earlier age. However, as the roles of government increased and expanded and public policies grew more complex, politics and administration became thoroughly intertwined.

Today the federal bureaucracy is at the core of American government and a dominant force in the political system. The executive, legislative, and judicial branches of government are also becoming bureaucratic institutions in their organization and behavior, partly as a response to the growing power of the federal bureaucracy. Thus the political power of elected and politically appointed* authorities is diminishing relative to that of the administrators and staffs of governmental organizations. Not only do administrators implement public policies; they also play a major role in policymaking.

Political parties and interest groups, the traditional links between government and citizens, are also in a period of transition and change. Party activists are being replaced by campaign managers, organization specialists, and media experts. Candidates for office rely more and more on their personal organizations rather than on their parties. And after the campaign is over, elected candidates tend to carry their personal staffs into office with them. As for interest groups, they are increasingly organized

* Drawing a line between political and nonpolitical appointees is obviously difficult. Essentially, by "political appointees" we mean those appointed by one branch of government with the advice and consent of another. Many nonpolitical appointments are nonpartisan as well.

bureaucratically, with power becoming concentrated among the professional executives and the operating administrators.

No longer can we understand American government without a careful examination of bureaucracy and its dominant position in the political system. But first we need to know something about the nature of power, its shifting bases, and its concentration.

POWER AND AUTHORITY

One of the most important characteristics of a society is the way it organizes power. For power, the medium of exchange in politics, is a key to the public life and government of any nation. Indeed, this proposition has been central to Western political thought since the days of Plato and Aristotle.

What is power? Robert Dahl defines it as follows: "A has power over B to the extent that he can get B to do something B would not otherwise do."[1] Thus power has to do with the relationships between two or more actors (individuals, groups, organizations, or nations) when one of them can affect the behavior of another. Richard Emerson further suggests that power resides "implicitly in the other's dependency," that is, actors in a power relationship are tied to each other by mutual dependency:

> Social relations commonly entail ties of mutual dependence between parties. A depends upon B if he aspires to goals or gratifications whose achievement is facilitated by appropriate actions on B's part. By virtue of mutual dependency, it is more or less imperative to each party that he be able to control or influence the other's conduct. At the same time, these ties of mutual dependence imply that each party is in a position, to some degree, to grant or deny, facilitate or hinder, the other's gratifications. Thus, it would appear that the power to control or influence the other resides in control over the things he values, which may range all the way from oil resources to ego-support, depending on the relation in question.[2]

Max Weber (1864–1920) drew an important distinction between power and authority. Power may involve force or coercion. Authority, on the other hand, is a form of power that does not imply coercion; it involves a "suspension of judgment" on the part of its recipients. People follow the orders given by someone in authority because they believe that they should. Their compliance is voluntary. To comply, however, they must have a common value system. When the members of a society do not accept the same values, other forms of power, such as coercion, become dominant. A society's value system legitimizes authority as a means of exercising power.

Weber further distinguished between three "ideal types" of authority: charismatic, traditional, and rational-legal. He describes the evolution of polities in terms of the type of authority relations within them. The earliest of the three is the *charismatic* authority that "rests on the affectual devotion of the follower to the lord and his gifts of grace (charisma). They comprise especially magical abilities, revelations of heroism, power of the mind and speech. . . . The purest types are the rule of the prophet, the warrior hero, the great demagogue."[3] The positions of the followers who depend upon their leader's charisma are most threatened at times of leadership succession. To secure their positions and prerogatives, they may institutionalize and routinize the process of selecting successors. This creates the *traditional* type of authority. Traditional authority, in Weber's words, "rests on the belief in the sacredness of social order and its prerogatives as existing yore. . . . The body politic is based on communal relationships, the man in command is the 'lord' ruling over obedient 'subjects.' People obey the lord personally since his dignity is hallowed by tradition; obedience rests on piety."[4]

BUREAUCRATIC POWER

Modern society, according to Weber, is based upon *rational-legal* authority. This type of authority

> rests on enactment; its pure type is best presented by bureaucracy. The basic idea is that laws can be enacted and changed at pleasure by formally correct procedure. The governing body is either elected or appointed and constitutes as a whole and in all its sections rational organizations. . . . Obedience is not owed by anybody personally but to enacted rules and regulations which specify to whom and to what rule people owe obedience.[5]

Yet even in modern society, Weber said, charismatic leaders may emerge in times of crisis and emergency, and charismatic authority may become institutionalized. Charismatic patterns of authority may coexist with rational-legal authority, as is the case with the American presidency and in some modern organizations.[6] Similarly, traditional authority can be found in modern rational-legal organizations. We are all familiar with voluntary compliance that is evoked by statements like "The Old Man wants it that way." But on the whole, rational-legal authority is the preponderant type of authority around which political life is organized in the United States.

Since Weber's time there have been several attempts to classify the concept of power in greater detail. One typology, developed by John French and Bertram Raven, is based on the nature of the relationship between the power holder and the power recipient.[7]

- *Reward* power, or "power whose basis is in the ability to reward," can appear in situations where the reward is meaningful for the power recipient.
- *Coercive* power is based on the recipient's perception of the ability of the power holder to distribute punishments.
- *Legitimate* power operates when the recipient acknowledges that the power holder has the right to influence him and that he has an obligation to comply.
- *Referent* power is observed when a power recipient identifies with a power holder and tries to behave in the same way. (In these situations, power holders may not even be aware that they have power.)
- *Expert* power is based on the special knowledge attributed to the power holder by the recipients. They believe that the holder possesses knowledge which they need but do not have. The obvious example is a professional-nonprofessional relationship, such as that of doctor and patient.

All these forms of power are found in modern society. All are also part of the legitimate authority system. But recent research has demonstrated that legitimate and expert power are more prevalent in American society than referent, reward, and coercive power.[8] This fact is important in accounting for the concentration of power among our nonelected authorities.

CONCENTRATION OF BUREAUCRATIC POWER

Power relationships are found in most aspects of life. At a very early age children learn what positions have authority over other positions and when and where different authority relations are binding. A major reason for the prevalence of power relations is that they reduce the individual's sense of complexity by increasing the predictability of the patterns of people's behavior.

Ours is often called a complex society, and much of our behavior consists of attempts to organize and manage this complexity. If "there is a unique quality to the modern era, it is that the conditions of existence have changed to such a degree that something explicitly recognized as 'complexity' now continually forces itself into our awareness."[9] The changes that have created complexity were brought on by the growth of modern science, the emergence of a large-scale technological environment, and the proliferation of immense social and political organizations that include more and more individuals. We are currently experiencing an unprecedented rate of change, and one accelerating so rapidly that it has become exponential. (An example of exponential growth is a town whose population trebles every ten years—3,000 in 1960, 9,000 in 1970, 27,000 in 1980, and so on.[10]) Many scientific, technological, and social processes are exponential in their patterns of growth. A good example is computer technology. Moreover, the actual number of scientific and technological developments impinging on society each year continues to grow so much that the developments become metaphors of human activity.

These changes take place in a highly differentiated, fragmented, and specialized environment. Indeed, knowledge itself has become fragmented and specialized:

> Modern science is characterized by its ever-increasing specialization, necessitated by the enormous amount of data, the complexity of techniques and of theoretical structure within every field. Thus science is split into innumerable disciplines continually generating new subdisciplines. In consequence, the physicist, the biologist and the social scientist are, so to speak, encapsulated in their private universes, and it is difficult to get from one cocoon to the other.[11]

Closely related to differentiation and fragmentation is the problem of interdependence. Before collective action can be taken, all the fragments of knowledge about that action must be brought together. But the process of integrating the fragments is often so difficult that it can result in "decreased efficiency of operation, neglect of creative combinations, erratic behavior in a climate of uncertainty, unpredictable breakdowns in the system, and at the extreme, disintegration of the organization itself."[12]

Today it is more and more difficult for individuals (including political decision makers) to comprehend any system as a whole. Whereas the knowledge required to understand both the separate components and their interdependence is rapidly increasing, the knowledge that is actually available grows relatively slowly. While he was in the Senate, Walter Mondale introduced the Full Opportunity and Social Accounting Act of 1967 in a speech that reviewed a variety of social programs. He concluded: "Our intentions are good, but we lack a systematic and integrated approach to social problems. When they miss their mark, we may not even realize it. If they are damaging, it may be years before we know it. Our successes are difficult to document; they suffer the attacks of the ignorant while we in our ignorance have no way to defend them."[13]

Power reduces the problems posed by the gap between the required and the available knowledge. In the economic arena, John Kenneth Galbraith points out, many large firms have given up trying to comprehend the uncertainties of the markets of supply and demand. Instead, they set out to influence the behavior of the markets: "This consists of reducing or eliminating the independence of action of those to whom the planning unit sells or from whom it buys. Their behavior being subject to control, uncertainty as to that behavior is reduced."[14] The basic motivation of the large corporation is no longer simply to maximize profits per se but to minimize uncertainties: "The firm is required . . . to control or to seek to control the social environment in which it functions—or any part which impinges upon it."[15] The result is that fewer and fewer corporations control a greater share of the market, and more and more individuals are employed in these fewer corporations. In the mid 1970s the 500 largest industrial corporations in the United States had a net worth of over $600 billion, employed over 14 million people, and held total assets of $44 billion (Exxon) to $1.5 billion (Lockheed Aircraft).[16] Some observers estimate that about 5 percent of all private and public organizations account for over 60 percent of employment.[17]

Ability to control the environment does help to overcome the uncertainties inherent in complexity. But it does not always guarantee success, and it creates additional problems. Differentiation is further accelerated, bringing increased needs for interdependence, which in turn raises the level of complexity. In such situations, power rests with those who can reduce the decision makers' *sense* of complexity.

It is often said that specialized bureaucratic skills are needed in government in order to manage the complexity of our environment. Complexity poses a serious problem for public policy. The demands made on government are increasing rapidly; problems that used to be handled in other ways now come under governmental jurisdiction. Consequently the number of areas that public policy is supposed to affect has been expanding. In the economic realm, for instance, the variety of national and multinational corporations that governments regulate in order to effect coherent policy has markedly grown. The interdependence among various corporations and their motives, markets, resources, and so on, creates a highly uncertain environment that government can only manage through further organization, regulation, and coordination. These activities have produced a new locus of power—bureaucratic power.

In the early 1920s Thorstein Veblen predicted that there would be a revolution in which power would become concentrated in the hands of scientists and engineers.[18] In the 1930s Harold Laski believed that power would shift to experts.[19] In the early 1940s James Burnham declared, "Managers . . . will be the ruling class in society . . . their preferential treatment in distribution will be alloted to them in terms of status in the political-economic structure."[20] In the 1950s Lasswell, Lerner, and Rothwell said that the revolution of our time is a shift in influence from "specialists in bargaining" to intellectuals ("symbol specialists" or "masters of persuasion"), to "specialists in violence," or to those with "administrative and police skills."[21] These strategic elites were expected to cope with uncertainty and to reduce the decision makers' sense of complexity. Just as traditional societies developed the roles of warriors to control their environments, modern society has created specialized roles to manage complexity. Individuals occupying these roles have become irreplaceable and central to the functioning of modern economic, social, and political organizations. In the process, their power has increased relative to other groups.

The new locus of power lies in bureaucracies, and the power of bureaucrats as a group has expanded: "Often possessing little technical knowledge beyond a somewhat intangible ability to organize others, administrators now control the allocation of the organization's resources."[22] Harold Wilensky, studying problems of knowledge and policy in government and industry, concluded:

> The managerial revolution has taken place but its form is less dramatic than that envisioned by Max Weber and Thorstein Veblen and popularized by James Burnham. Instead of scientists, engineers and other technical staff coming to power by virtue of their indispensability, there is a shift of power to administrative leaders.[23]

In political institutions, forms of dual authority frequently emerge. Public officials run for election and fulfill expressive functions, such as voicing the public's needs, preferences, and moods. In contrast, bureaucratic staffs concentrate on dealing with complexity by managing information, organizing and coordinating productive efforts, setting agenda, controlling resources, and formulating and implementing public policies. The authority of elected officials and that of bureaucrats interact and may overlap, but they are nevertheless distinct. Furthermore, as the elected and politically appointed officials become more dependent on administrators, the latter's power expands. Power, as Robert Michels argued, has a self-perpetuating aspect.[24] Those who have power tend to remain in power, since they have the resources to do so. The very fact that legitimacy is such an important consideration in democratic regimes means that existing power distributions can be perpetuated.

THE FORMAT OF THIS BOOK

Power relationships are prevalent in many aspects of life, and the ways in which power is distributed and legitimized affect the nature of public policy and the public's well-being. In the United States, large-scale bureaucracies increasingly take over functions previously carried out by individuals, families, and neighborhoods. Within these bureaucracies, the locus of power has shifted from expressive authorities who speak to popular aspirations into the hands of administrators. The American polity, like American business, places power in organizations that are becoming increasingly bureaucratic in terms of structure, process, and behavior. Power is bureaucratized, and bureaucrats emerge as major power holders. The following chapters develop these propositions.

Specifically, Chapter 2 deals with the key features of bureaucratic organization and behavior and their impact on individuals and democracy. Chapter 3 focuses on the organization, expansion, and growing power of the federal bureaucracy. Chapter 4 deals with the imaginary and real powers of the presidency, and views the gap between these two as a major reason for the bureaucratization of that office. Chapter 5 discusses Congress's response to complexity: increased bureaucratization in the form of hierarchy, specialization, routinization, and the development of a sizable administrative component. This transformation reduces Congress's representative qualities. Chapter 6 argues that in terms of structure and process, the judicial branch displays most of the attributes of bureaucracy. Yet the most pronounced changes in the judiciary involve process rather than structure. One consequence of the bureaucratization of justice is that the jury, the most democratic feature in the judicial process, has been reduced in importance by the process of "plea bargaining."

American political parties are an exception to the increased tendency toward bureaucratization. But by retaining their traditional character, the national political parties have become weaker in relation to other, more bureaucratically organized political organizations. Chapter 7's thesis is that parties in general have become weaker links between citizens and government, and that party organizations are being replaced by candidate-centered organizations in which power is concentrated in the staff. Chapter 8 discusses interest groups, their tendency to become bureaucratically organized, and the concentration of power in the hands of their professional and administrative staffs. The consequences of bureaucratization and the expansion of bureaucratic power are the focus of Chapter 9. Its conclusion is that many Americans no longer believe that they can control government and politics through democratic processes such as elections. The increase of nonvoting may represent the citizens' response to the emergence of bureaucratic government.

NOTES

1. Robert A. Dahl, *Modern Political Analysis* (Englewood Cliffs, N.J.: Prentice-Hall, 1963), p. 40.
2. Richard M. Emerson, "Power Dependence Relations," *American Sociological Review*, 27 (February 1962), 32.
3. Max Weber, "The Three Types of Legitimate Rule," in Amitai Etzioni, ed., *A Sociological Reader on Complex Organizations*, 2nd ed. (New York: Holt, 1969), p. 12.

4. Ibid., p. 9.

5. Ibid., p. 7.

6. See, for example, Victor Thompson, *Modern Organizations* (New York: Knopf, 1961), p. 439.

7. John R. P. French and Bertram Raven, "The Bases of Social Power," in Dorwin Cartwright and Alvin Zander, eds., *Group Dynamics*, 3rd ed. (New York: Harper & Row, 1968), pp. 259–269.

8. See, for example, Curt Tausky, *Work Organizations*, 2nd ed. (Itasca, Ill.: Peacock, 1978), p. 138, and Guy Benveniste, *The Politics of Expertise* (San Francisco: Glendessary, 1972).

9. Langdon Winner, "Complexity and the Limits of Human Understanding," in Todd R. La Porte, ed., *Organized Social Complexity: Challenge to Politics and Policy* (Princeton, N.J.: Princeton University Press, 1975), p. 41.

10. In general, exponential models are formed by a series of points in fixed intervals, each of which represents the same base raised to a higher power each time, e.g., $3, 3^2, 3^3 \ldots 3^n$.

11. Ludwig von Bertalanffy, *General Systems Theory* (New York: Braziller, 1968), p. 30.

12. Winner, "Complexity and the Limits of Human Understanding," p. 63.

13. U.S. Senate, 90th Congress, Hearings before the Subcommittee on Government Research of the Committee on Government Operations, *Full Opportunity and Social Accounting Act Seminar* (Washington, D.C.: Government Printing Office, 1967), p. 34.

14. John Kenneth Galbraith, *The New Industrial State* (New York: Signet, 1968), p. 39.

15. John Kenneth Galbraith, *Economics and the Public Purpose* (Boston: Houghton Mifflin, 1973), p. 39.

16. *Fortune* (May 1976), p. 318.

17. Tausky, *Work Organizations*, pp. 2–3.

18. Thorstein Veblen, *The Engineers and the Price System* (New York: Viking, 1921).

19. Harold J. Laski, *The Limitations of the Expert* (London: Fabian Society, 1931).

20. James Burnham, *The Managerial Revolution* (Bloomington, Ind.: Indiana University Press, 1960), pp. 70, 72, 80.

21. Harold D. Lasswell, Daniel Lerner, and E. C. Rothwell, *The Comparative Study of Elites* (Stanford, Calif.: Stanford University Press, 1952), esp. pp. 16–18.

22. Robert Presthus, *The Organizational Society*, rev. ed. (New York: St. Martin's, 1978), p. 16.

23. Harold L. Wilensky, *Organizational Intelligence* (New York: Basic Books, 1967), p. 173.

24. Robert Michels, *Political Parties* (Glencoe, Ill.: Free Press, 1949). See also Charles P. Snow, *Science and Government* (Cambridge, Mass.: Harvard University Press, 1960), and Suzanne Keller, *Beyond the Ruling Class* (New York: Random House, 1963).

2

Bureaucracy: Structure and Behavior

Chapter 1 contended that complexity and power in contemporary America have created a situation in which the administrative staffs of elective and appointive political authorities largely run our government institutions. This chapter will analyze bureaucracy as a certain type of organization that behaves in certain ways.

THE ORGANIZATION OF BUREAUCRACY

People often apply the word "bureaucracy" to incompetent organizations and administrative behavior. As a result the term has caused such confusion that some political scientists have seriously suggested avoiding using it even when they are studying bureaucratic institutions.[1] Ignoring the word, however, will not bring us any closer to an understanding of the organizational reality behind it. Some sort of definition is necessary. First let us say what bureaucracy is *not*. It should not be used in serious research as a synonym for inefficient organization or ineffective administration.* Efficiency[2] and effectiveness can be found in virtually any setting; there is nothing to be gained by calling poor work "bureaucratic" and competent work "nonbureaucratic." There is a related tendency in the United States to call all public organizations "bureaucracies." This practice is not helpful either. Given the diversity in types of public organizations and organizational structures, and the fact that many private or-

* Efficiency generally refers to the accomplishment of a task at the lowest feasible cost. Effectiveness concerns the attainment of objectives.

ganizations can also legitimately be described as "bureaucratic," there is little reason to use the term as a synonym for the less confusing word "public."

Once these definitional approaches are discarded, it becomes possible to identify the core of structural features that constitute bureaucratic organizations:[3]

1. *Hierarchy*. This is the hallmark of bureaucracy. It consists of a ranking of roles and a system of status. Those who are higher up in the organization are termed *superordinates*; those who are lower down are *subordinates*. Hierarchy carried to its logical extreme is pyramidal in shape, with one position at the head. Information flows up the hierarchy; direction and control flow downward. Generally, superordinates enjoy privileges unavailable to their underlings. While rank in a hierarchy may be attached to a person, in civilian public bureaucracies in the United States it is usually attached to the position itself. Where hierarchies are rigid, they condition virtually all human interaction within them. Indeed, some social scientists say that an individual's position in a hierarchy can modify his or her self-characterization.[4]
2. *Specialization* (differentiation). Bureaucratic organizations have a well-developed division of labor. Tasks and jurisdictions are parceled out among various offices. This enables officeholders to concentrate on limited spheres of activity. Consequently bureaucratic organization tends to produce high levels of expertise in narrow areas. Often, but not always, the duties of officials and bureaus are spelled out in detailed written form. (In the federal bureaucracy there is a position description covering each of its 2.8 million slots.) The multitude of specialized functions must be coordinated; typically this is the task of the hierarchy. There is an inherent tension, however, between the authority based on the specialist's knowledge and the formal organizational authority of superordinates.[5] Those at the top find it difficult to control specialists throughout the ranks.
3. *Formalization*. Communication in bureaucracies tends to be in writing. Because the organizations are designed to continue even though individuals come and go, communication takes the form of memos written from one position or office to another. The memos are stored in files, whose maintenance and control are vital to the organization. In addition, many aspects of organizational life are set forth in formal written fashion: not only position descriptions but also aspects of the personnel's behavior such as the kinds of clothes and the hairstyles that may and may not be worn to work. The principal object of formalization is clarity. (Sometimes, however, the desire to specify what is to be done under all possible circumstances produces language that is gobbledy-

gook even to the bureaucrat.) Formalization acts as a constraint on individual discretion by specifying what the organization demands in various situations. Sometimes formalization is the prime cause of "red tape,"[6] but by the same token it generally assures uniform treatment of identical cases.

4. *Merit and Seniority*. Bureaucratic organizations make use of the principles of merit and seniority in their personnel systems. Merit is the ability to perform tasks well and is supposed to be measured or estimated in some evenhanded fashion.[7] Typically, merit is the primary criterion for entrance into a bureaucratic organization, with the "best"-qualified being selected first. Promotions may also be according to merit, but seniority commonly plays a role here as well. Although the achievement orientation found in bureaucracies is second nature to us today, it is not the only value system in organizations. In the past, and even today in nonbureaucratic personnel systems, criteria such as kinship, race, and religion have been used to hire and promote people.
5. *Size*. In order to be fully bureaucratized, most organizations must be large. Anthony Downs suggests that an organization has reached the right size to become truly bureaucratic when the highest-ranking members know less than half of the other members.[8] Bigness reinforces the need for hierarchy and formalization and is likely to be associated with a high degree of specialization as well.[9]
6. *Nonmarketable Output*. Typically the output of public bureaucracies is unassessable in the marketplace. They generally do not produce a product that can be freely bought and sold. Although price tags may be attached to bureaucratic services, they are not established by market mechanisms. They are really budgetary devices (as in the Department of Defense, for example) or monopolistic transactions (as in the Postal Service). Agencies may show surpluses or deficits, but these should not be confused with profit and loss. Hence a bureaucracy's output and efficiency cannot be evaluated by the simple question: does it make a profit? One consequence is that bureaucracies tend to judge themselves by the quantity rather than the quality of their work.[10]

In order to be considered a true bureaucracy, an organization must have all six characteristics in this list. Although it can be useful to think of bureaucratization as a continuum on which some organizations are more and some less bureaucratic, it is important to distinguish between true bureaucracies and organizations that simply have a few bureaucratic qualities. Those that fulfill the six criteria tend to show similar forms of behavior. And this behavior makes them different in nature and in operations from other organizations.

THE GROWTH AND DOMINANCE OF BUREAUCRACY

One of the outstanding features of bureaucracy is that it tends to engulf and dominate an increasing number of social, economic, and political activities. For instance, citizens in contemporary America are involved with bureaucratic organizations throughout their lives. We are born, and often die, in hospitals—the larger of which are bureaucratic organizations. Our births and deaths must be officially registered. Knowledge and culture are transmitted to us through educational bureaucracies. Many of us work for bureaucracies. To people in almost any walk of life, the power position of bureaucracy is "overtowering."[11] Indeed, it has been said that bureaucracy has the same relation to nonbureaucratic organizations that the machine does to nonmechanical modes of production.[12] So pronounced has the trend toward bureaucracy been in the twentieth century that some social scientists have spoken of "the bureaucratization of the world."[13]

Why has bureaucracy spread so far so fast? Although we often think of bureaucracies as inefficient by definition, in reality they have technical advantages over other forms of organization. Hierarchy enables the bureaucracy to speak largely with one voice and to maintain a unified system of command. Some bargaining and compromise take place within the hierarchy, but nothing like the give-and-take that characterizes organizations where all members have an equal voice. Centralized command yields speed and projects unity. Moreover, since bureaucracies develop expertise through specialization, many decisions can be made without widespread consultation throughout the organization. Hierarchy, specialization, and formalization give bureaucracies a life of their own, apart from that of the individuals who staff them. Indeed, it has been said that individual bureaucrats are nothing more than "cogs" in a machine whose direction they cannot control.[14] Individuals enter and leave the organization, but it remains an entity with a "personality" and "culture."[15] Finally, the bureaucracy's formalization provides the great advantage of precision.

In turn, other forms of organization offer some advantages that bureaucracy lacks: for example, more participation, personal freedom, and individualism. It is reasonable to assume that different types of organizational structures are best suited to different kinds of tasks. Bureaucracies can process large numbers of cases with little deviation in routine. Thus they serve to reduce complexity and make modern life more manageable. The individual bureaucrat is directed through hierarchy, formalization, and specialization. The client is also constrained by the organizational rules and becomes a "case" that gets processed. If the client does not like the result, the case can be appealed. However, it is very difficult for a person to break through the standard bureaucratic process and transform the "case" back into the individual. Most people who are dissatisfied with a bureaucracy's treatment of their case eventually come to accept the result. This is the nature of rational-legal authority as exercised by public bureaucracies.

Bureaucracy is an organizational form well suited to regulating human behavior. The Internal Revenue Service (IRS), the motor vehicle departments, police forces throughout the country, the Department of Agriculture, the Department of Health, Education, and Welfare, and so on all have a major impact on citizens' lives. Often their regulation is indirect, as in the case of rules that affect home owning, retirement, marriage, and divorce. Sometimes, as in the case of the police, control is direct, highly visible, and coercive. Ironically, bureaucracies are also service organizations. This paradoxical quality was expressed in the title of the old military draft bureaucracy, the Selective Service System. Indeed, the federal bureaucracy is often called the federal "service." Bureaucracies do render service, but we must remember that usually they are also engaged in regulation. So when we criticize them for giving us inefficient *service,* we may be overlooking the major part of their work. For instance, people who complain about the Postal Service usually speak as if its only duty is to handle first class mail. They do not consider the impact of its regulations on the mail order, advertising, and publishing businesses.

IMPERSONALITY

The dual function of bureaucracies in providing both regulation and service has led to different evaluations of their behavior. Some authorities, including Max Weber, have spoken of their superiority and efficiency; others, such as Victor Thompson, have stressed pathological elements of bureaucratic behavior. In part this is because the first approach views bureaucracy as an instrument of regulation, while the second judges it by the services it renders. Yet both schools agree on at least two aspects of bureaucratic behavior. One is its dehumanizing or impersonal quality. The other is the political unresponsiveness of public bureaucracy, which will be discussed later in this chapter.

It has been said that the "special virtue" of bureaucracy is "dehumanization"—the elimination of emotions, personal biases, and idiosyncracies from the performance of individual bureaucrats.[16] Today the term "impersonality" is generally used in referring to this quality of bureaucratic behavior. In the prebureaucratic past, administration was rife with nepotism, personal subjugation, and capricious and uninformed judgment. Against that background impersonality certainly seems a step in the direction of efficient and effective administration.

Impersonality has at least three consequences. First, it increases organizational effectiveness by enabling administrators to accomplish regulatory tasks which might otherwise prove too expensive in human costs. In the course of their normal functioning, organizations may create considerable hardship for individuals. This is especially true of public organizations, which are often engaged in punishment, taxation, conscription, the withholding of benefits, or generally coercive measures. Impersonality makes it easier for bureaucrats to accomplish these functions; the elaborate hierarchy and formalization of a bureaucratic organization provide a rationalization for disrupting and even destroying individuals' lives. In addition, the decision makers of a bureaucracy are often isolated from the human consequences of their choices, since their orders are carried out by employees far down the ladder.

A second consequence of impersonality flows from the possibility that "efficiency also suffers when emotions or personal considerations influence administrative decisions."[17] Wherever recruitment and promotions are based on personal preference or on criteria other than competence, administration is generally less efficient.[18] From the organization's point of view, hiring and promotion by merit are advantageous for both regulatory and service functions.

Third, impersonality tends to produce relatively evenhanded application of the rules. Consequently it assures procedural justice, if not necessarily justice in terms of substance. Especially in a bureaucracy's service activities, employees who "go by the book" give equal treatment to people in the same categories, no matter who they are. Although the classic bureaucratic refrain, "If I do it for you, I'll have to do it for everyone," may not make sense in specific applications, it epitomizes the spirit of impersonality.

In turning the individual into a "case," impersonality also creates difficulties for the bureaucracy. Obviously individuals are not cases, and they may resent being treated as such. Thus bureaucratic behavior may ensure procedural justice while falling short of substantive justice. Bureaucrats do not generally deal with wide aspects of their clients' lives but only with the limited and specific facts which brought the client and the bureaucrat together in the first place. Hence the decisions reached or rules applied may fail to fit the client's true situation. At one time or another, virtually everyone feels that a bureaucracy's rules are inappropriately applied in his or her case. Exceptions do occur, but bureaucrats are likely to ignore them, even when they are recognizable. The code of impersonality is so strong that bureaucrats may apply established rules and procedures even when they realize that these are not reasonable or just in a specific instance. Means and ends are inverted as the rules become more important than the underlying objectives.

Moreover, the transformation of individuals into cases may arouse hostility toward bureaucracy—often expressed in complaints about "bureaucracy" and "red tape." Analysis has shown that people dislike impersonality because: (1) Their claims are not taken at face value but must be proved by the individual or investigated by the bureaucracy. (2) Consequently the individual's "worth is questioned, his status is impugned." (3) Seemingly irrelevant questions are asked about the individual's private life. (4) There is a built-in imbalance of power; the individual is dependent on the bureaucracy, but the bureaucrat sees the individual as simply another case. (5) Individuals may feel that no one cares about their situation, and they may be forced to cut through many hierarchical layers to find someone who will turn the "case" back into the individual.[19]

THE BUREAUCRATS

Impersonality not only arouses the hostility of clients; along with other features of bureaucracy, it may wreak havoc upon the bureaucrat's psyche. It has long been thought that immersion in a bureaucracy can lead to personality disorder.[20] Its employees are "provided minimal control over their work-a-day world," and they are "expected to be passive, dependent, subordinate."[21] The psychological needs of the individual are in conflict with the organizational needs of bureaucracy. According to Abraham H. Maslow, the hierarchy of human needs, from highest to lowest, is as follows:[22]

1. *Self-actualization*, or the ability to do what one is "fitted" for. Self-actualization is denied when a person cannot be what he or she "must" be.
2. *Self-esteem*, or the need to value oneself highly and think positively of oneself.
3. *Social* ("love") needs; a sense of belonging, affection, and friendship.
4. *Safety* needs, such as the need for shelter and protection.
5. *Physiological* needs, including the need for food and drink.

Clearly, bureaucracy does not allow its employees to attain the higher needs. Hierarchy, for instance, militates against self-actualization and self-esteem. It prevents people from choosing and structuring their own work, and it leads adults to act and react in childlike patterns.[23] It can also thwart the social needs by making personal and social interaction conditional upon organizational status. Similarly, specialization makes self-actualization and self-esteem difficult. It often requires that only a small and even superficial aspect of the whole person be tapped by a narrow job. Formalization replaces oral communication with written memos and thereby makes it difficult to fulfill social needs on the job. So do the bureaucracy's large size and impersonality. Other features, such as the absence of markets in which a person's work can be evaluated, also hinder the development of a healthy adult personality.

So pervasive are the conflicts between bureaucracy and the individual psyche that one authority has argued: "The bureaucrat's personality is devastated. It is no longer possible to easily speak of the individual's personality as 'belonging' to him."[24] Yet it has also been said that there is a generalized collective bureaucratic personality, in which "the bureaucrat surrenders his or her internalized superego to domination by an externalized superego."[25] In everyday language this means that the bureaucrat's individual conscience is replaced by a collective organizational conscience. Bureaucrats do what the organization tells them to and feel guilty about their actions only when the organization has failed in some fashion.

This line of reasoning fits the notion that bureaucrats are simply "cogs" in a machine over which they exercise limited control. But there is some doubt as to whether people's individuality can be so thoroughly destroyed. Informal groups and other nonbureaucratic elements can be found within bureaucratic organizations.[26] Several analysts have argued that while bureaucracy obviously places constraints on individual bureaucrats, they still retain elements of humanity and individuality.[27] In its political context, this approach is generally put forward under the labels of "representative bureaucracy" and "participatory bureaucracy."[28]

The belief that a civil service can be representative of anything other than itself has been with us since the days of Presidents Thomas Jefferson and Andrew Jackson. More recently, social scientists have applied the concept of representative bureaucracy in an effort to explain the behavior of bureaucracies. Although controversial, the basic idea of this concept is that dehumanization is rarely complete.[29] In other words, bureaucrats continue to be influenced by factors stemming from their social backgrounds. The most important of these are class, race, ethnicity, religion, and gender. According to this line of thought, the personnel of a public bureaucracy can be recruited to reflect the values of specific groups or of the whole society. It follows that a public bureaucracy could become a representative branch of government which is responsive to the citizenry as a whole.

The importance of the concept of representative bureaucracy is immense. Research has not yet shown conclusively that the social background of bureaucrats influences their *behavior* in a wide variety of settings. However, studies of public bureaucrats in the United States, Canada, and Israel have demonstrated that values stemming from one's social background may be modified but not eliminated by a bureaucracy.[30]

Consequently bureaucrats cannot be fully dehumanized, nor the bureaucracy fully homogenized, if the bureaucrats come from different backgrounds. But so far, no one knows how these differences actually affect bureaucratic decisions and behavior. Some research has been done in the United States on minority bureaucrats who want to help their own groups. The results show that these bureaucrats feel a greater sense of success when they help individuals of their groups get jobs than when they work to develop policies which will affect their group as a whole.[31] This is understandable, since it is easier to have an influence on a personnel system than on the society's economic, political, and social systems.

Nevertheless, the notion remains that if enough people from a diversity of social groups were present in the higher levels of a public bureaucracy, the wide representation would be reflected in the policies made by the bureaucrats. A democratic political system could then pay less attention to traditional notions concerning the control and accountability of bureaucrats,[32] and begin to treat bureaucracy as a representative branch of government. In other words, one could move beyond the notion of public bureaucracy as a kind of business organization and treat it as the reality which it is: a powerful political instrument. For example, the United States Congress with its two overlapping bodies is surely not among the most *efficient* national legislatures. Yet rarely does anyone propose to eliminate duplication by abolishing of the House or the Senate. The basic assumption is not that Congress should be efficient, but that it should be representative. The same approach might well be taken with regard to the federal bureaucracy as a whole. Of course, it would still be desirable to maintain checks upon public bureaucrats, as is done with regard to Congress and the other branches of government.

Regardless of how much weight one gives to the concept of representative bureaucracy, the view of bureaucrats as virtually identical "cogs" seems difficult to sustain. Several scholars have argued that there are different types of bureaucrats:[33]

- CLIMBERS; UPWARD MOBILES Bureaucrats who seek to maximize their own position, income, power, and prestige. They are forever searching for ways to expand their domain. When climbers are in the top positions of a bureaucracy, the entire organization will try to extend control over more and more areas.
- CONSERVERS; INDIFFERENTS Bureaucrats who seek to maximize their own security. They attempt to avoid change and do not identify with the organization.
- AMBIVALENTS Bureaucrats who seek advancement within the organization but are unable to accept its values and demands upon them. These bureaucrats find life in the bureaucracy singularly unrewarding.

- ZEALOTS Bureaucrats who are convinced that their own objectives are synonymous with the public interest, regardless of competing programs and values. Like climbers, they tend to promote everything under their control, but for more altruistic reasons.
- ADVOCATES Like zealots, advocates promote programs they believe in, but they tend to be more moderate and more open to influence from superordinates and other coworkers and associates.
- STATESMEN Bureaucrats who are interested in serving the society as a whole rather than themselves or a narrow constituency. They retain a general outlook and are capable of placing programs and actions in perspective while seeking to exercise their own responsibilities competently.
- POLITICOS Bureaucrats who are oriented toward "office politics" as a means of advancing their own interests.[34]

Other bureaucratic types have been noted as well. These relate to the bureaucrat's technical specialty or bias toward an outside group.[35] In passing it should be noted that zealots, advocates, and ambivalents often effectively play the role of "change agent," thereby lending an element of dynamism to bureaucracy. What, then, can be said about the bureaucrat? First, many bureaucrats obviously suffer strain from working in bureaucracy. Their individuality is diminished, and their opportunity to develop a full, healthy, adult personality on the job is all but denied. These are genuine occupational hazards, but they are far less visible than, say, black lung disease. At the same time, however, some individuals thrive in bureaucratic organizations. Second, bureaucrats are not identical in their personal, social, and political values. Factors such as social background and past experience are likely to have an enduring influence on their viewpoint, despite bureaucratic socialization. To speak of "the" bureaucrat, or of bureaucrats as "cogs," is to seize upon a fact and overstate it. Finally, there is good reason to believe that bureaucrats also differ in behavior, but here the organizational constraints are more powerful and the observable cases far fewer.[36] All in all, working in a bureaucracy may be frustrating, and may generate a hostility which the bureaucrat takes out on subordinates or clients.[37]

BUREAUCRATIC BEHAVIOR

Like human behavior, the behavior of a bureaucracy is too complex to be described by a few laws, such as Parkinson's Law (Work expands to fill the time available) or Peter's Principle (In a hierarchy each individual tends to rise to the level of his own incompetence).[38] More often than not, such descriptions are worth more for their wit than their accuracy. But some behavioral characteristics of a bureaucracy are so frequently seen that they do serve to describe the general tendencies of these organizations. Even so, they are not found in every bureaucracy, despite the tendency to call them "laws." Perhaps the most comprehensive set of propositions about bureaucratic behavior has been presented by Anthony Downs, who derived them theoretically rather than empirically.[39]

- Law of Increasing Conservatism "All organizations tend to become more conservative as they become older, unless they experience periods of very rapid growth or internal turnover."[40] Bureaucracy stresses routine, and routine breeds reluctance to accept new approaches and new ways of thinking. Bureaucracy is also a hierarchy of vetoes: a proposal has to cross several points of decision on its way to the top leadership of the organization, and it may be stopped at any point. Bureaucrats tend to know all the reasons why something new *cannot* be done.
- Law of Increasing Conserverism This is a corollary of the previous law. "In every bureau, there is an inherent pressure upon the vast majority of officials to become conservers in the long run."[41] Once people have invested their careers in a bureaucracy, have learned its way of doing things, have come to identify with it, and have contributed to its development, they are likely to resist change and prefer to hold onto what has already been attained.
- Law of Imperfect Control "No one can fully control the behavior of a large organization."[42] Bureaucratic outcomes are sometimes unanticipated and unplanned by those at the top of the hierarchy. Decisions, policies, information, and communication can become distorted as they are acted upon up and down the ranks. Moreover, "the larger any organization becomes, the weaker is the control over its actions exercised by those at the top."[43]
- Law of Countercontrol This is a corollary of the previous law. "The greater the effort made by a sovereign or top-level official to control the behavior of subordinate officials, the greater the efforts made by those subordinates to evade or counteract such control."[44] This proposition suggests that since power has come into the hands of bureaucrats in the American political system, efforts to restore it to the control of elective and appointive political authorities will be difficult. Once having gained power, bureaucrats are likely to oppose relinquishing it.
- Law of Control Duplication "Any attempt to control one large organization tends to generate another" organization.[45] In a sense, the bureaucratization both of Congress and of the presidency can be seen as

an effort to control the federal bureaucracy. To take just one instance, the desire to give the president control of the federal bureaucracy caused the shifting of the Bureau of the Budget from the Treasury Department to a newly created Executive Office of the President in 1939. In 1974, in an effort to reassert its control, Congress created its own Budget Office.

Several more general aspects of bureaucratic behavior have a significant effect on the work turned out by bureaucracies. First, they show pathologies, or self-defeating tendencies.[46] The most important is "goal displacement," a common tendency that can take several manifestations. The simplest is the substitution of means for ends: the desire for routinization sometimes causes bureaucrats to give the routines precedence over the objectives for which they were created. Goal displacement is also manifested in "quantitative compliance." Because bureaucracies do not offer a product for sale in free market transactions, it is difficult to judge the worth of their outputs. Consequently efficiency or output is often assessed in terms of what can be most easily measured. This may be the number of cases processed regardless of the content of the decisions, the number of reports issued regardless of their quality, the number of arrests made regardless of the number of convictions, the number of bills disposed of, and so forth.[47]

Goal displacement sometimes takes the form of absurdities which are perhaps best called "back think." They are cases where priorities (goals) become so distorted that the bureaucratic outcome is useless to the organization and the client. For instance, in Mexico the Ministry of Tourism reportedly prints road maps with nonexistent roads marked on them. The bureaucratic rationale is that the roads will eventually be built, and the government will save money by having accurate maps already available. The driver who comes to a clearly marked nonexistent intersection is not the bureaucrat's problem.

Goal displacement also has a more serious and complex side. Typically, the first and foremost goal of a bureaucracy is its own survival. Thus the bureaucracy's real goal is unlikely to be the formally stated one. A public bureaucracy cannot justify itself simply by indicating that it desires to remain in existence. Public bureaucracies consequently develop ideologies and adapt to the political nature of the times.[48] Their adaptation may involve a succession of goals. Once a goal is accomplished or it becomes clear that its attainment would be undesirable, the bureaucracy chooses another objective. For example, the United States Coast Guard, which was originally created to combat smuggling and piracy, may come to request a bigger budget to counteract oil spills. More problematic from the perspective of the public interest, an agency created to regulate an economic activity may come to be dominated by those it is supposed to regulate. Thus rather than regulating railroads and truckers, the Interstate Commerce Commission has sometimes been a spokesman for them. Indeed, back in the 1930s the airlines actively sought a regulatory agency of their own for the purpose of making it their spokesman. More recently the Environmental Protection Agency has provided unrealistic miles per gallon figures which underestimate the cost of running vehicles, thereby helping the automobile industry sell more cars rather than protecting the environment or informing the consumer. (See Chapter 3 for more discussion of regulatory agencies.)

Bureaucratic behavior, of course, includes the use of jargon. It is a standard (and tired) joke to poke fun at the "federalese" spoken by federal bureaucrats. All bureaucracies create their own language, and persons who do not speak it cannot easily deal with the bureaucrats. Indeed, where matters of importance are involved, clients may have to hire professional interpreters such as lawyers or accountants.

The development of bureaucratic languages can be partially attributed to specialization and the desire for precision. When someone seeks to write rules covering every conceivable eventuality, the language is likely to be cumbersome, wordy, and specialized. However, bureaucratic language is also used for purposes of control. Clients who cannot understand the jargon are usually more pliable and less assertive, simply because they do not comprehend their rights. Moreover, the purpose of bureaucratic language is sometimes less to furnish information than to provide directions or orders. Unlike language in most social settings, it is not supposed to create a give-and-take situation. It is a one-way street, with the bureaucracy giving or taking when it sees fit. In Hummel's words, "The function of bureaucratese is fundamentally to make outsiders powerless":

> Because we are trained to do so in society, in our attempts to talk back to bureaucracy, we naturally look for a *person* to talk back to. In bureaucracy, because of the way it is designed, communication is naturally not personal, but impersonal. That means if there is anything to talk back to at all, it is a *structure*, not a person.[49]

To summarize, bureaucratic behavior is substantially different from social behavior in general. Language and personality take on new meanings and forms in bureaucracy. The emphasis is on precision, stability, discipline, reliability, calculability of results, formal rationality, formalistic impersonality, and formal equality of treatment. In contrast, the larger society attaches greater importance to such elements as justice, freedom, happiness, emotion, illness, death, depression, and oppression.[50] Several misunderstandings result from this divergence. While much of the public thinks of bureaucracies solely as service institutions dealing with people, in reality they are also regulatory institutions processing cases. It is convenient to regard the bureaucrat as just a "nice guy with a bad job," but the bureaucrat's behavior on the job is likely to be fundamentally distinct from people's behavior in society at large. Bureaucrats share many concerns with the general population, but bureaucracies also have different values and a different set of priorities. Bureaucratic language is not simply odd or different; it is a tool of bureaucratic regulation. As Hummel sees it, "The *cultural* conflict between bureaucracy and society is between systems needs and human needs,"[51] and the great threat of increasing bureaucratization is that human needs will eventually be ignored altogether. The means and tool may become the end and master. Consequently the nature of bureaucratic decision making is of fundamental importance in the bureaucratized society.

BUREAUCRATIC DECISION MAKING

Decision making is a key activity for many bureaucracies, especially those in the public sector. Although it was once common to think of public administration as nothing more (or less) than a "science of means," in recent years it has been realized that the "means" are often as politically important and sensitive as the ends. For example, the strategy of "affirmative action" as practiced in the United States in the 1970s was developed and enforced by bureaucratic agencies rather than by elective institutions such as Congress or the president. Yet the means of promoting equal opportunity has been far more controversial than the goal of equal opportunity itself. Just as it is erroneous to believe that the formal heads of bureaucracies actually control all that goes on in their organizations, it is equally inappropriate to deny that public bureaucracies are deeply immersed in politics and are making some of the most important political decisions in the United States.

THE RATIONALIST APPROACH

There is a wealth of scholarship concerning decision making.[52] But most of it deals with how decisions *should* be made, not how they are made in practice. After all, social scientists do not often have the opportunity to observe bureaucratic and other officials in the process of making decisions. Among the various scholarly approaches, one is the "rationalist" approach to decision making.[53] According to administrative thinking in the earlier part of this century, bureaucratic decision making can be highly rational. Rationalists contend that it is possible to identify objectives and then choose the most efficient or effective method of attaining them.[54] In one way or another this notion underlies most of the fads currently being tried in an effort to reform and rationalize public bureaucracy in the United States. Examples are PPBS (Planning, Programming, Budget System—now no longer required at the federal level)[55] and ZBB (Zero Base Budgeting).[56] While it is an appealing idea, rationalist decision making cannot be dominant in American public bureaucracies as they are currently set up.

At the federal level, a plethora of bureaucratic organizational entities are involved in the decision-making process. Some are part of the legislature, others are attached to the presidency, and most can be found within the huge and fragmented federal bureaucracy. The large number of organizational participants in government has several consequences. First, they require coordinating bodies. In the federal service there are hundreds of interagency committees and related organizational forms for this purpose. Given the many units, redundancies and overlaps are inevitable. It is not unusual to find more than a dozen agencies involved in aspects of the same policy area, such as health or education. Second, organizational units tend to multiply. A new problem or policy area, such as the environment or energy, often leads to the creation of a new agency to deal with it. This is because old agencies have their established outlooks and ways of doing business and do not rapidly adapt to new conditions and new priorities. (Remember the Law of Increasing Conservatism.) Fragmentation makes it difficult for political authorities, sitting at the heads of bureaucracies for relatively short periods of time, to gain much control over their agencies. Indeed, many cabinet departments are more like holding companies of several bureaus than single pyramidal organizations, and keeping the various parts from going off in separate directions is a difficult task in itself. (This will become more evident in Chapter 3.)

These structural aspects of federal bureaucracies have two direct effects on bureaucratic decision making. First, the competition and overlapping jurisdictions between agencies encourage bureaucrats to stress interunit relations as opposed to substantive questions of public policy.[57] Government therefore becomes heavily procedural. Formal rules are adopted to govern the interaction among units in an effort to reduce the uncertainties of unrestrained competition. Second, and resulting from this, fragmentation encourages reliance on budget makers and lawyers.[58] Budgetary decisions become surrogate policy decisions, and lawyers are called on to integrate diverse viewpoints and interests. Thus whereas the multitude of bureaucratic organizations increases the incidence of conflict, it may also decrease its intensity.[59]

The "rationalist" approach cannot be implemented well under these conditions. Objectives cannot always be expressed with great clarity or without some political risk. To the extent that goal displacement occurs, it may not be politically advisable to state an agency's true objectives. Moreover, given the importance of procedure, there are some agency activities and programs without any genuine objectives except to maintain a stable set of relationships with other agencies and client groups. Indeed, at times public programs may be little more than symbolic, with no clear-cut objectives.[60] Others have competing objectives. For example, the objective of equal opportunity in several areas of life was broadly endorsed by the Civil Rights Act of 1964 and the Equal Employment Opportunity Act of 1972. Several agencies, including Health, Education, and Welfare, the Equal Employment Opportunity Commission, and the Civil Service Commission were given major responsibility for carrying out the acts. The legislation requires equal opportunity, but it also speaks of "affirmative" programs for reaching this state of affairs. For an agency like the old Civil Service Commission, whose primary task was to administer the federal merit system, any form of discrimination in favor of minorities raised an obvious and potentially serious conflict. This did not go unnoticed by the agency in its formulation of policy.[61] The official "mission description" for the Department of the Interior, provided in Box 2-1, illustrates the complexity of bureaucratic objectives.

THE INCREMENTALIST APPROACH

The rationalist approach is opposed by those who stress the "incremental" nature of bureaucratic decisions.[62] While incrementalism is less

BOX 2–1

Objectives of the Department of the Interior

In formulating and administering programs for the management, conservation, and development of natural resources, the Department pursues the following objectives: the encouragement of efficient use; the improvement of the quality of the environment; the assurance of adequate resource development in order to meet the requirements of national security and an expanding national economy; the maintenance of productive capacity for future generations; the promotion of an equitable distribution of benefits from nationally-owned resources; the discouragement of wasteful exploitation; the maximum use of recreational areas; and the orderly incorporation of Indian and Alaska Native people into our national life by creating conditions which will advance their social and economic adjustment.

SOURCE: *United States Government Organization Manual 1972/73* (Washington: Government Printing Office, 1973), p. 251.

appealing than the rationalist model, it provides a more accurate description of day-to-day decision making by federal bureaucracies. The incrementalist argues that ends cannot be set in the absence of a consideration of means. Rather than stating an objective and selecting the best technique for attaining it, incremental decision making looks at a general problem or policy area and a number of means-ends proposals for having an impact on it. Most importantly, incrementalists recognize that to state explicit ends may weaken the political coalition that was responsible for creating a policy or program in the first place. Incremental decision making in a fragmented bureaucracy is concerned with generating political and organizational consensus. In this sense, bureaucratic programs and actions are not unlike political party platforms. They may include something for everyone without setting explicit priorities. The Food Stamp Program provides a good illustration. It was put together by a coalition of those supporting low-income and poverty groups, farmers, food processors, and supermarkets. All these groups receive a direct or indirect federal subsidy from the program, which is sponsored by the Department of Agriculture (USDA). Now, suppose the USDA had explicitly stated that its chief interest was in subsidizing farmers and had taken steps to further this aim. For example, suppose it had limited the products which could be bought with food stamps to those for which a greater demand would benefit farmers. Then the "welfare" segment of the coalition would have protested and might have succeeded in shifting the program to, say, the Department of Health, Education, and Welfare. On the other hand, if some effort had been made to neutralize the subsidy for farmers by retracting other benefits they receive, the program might have lost their support. Given the disparate interests involved, incremental decision making is well suited to holding the necessary coalition together in order to support a program.

Incremental decision making involves selecting the most desirable combination of means and ends. If the means are politically undesirable or unfeasible, then incrementalism argues that the end is also undesirable or unattainable. But what is the test of a "good" decision or policy under these conditions? Simply put, the yardstick is the amount of agreement and consensus for the decision or policy. An effective political platform is the one that gets the most votes; an effective bureaucratic decision is the one that generates the most support. Decisions and policies are not tested against objectives, but rather against political consensus.

A corollary to the incremental approach is that programs may be politically desirable even if they do not work well. For example, it might be argued that in terms of unemployment and income levels, blacks have made few substantive gains in the United States during the past three decades.[63] The problem may be intractable, but would this be grounds for dismantling all the federal bureaucratic machinery aimed at its solution?

If nothing else, the machinery testifies to society's recognition that something should be done. Politically, this is important in itself. Symbolism is at the very heart of some federal programs. Consider the Federal Deposit Insurance Corporation, for example. It is an agency whose goal can be fulfilled only if it is not made explicit. Its true objective is to prevent a run on banks by *convincing* savings depositors that their money is fully insured. To do this, it tells the depositor that every cent up to a specified maximum is insured and will be repaid if the bank should fold. However, in the event of massive bank failures, under the present program the FDIC would be unable to repay all insured sums. This is a subtle use of symbols to influence the population's behavior.

Seen in terms of programs without clear, statable objectives, means that are more important than ends, and consensus as the test of a decision's desirability, the world of bureaucratic politics becomes far more lucid. Bureaucratic decisions take on a gamelike quality, with the various players sitting in different positions. The players' moves may be predicted less by their personalities (for bureaucracy is largely impersonal) than by their agencies. It has been said: *Where one stands depends upon where one sits*.[64] Bureaucrats' priorities are likely to be parochial and to focus on their impact on the agency and, sometimes, on the individual decision makers. Decisions are not generally made in a detached, rational fashion, but rather worked out under the pressures of deadlines and limited information. Bureaucratic agencies are by and large reactive instead of proactive, but since they are often reacting to one another, the whole system appears to be in motion.[65] Given the Law of Incomplete Control, bureaucratic decisions are not synonymous with bureaucratic outcomes. Therefore intention and action are two separate elements, and the former cannot necessarily be deduced from the latter. In other words, "policy" is often the accretion of events rather than the outcome of a decision process.

IMPLEMENTATION OF PUBLIC POLICY

Some public bureaucracies have no responsibilities for programs, but to a large extent contemporary bureaucratic power is intertwined with the implementation of public policy. Traditionally, the terms "line" and "staff" have been used to make this distinction. Line agencies manage programs, and staff agencies serve the needs of line agencies—the needs of political authorities for personnel, information, budget making, and the like. In practice, however, the distinction often becomes blurred. But for agencies with program responsibilities, the implementation of public policy is paramount.

It is important to recognize that implementation is not simply a matter of paying attention to details, filing reports, reading applications, processing individual cases, and so on. It often involves some very controversial questions, as noted above in connection with affirmative action. Indeed, controversial questions are often left to public bureaucracies for resolution. Congressmen and presidents are reluctant to make controversial choices for which the voters may blame them. They would much rather berate "the bureaucracy" for being power-hungry, inefficient, and ineffective. Neither Congress nor the president is by any means powerless, but it is the government's unelected, bureaucratic component that often determines what is actually to be done about crucial and emotional issues. Even in less controversial areas, statutes and directives often state very broad objectives and then delegate the authority for reaching them to various bureaucratic agencies.

Given the nature of bureaucratic decision making, it is not surprising that the implementation of policy often appears haphazard. Despite the hue and cry against "dictatorial bureaucracies," observers tend to be struck by how little information and knowledge bureaucracies have about how well their programs are working. In the words of Elizabeth Drew:

> Those who picture Washington as one mass of files and computers containing more information than they would like will be comforted by the experiences of program-planners in attempting to evaluate on-going programs. Whatever the files and computers do contain, there is precious little in them about how many and whom the programs are reaching, and whether they are doing what they are supposed to do.[66]

Bureaucracies are regulatory instruments. When it is they who are doing the regulating, there is no limit to the number of forms, certificates, and procedures they may require. But when there is a possibility that the information collected may be used to control the bureaucracy itself, the agency may well decide not to collect it. There are at least two reasons for such a decision. First, some programs by their very nature cannot succeed. They may be the product of a political coalition with different and conflicting objectives. They may be politically desirable but largely unachievable through government action; for example, programs to eliminate racism, unemployment, and inflation in the United States. Second, agencies may be saddled with programs that they do not particularly want to implement. This was the case with the Federal Equal Employment Opportunity Program in the Civil Service Commission.[67] An agency that does not favor a program, but fears the political consequences of transferring it to a competitor agency, may carry it out in such a way that it is bound to fail. For the agency to supply information revealing that failure would obviously be self-defeating.

Another feature of the implementation of public policy by bureaucratic agencies is that those with overlapping missions generally do not coordinate their dealings with the same clientele. Hence the "consumer" of bureaucratic programs is required to meet the different requirements of each agency involved. To take a trivial example, suppose that you want to import parrots into the United States. You could bring them to some ports under regulations of the Customs Bureau, but these are not necessarily the same ones allowable under the rules of the departments of Agriculture and the Interior. Such difficulties are commonly encountered by people seeking various government benefits, whether in agriculture, small business, urban renewal, or some other area. In 1979 Sears, Roebuck and Company filed a well-publicized suit against the federal government on the grounds that its antidiscrimination regulations were hopelessly contradictory.[68]

Where the issue is not direct regulation, implementation may also appear irrational and disorganized. This can occur when (1) the process of control is indirect and benefits are conditional upon compliance with bureaucratic regulations or (2) the agency is struggling to resolve intractable problems. Indeed in recent years, as social scientists became more interested in "policy evaluation," many studies failed to trace the impact of bureaucratic activities upon the policy area involved. The influence of bureaucratic agencies on the outcome of a policy is great, but that influence is not a rational effort at obtaining specified objectives.

Coming back to the major theme of this book, bureaucratic implementation, like bureaucratic decision making, makes control by outsiders extremely difficult to establish. Indeed, although an agency may be in control of itself in some sense, none of its officials may be in control of the agency. The organization is the actor. Whenever individuals and even outside organizations try to control a well-developed bureaucracy, it is like hitting a featherbed, as President Franklin D. Roosevelt once said in exasperation.[69]

Conclusion Democracy and Bureaucracy

It has been evident since the earliest days of social scientific analysis of bureaucracy that it inherently and inevitably conflicts with democracy. As Weber observed, although middle-class dissatisfaction with aristocracy often brought both bureaucracy and democracy into being, eventually the bureaucratization of government and politics clashes with the idea of popular rule.[70] Indeed, in a fully developed bureaucratic political system, rule would be by bureaucratic organizations rather than by individual bureaucrats. The inherent tension between the two forms of organization is obvious when their requirements are compared:

Democracy Requires	Bureaucracy Requires
Plurality	Unity
Equality	Hierarchy
Liberty	Command
Rotation in office	Duration in office
Openness	Secrecy
Equal access to participation in politics	Differentiated access, based on authority
Election	Appointment

Given these divergencies, it is an open question whether bureaucracy and democracy can reach a harmonious accommodation.

The primary difficulty in integrating bureaucratic government into a democratic political framework is that control of public bureaucracies by elective and appointive political authorities is highly problematic. True, bureaucrats can be influenced, but it is virtually impossible to dominate all of them over a long period. Traditional notions about accountability and responsibility to political authorities are largely inappropriate in the modern bureaucratized state.[71] For instance, the rapid unionization of public employees in the past decade is based on the idea that public employees are an independent group with whom the government must bargain.[72] Similarly, budgeting and reorganizational schemes are not equal to the task of changing the bureaucracy. Budgetary approaches have succeeded more in reorganizing budget bureaus than in giving elective and appointive political authorities greater control over public bureaucracies. Likewise, reorganizations do not necessarily resolve problems of substance nor enable political authorities to exert greater influence over bureaucratic agencies.[73] In addition, as Weber argues, bureaucratic specialization and expertise often place "the 'political master' . . . in the position of the 'dilettante' who stands opposite the 'expert,' facing the trained official who stands within the management of administration."[74]

If public bureaucracies cannot be made responsive to outside control by individuals, can they instead be held accountable to the rule of law? Not without difficulties. Statutes in the United States allow administrative agencies a great deal of discretion and thereby delegate authority and power to them. Why is this the case? In part it is due to electoral politics and the reluctance of elected officials to take clear-cut operational stands on controversial issues. But it is also due to the fact that bureaucratic agencies have a great deal of expertise which can improve the implementation of programs. In short, although bureaucracies are far from perfect, they often have the know-how that government requires. Individual bureaucrats can take a less partisan view of policy and act as impartial, expert judges.[75] Moreover, any effort to try to legislate in such a way as to cover all possible contingencies in today's complex and fast-paced world of permanent crisis would be doomed to failure. The legislative process can only give broad direction to most governmental programs or else veto them entirely.

As the power of bureaucrats and bureaucratic organizations grows, the political influence of the general citizenry inevitably declines. Elections are still important, especially as a means by which the voters can pass judgment on government performance and contribute to the formulation of broad national objectives. But at best, elections can only indirectly influence the behavior of public bureaucrats, and at the federal level an election rarely provides the public with specific policy options. Paradoxically, since changing the elected officials does not normally lead to far-reaching changes in the government bureaucracy, the citizen's most forceful legal protest against the bureaucratic polity may lie in *not* voting—that is, in refusing to legitimize the state of affairs with his or her vote.[76] Thus the tension between bureaucracy and democracy goes beyond the relations among politicians and bureaucrats; it engulfs the citizenry and militates against their participation in political life (see Chapter 9).

NOTES

1. Martin Albrow, *Bureaucracy* (New York: Praeger, 1970), p. 125.
2. The concept of efficiency is at the heart of bureaucratic and other Western work organizations. In the view of some, efficient production is far more important than the impact of work processes on workers. See Frederick Taylor, *The Principles of Scientific Management* (New York: Harper and Brothers, 1911), for a classic statement on efficiency.
3. For more elaborate definitions of bureaucracy see Albrow, *Bureaucracy*; Max Weber, *Essays in Sociology*, trans. and ed. by H. H. Gerth and C. W. Mills (New York: Oxford University Press, 1958); Anthony Downs, *Inside Bureaucracy* (Boston: Little, Brown, 1967); Ferrel Heady, *Public Administration: A Comparative Perspective* (Englewood Cliffs, N.J.: Prentice-Hall, 1966); and Victor Thompson, *Modern Organizatton* (New York: Knopf, 1961) among numerous others.
4. Thompson, *Modern Organization*, p. 73.
5. Thompson, ibid., argues that this is the basis for several pathological aspects of bureaucracy; see especially pp. 23–24.
6. For a discussion see Herbert Kaufman, *Red Tape* (Washington, D.C.: Brookings Institution, 1977).
7. This is often highly problematic. See D. Rosenbloom, "Public Personnel Administration and Politics," *Midwest Review of Public Administration*, 7 (April 1973), 98–110. Reprinted in J. A. Uveges, Jr., *The Dimensions of Public Administration*, 2nd ed. (Boston: Holbrook, 1975).
8. Downs, *Inside Bureaucracy*, pp. 24–25.
9. In recent years some efforts have been made to organize small work groups within large bureaucracies to reduce these consequences of large size. In the United States, however, such an approach remains the exception. See George Berkley, *The Craft of Public Administration* (Boston: Allyn and Bacon, 1975), and *The Administrative Revolution* (Englewood Cliffs, N.J.: Prentice-Hall, 1971), for a discussion.

10. Thompson, *Modern Organization*, pp. 160–161.

11. Weber, *Essays in Sociology*, p. 232.

12. Ibid., "Bureaucracy."

13. Henry Jacoby, *The Bureaucratization of the World* (Berkeley; Calif.: University of California Press, 1973).

14. Weber, *Essays in Sociology*, p. 228.

15. Harold Seidman, *Politics, Position, and Power* (New York: Oxford University Press, 1970), p. 18.

16. Weber, *Essays in Sociology*, p. 216.

17. Peter Blau and Marshall Meyer, *Bureaucracy in Modern Society* (New York: Random House, 1971), p. 9.

18. But impersonality may impair efficiency in other contexts. See Thompson, *Modern Organization*, chap. 8.

19. Alvin Gouldner, "Red Tape as a Social Problem," in R. K. Merton et al., eds., *Reader in Bureaucracy* (New York: Free Press, 1952), pp. 410–418.

20. Chris Argyris, "The Individual and Organization: Some Problems of Mutual Adjustment," *Administrative Science Quarterly*, 2 (June 1957), 1–24.

21. Ibid., p. 18. See also R. K. Merton, "Bureaucratic Structure and Personality," in Merton et al., eds., *Reader in Bureaucracy*, pp. 361–371.

22. See Abraham H. Maslow, "A Theory of Human Motivation," *Psychological Review*, 50 (July 1943), 370–396.

23. Thompson, *Modern Organization*, especially chap. 9.

24. Ralph P. Hummel, *The Bureaucratic Experience* (New York: St. Martin's, 1977), pp. 129–130.

25. Ibid., p. 135.

26. These aspects form the core of the "human relations" approach to organization. See A. Etzioni, *Modern Organizations* (Englewood Cliffs, N.J.: Prentice-Hall, 1964) for a concise discussion.

27. For a forceful statement by a bureaucratic official see V. A. Pai Panandiker, "Developmental Administration," in N. Raphaeli, ed., *Readings in Comparative Public Administration* (Boston: Allyn and Bacon, 1967), pp. 199–210.

28. For useful descriptions see Samuel Krislov, *Representative Bureaucracy* (Englewood Cliffs, N.J.: Prentice-Hall, 1974), and Harry Kranz, *The Participatory Bureaucracy* (Lexington, Mass.: Lexington Books, 1976).

29. See ibid.; D. Nachmias and D. Rosenbloom, "Bureaucracy and Ethnicity," *American Journal of Sociology*, 83 (January 1978), 967–974; D. Rosenbloom and J. Featherstonhaugh, "Passive and Active Representation in the Federal Service," *Social Science Quarterly*, 57 (March 1977), 873–882.

30. Ibid., and Seymour M. Lipset, "Bureaucracy and Social Change," in Merton et al., eds., *Reader in Bureaucracy*, pp. 221–232.

31. D. Rosenbloom and D. Kinnard, "Bureaucratic Representativeness and Bureaucrats' Behavior," *Midwest Review of Public Administration*, 11 (March 1977), 35–42.

32. For a discussion of accountability, see D. Rosenbloom, "Accountability in the Administrative State," in S. Greer et al., eds., *Accountability in Urban Society, Urban Affairs Annual*, vol. 15 (Beverly Hills, Calif.: Sage, 1979).

33. See Downs, *Inside Bureaucracy*; Robert Presthus, *The Organizational Society*, rev. ed. (New York: St. Martin's, 1978); Leonard Reissman, "A Study of Role Conceptions in Bureaucracy," *Social Forces*, 27 (March 1949), 305–310, upon which the remainder of this paragraph is based.

34. D. Nachmias and D. Rosenbloom, *Bureaucratic Culture* (London and New York: Croom Helm and St. Martin's, 1978).

35. Reissman, "A Study of Role Conceptions," *Social Forces* 27.

36. Lipset, "Bureaucracy and Social Change," in Merton et al., *Reader in Bureaucracy*.

37. It should be noted that many employees of bureaucracies are professionals such as doctors, engineers, scientists, and lawyers rather than administrators per se (see Chapter 3). While not "bureaucrats" in all senses of the word, such individuals are subject to many of the same pressures. See Frederick Mosher, *Democracy and the Public Service* (New York: Oxford University Press, 1968), for a discussion with reference to the federal bureaucracy.

38. C. Northcote Parkinson, *Parkinson's Law* (Boston: Houghton Mifflin, 1957); Lawrence J. Peter and Raymond Hull, *The Peter Principle* (New York: William Morrow, 1969).
39. Downs, *Inside Bureaucracy*.
40. Ibid., p. 262.
41. Ibid.
42. Ibid.
43. Ibid. Downs refers to this as the Law of Diminishing Control.
44. Ibid.
45. Ibid.
46. See Thompson, *Modern Organization*, for a comprehensive discussion. The remainder of the paragraph draws upon this source.
47. For a discussion of the problems of such measures, see D. Nachmias, *Public Policy Evaluation* (New York: St. Martin's, 1979).
48. Downs, *Inside Bureaucracy*, chap. 19.
49. Hummel, *The Bureaucratic Experience*, p. 147.
50. See ibid., chap. 2, for an extended discussion.
51. Ibid., p. 56.
52. See David Braybrooke and Charles E. Lindblom, *A Strategy of Decision* (New York: Free Press, 1970); Alan A. Altshuler and Norman Thomas, eds., *The Politics of the Federal Bureaucracy* (New York: Harper and Row, 1977), chap. 3; Donald W. Taylor, "Decision Making and Problem Solving," in James G. March, ed., *Handbook of Organizations* (Chicago: Rand McNally, 1965), pp. 48–86; Herbert Simon, *Administrative Behavior*, 2nd ed. (New York: Free Press, 1957); and Graham T. Allison, "Conceptual Models and the Cuban Missile Crisis," *American Political Science Review*, 63 (September 1969), 689–718.
53. See Charles E. Lindblom, "The Science of 'Muddling Through,' " *Public Administration Review*, 19 (Spring 1959), 79–88, for a discussion.
54. The influential L. Gulick and L. Urwick, eds., *Papers on the Science of Administration* (New York: Institute of Public Administration, 1937) is very much in this vein.
55. See Alan Shick, "A Death in the Bureaucracy," *Public Administration Review*, 33 (March/April 1973), 146–156.
56. See P. Pyhrr, "The Zero-Base Approach to Government Budgeting," *Public Administration Review*, 37 (January 1977), 1–8.
57. See Ira Sharkansky, *Public Administration* (Chicago: Rand McNally, 1975), chap. 3.
58. Ibid.
59. Ibid.
60. For several years this was true, for example, of the federal equal employment opportunity program. See D. Rosenbloom, *Federal Equal Employment Opportunity* (New York: Praeger, 1977). For a time before its demise, the Subversive Activities Control Board was left without substantial authority as a result of Supreme Court decisions affecting its original mission.
61. Ibid.
62. Lindblom, "The Science of 'Muddling Through.' "
63. See *New York Times*, Feb. 28, 1978, p. 22; April 2, 1978, p. 18; Feb. 26, 1978, p. 1. However, some groups within the black population have fared better than others.
64. Seidman, *Politics, Position, and Power*, p. 19.
65. See Louis Gawthrop, *Bureaucratic Behavior in the Executive Branch* (New York: Free Press, 1969), especially chap. 8.
66. Elizabeth Drew, "HEW Grapples with PPBS," *Public Interest*, 8 (Summer 1967), 9–27, at p. 11.
67. Rosenbloom, *Federal Equal Employment Opportunity*.
68. Letter of Mr. E. Telling, Chairman, Sears, Rosebuck and Co., to the *New York Times*, Feb. 2, 1979.
69. See Sidney Hyman, ed., *Beckoning Frontiers* (New York: Knopf, 1951), p. 336.
70. Weber, *Essays in Sociology*, especially pp. 224–235.
71. Rosenbloom, *Urban Affairs Annual*, 15.
72. See Jay M. Shafritz et al., *Personnel Management in Government* (New York: Marcel Dekker, 1978), part V; for a discussion in the European context see Brian Chapman, *The Profession of Government* (London: Unwin University Books, 1959).

73. Seidman, *Politics, Position, and Power*.

74. Weber, *Essays in Sociology*, p. 232.

75. Herbert J. Storing, "Political Parties and the Bureaucracy," in R. Goldwin, ed., *Political Parties, U.S.A.* (Chicago: Rand McNally, 1964), pp. 137–158.

76. See Theodore Lowi, "A 'Critical' Election Misfires," *The Nation*, December 18, 1972, for an argument that "abstentionism" (nonvoting) is the only untried route to political change in the United States. Some, such as Alan Wertheimer, would close this route by making voting compulsory: "In Defense of Compulsory Voting," *Nomos XVI, Participation in Politics*, J. Pennock and J. Chapman, eds. (New York: Leiber-Atherton, 1975). See also Frederick Thayer, *An End to Hierarchy! An End to Competition!* (New York: New Viewpoints, 1973), chap. 2.

Part II

THE BUREAUCRATIZATION OF THE FEDERAL GOVERNMENT

3

The Bureaucratic "Fourth Branch" of Government

The expansion of political power in the hands of nonelected and non-politically appointed public officials is most evident in the federal bureaucracy. This institution consists of a vast and complex set of organizational arrangements. It is composed of an array of structural units with varied, although often overlapping, missions. While very few aspects of American life are not at least indirectly affected by the federal bureaucracy, the public generally misunderstands its nature, structure and behavior. One reason is that the workings of bureaucratic organizations are not open to public view; another is that popular dislike of bureacracy is fostered by our political rhetoric and journalism. Given the power of the federal bureaucracy in day-to-day governance, however, it is crucially important to have an accurate knowledge of this "fourth branch" of government.

DEVELOPMENT OF THE FEDERAL BUREAUCRACY

A large, powerful federal bureaucracy was not anticipated by the founding fathers; it developed and expanded in response to needs of the political system.[1] As a result it grew haphazardly, reflecting the political climates of various periods. Nor has it been fully integrated into the scheme of constitutional government. Although there were administrative structures under the government of the Articles of Confederation, the founders had little desire to perpetuate these when the Constitution went into effect in 1789. Indeed, President Washington wanted to wipe the administrative slate clean in an effort to place the new government on a firm foundation. He thought that administrative precedents would be among the most important that he could set for the new regime. In his first year as president, the departments of State, Treasury, and War were organized. The position of postmaster general was established, and by the turn of the eighteenth century, the Department of the Navy was created. An office of Attorney General was also set up under Washington, but the Department of Justice did not come into existence until 1870.[2]

As Table 3–1 shows, in the early days of the republic the federal "bureaucracy" was a small-scale affair. The Jeffersonians, who replaced the Federalists at the head of the national government in 1801, had little desire for administrative supervision of the life of the society. By 1821 the fledgling bureaucracy consisted of slightly less than 7,000 employees. However, developments over the next several decades drastically changed this picture.

In 1829 one of the most momentous events in the history of the federal bureaucracy took place. President Andrew Jackson was inaugurated. Calling for reform of the federal bureaucracy in virtually his first words as president, Jackson sought two changes in federal personnel policy: (1) the political selection of federal administrators, and (2) their rotation in office.[3] These changes would resolve the problem of superannuation which was beginning to plague the bureaucracy and would let the common people into what had previously been largely an

TABLE 3–1

Growth of Federal Employment

YEAR	NUMBER OF EMPLOYEES
1821	6,914
1831	11,491
1841	18,038
1851	26,274
1861	36,672
1871	51,020
1881	100,020
1891	157,442
1901	239,476
1911	395,905
1921	561,143
1931	609,746
1941	1,437,682
1951	2,482,666
1961	2,435,808
1971	2,862,926
1977	2,724,000

SOURCES: Through 1951, U.S. Bureau of the Census and Social Science Research Council, *Statistical History of the United States from Colonial Times to the Present* (Stamford, Conn.: Fairfield Publishers, 1965), p. 710. Figures for 1961 and 1971 are from U.S. Civil Service Commission, *Annual Report,* pp. 78, 88, appendix A. The 1977 figure is from U.S. Bureau of the Census, *Statistical Abstract* (Washington, D.C.: Bureau of the Census, 1978), p. 278.

upper-class preserve.[4] In addition, they would give the political parties mass appeal and provide them with a large number of potential workers and contributors who hoped to be rewarded with a job in the federal service.

By the 1840s the spoils system was in full swing. The partisanship of the presidency changed almost every four years until Abraham Lincoln was reelected in 1864. Even when a single party controlled the presidency for more than one term, as the Democrats did in the 1850s, the faction that dispensed patronage within the party was rotated. The competitiveness of the parties produced strong pressures for the creation of new federal positions upon which the patronage machines could feed. Between 1831 and 1861 the number of federal employees more than tripled from about 11,000 to 37,000.[5] For the most part this was the result of adding positions to established agencies, but some new units were created, including the Department of the Interior in 1849.

By the outbreak of the Civil War, the spoils system had reached its peak. Twenty-two years later in 1883, legislation was adopted to depoliticize the civil service and to base the recruitment and selection of federal employees on "merit."[6] This reform worked so well that toward the end of the century, spoils were almost inconsequential. The demise of the spoils system coincided with (and was in fact linked to) the development of a larger federal role in the life of the society, especially in its economy. The thrust of federal policy became regulatory. Interstate commerce and antitrust legislation were the hallmark of the period. It had taken the federal service eighty-two years to acquire some 50,000 positions. In the decade from 1871 to 1881 another 50,000 were added, and yet another 50,000 in the following decade. Growth during this period was highlighted by the creation of the Department of Agriculture, the Department of Justice, and the Interstate Commerce Commission.

By the 1900s the pattern of bureaucratic growth appeared to be fairly well established. During the Progressive Era the government was anxious to take on more and more functions, and it needed increasing numbers of structural units and employees to implement new regulations and programs.[7] Among these were the Pure Food and Drug Act of 1906, the use of the Hepburn Act of 1906 to regulate telephone and telegraph rates, and the further regulation of transportation under the Transportation Act of 1920. The regulatory policy of the period between the Civil War and World War I was a prime contributor to bureaucratic growth, as were the wars themselves. Among the new units created during this period were the departments of Commerce and Labor in 1913.

The next major impetus to bureaucratic growth occurred during the New Deal. In 1931 there were some 600,000 federal employees; a decade later the number topped 1,400,000. President Franklin D. Roosevelt sought vigorous federal participation in the effort to bring about recovery from the Great Depression that began in 1929. By 1936 more than sixty new agencies had been created to help cope with the continuing crisis.[8] In a very real sense the contemporary federal bureaucracy dates from this time. Roosevelt was suspicious of old-line, established agencies and generally argued that a new function needed a new agency. Moreover, his personal style of organizing the presidency required overlaps among the various agencies and among his own staff assistants.[9] Significantly, the Executive Office of the President dates from this period (see Chapter 4). In many ways the New Deal contributed to the notion that real and intractable problems of substance demand the creation of new agencies or the reorganization of those that already exist.[10]

During World War II, as could be expected, the federal bureaucracy continued its rapid growth. Since that time the number of employees has fluctuated between about 2.5 million and 3 million. Today it appears to be relatively stable at around 2.8 million. In part the stability is because recent federal programs, such as revenue sharing, require less federal and more state administration. (This may have contributed to the phenomenal growth of state and local employment during the past two decades.)[11] In addition, much federal bureaucratic work is now contracted out to private firms. In any event, rapid growth of public bureaucracies is occurring today only on the state and local levels. In the post–World War II period the departments of Defense (1949), Health, Education, and Welfare (1953), Housing and Urban Development (1965), Transportation (1967), and Energy (1977) were among the new units created within the federal bureaucracy.

The number of employees in a bureaucracy is one indicator of its size. Another is the number of organizational entities it contains. Counting the entities in the federal bureaucracy, however, is harder than it sounds. During the 1976 presidential campaign, candidate Jimmy Carter promised to reduce some 1900 federal agencies to no more than 200.[12] Yet in its 1977 organizational chart of the government of the United States, the *U.S. Government Manual* showed only 55 agencies in the executive branch outside the Executive Office of the President and about a dozen within it. (A more recent version of government organization appears in Figure 3–1.) Why was there such a discrepancy? The difference stems from what definition of an agency is used.

When Carter made his campaign pronouncements, he was inflating the number of agencies by considering advisory committees, interagency committees, and some very minor units as full-fledged operating agencies.[13] This may have been good politics, but it was clearly

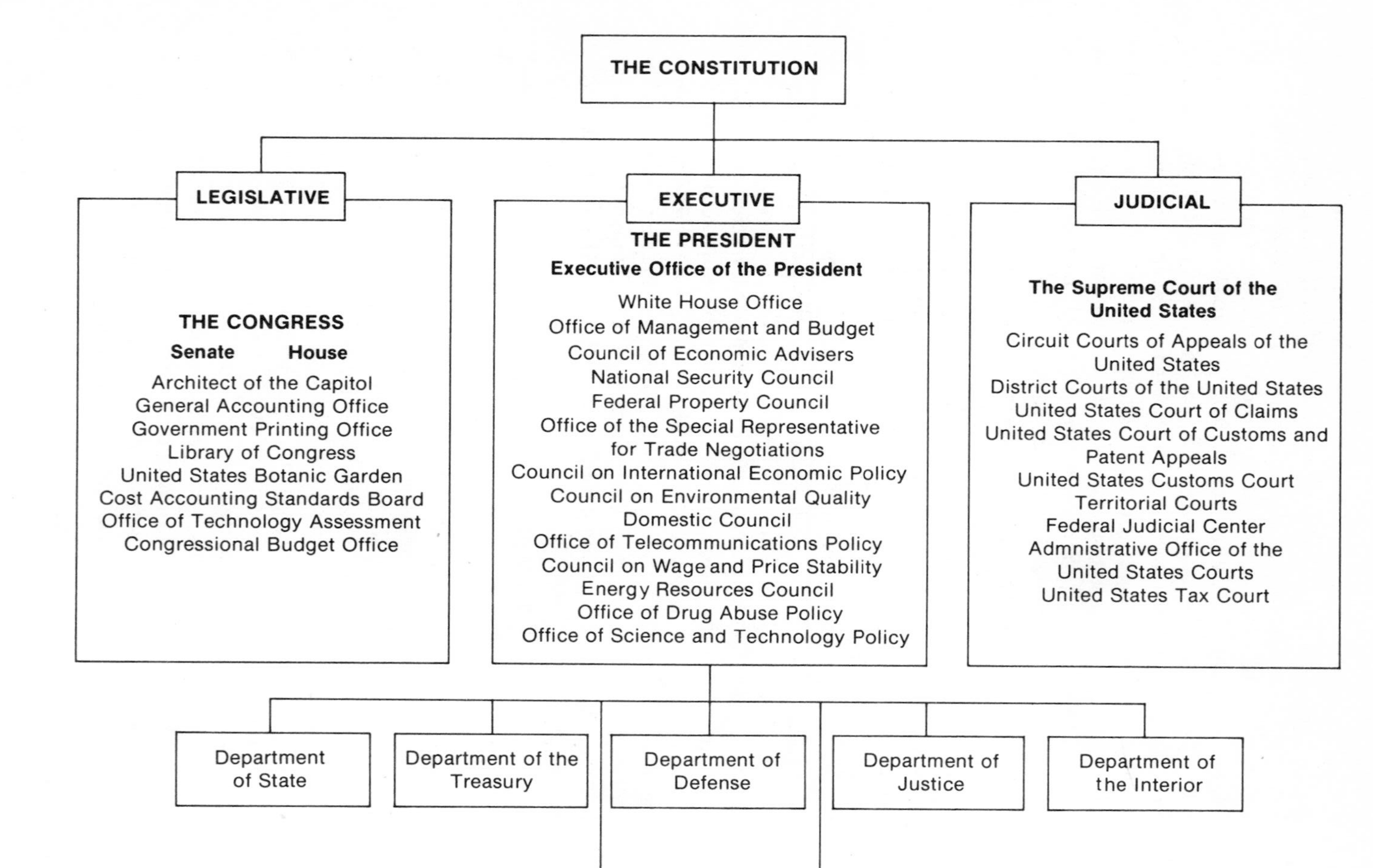
THE CONSTITUTION
LEGISLATIVE
THE CONGRESS
Senate House
Architect of the Capitol
General Accounting Office
Government Printing Office
Library of Congress
United States Botanic Garden
Cost Accounting Standards Board
Office of Technology Assessment
Congressional Budget Office
EXECUTIVE
THE PRESIDENT
Executive Office of the President
White House Office
Office of Management and Budget
Council of Economic Advisers
National Security Council
Federal Property Council
Office of the Special Representative for Trade Negotiations
Council on International Economic Policy
Council on Environmental Quality
Domestic Council
Office of Telecommunications Policy
Council on Wage and Price Stability
Energy Resources Council
Office of Drug Abuse Policy
Office of Science and Technology Policy
JUDICIAL
The Supreme Court of the United States
Circuit Courts of Appeals of the United States
District Courts of the United States
United States Court of Claims
United States Court of Customs and Patent Appeals
United States Customs Court
Territorial Courts
Federal Judicial Center
Admnistrative Office of the United States Courts
United States Tax Court
Department of State
Department of the Treasury
Department of Defense
Department of Justice
Department of the Interior

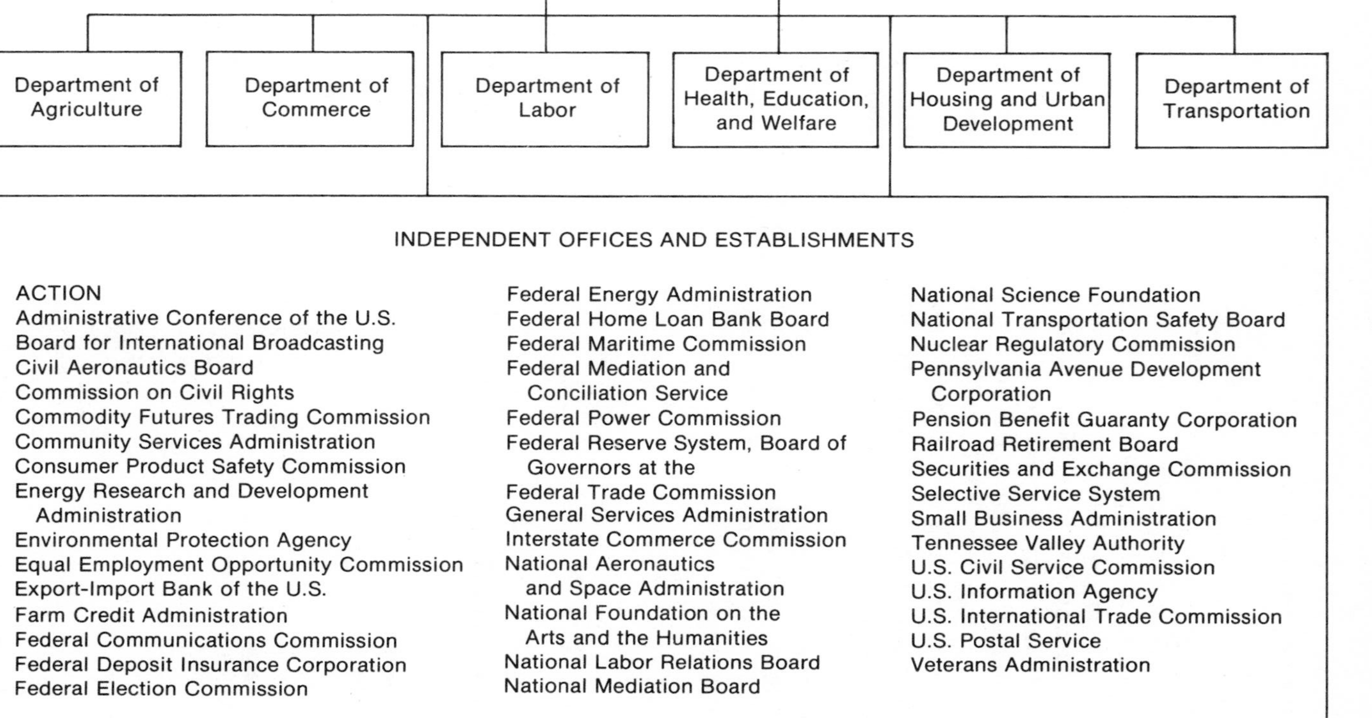

Figure 3–1 **The Government of the United States in 1977**

SOURCE: *U.S. Government Manual,* 1978–1979, p. 30.

misleading, as his administration conceded after taking office. Indeed, bringing the number of agencies to 200 would require not reduction, but the *addition* of about 100 units. For it is generally accepted that the number of actual operating agencies is about 90 to 100.[14] Yet Carter was not completely wrong in his estimate, because a unit that is considered a single agency in a legal sense may contain scores of semiautonomous "bureaus." These are the operational units of government, and although they may be strung together under one agency, many of them have long histories of their own and have been shifted from one agency to another in the past. Owing to problems of definition as well as a lack of adequate data, the number of distinct bureaus in the federal bureaucracy is unknown. One study, which excluded the Department of Defense, found that in 1973 the remaining *cabinet* departments and the Executive Office of the President contained 394 bureaus, and that the number had increased from 175 in 1923.[15] Hence it is not the number of personnel, but the number of reasonably distinct operating units that appears to be growing in the federal bureaucracy today. Table 3–2 presents the size and budget of cabinet departments, and Table 3–3 shows the occupations of federal employees. These tables make clear the scope and activity of the federal bureaucracy.

TABLE 3–2

Personnel and Budget of Cabinet Departments, 1978

DEPARTMENT	PERSONNEL	BUDGET OUTLAYS (IN BILLIONS)
Agriculture	114,000	$23
Commerce	39,000	5
Defense	982,000	105
Health, Education, Welfare	158,000	165
Housing & Urban Development	18,000	8
Interior	76,000	4
Justice	53,000	3
Labor	17,000	24
State	30,000	1
Transportation	74,000	14
Treasury	133,000	56
Energy	20,000	8

SOURCE: U.S. Bureau of the Census, *Statistical Abstract* (Washington, D.C.: Bureau of the Census, 1978), pp. 280, 263. Budget figures are estimates.

TABLE 3–3

White-Collar Full-Time Civilian Workers in the Federal Government, by Major Occupational Group, 1976 (In Hundreds)

OCCUPATIONAL GROUP	1976
Postal	469.6
General administration, clerical, and office service	471.7
Engineering & architecture	151.3
Accounting & budget	121.6
Medical, hospital, dental, & public health	120.5
Supply	60.0
Business & industry	69.0
Legal & kindred	64.3
Personnel management & industrial relations	44.4
Physical sciences	41.7
Biological sciences	46.2
Investigation	46.5
Social sciences, psychology, & welfare	53.1
Transportation	43.7
Education	28.7
Quality assurance inspection & grading	18.7
Information & arts	20.5
Equipment, facilities, & service	14.0
Mathematics & statistics	14.6
Library & archives	9.7
Other	71.3

SOURCE: U.S. Bureau of the Census, *Statistical Abstract* (Washington, D.C.: Bureau of the Census, 1978), p. 284.

DEPARTMENTS, AGENCIES, COMMITTEES, COMMISSIONS

Although bureaus are the working units of the federal bureaucracy, they are grouped together to form different types of structures. Departments are generally considered the most important. These are distinguished from other structures by the scope of their missions, their national importance, and their generally more frequent interaction with the president. The head of a department (the secretary) is by definition a member of the president's cabinet and has the highest executive-level rank (rank I). It should be emphasized that it is not the size of a unit but rather the nature of its mission that usually determines whether it will be a department or some other form of agency. Of course, like any other organizational decision concerning the federal bureaucracy, the decision to create a department is largely a political one.

Although all departments enjoy high formal status within the federal establishment, their structures and overall character vary markedly. Some, such as the Department of Labor, are relatively small (17,000 employees) and compact. In contrast, the Department of Defense, has close to a million civilian employees apportioned among several major structural units, including the (sub) departments of the Army, Navy, and Air Force. The Department of Health, Education, and Welfare (HEW) is a holding company of such units as the Social Security Administration, the Office of Education, and the Public Health Service (which includes the Food and Drug Administration, the National Institutes of Health, and other bureaus). The Department of Agriculture and the Treasury are also conglomerates with huge staffs, whereas other cabinet departments have less than 100,000 employees. For the most part, however, cabinet departments are clusters of separate bureaus, many of which tend to act in directions of their own regardless of efforts to coordinate them. For example, when the Federal Aviation Agency was put under the Department of Transportation, it was argued that this would not violate its independence or integrity and, indeed, it was given special legal status to assure that this would be the case.[16] The independence of bureaus is enhanced by their geographic dispersal and organization. Within a department such as Agriculture, for example, there may be as many as twenty different ways of dividing the country geographically, with the various bureaus having regional headquarters in different cities. Despite popular misconceptions, only about 10 percent of all federal employees are situated in the greater Washington, D.C., area. Most of the federal bureaucracy is located in the rest of the country and abroad.

Agencies are another structural form in the federal bureaucracy. There are two basic types: those that are formally accountable to the president and those that are formally "autonomous." Agencies of the first type include the Veterans Administration (VA), General Services Administration (GSA), and Small Business Administration. These may be sizable in number of employees—the VA has long had over a hundred thousand—and relatively complex in organizational structure. But the scope of their missions is limited to relatively distinct groups, or is considered of relatively minor importance to the nation as a whole, or is restricted to "overhead" functions intended to ensure the smooth working of the federal bureaucracy. The medium-sized GSA and some smaller agencies dealing with federal personnel administration are examples of "overhead" agencies.

Perhaps the best-known independent agencies are regulatory commissions. Among the most important are the Interstate Commerce Commission (ICC), Federal Communications Commission (FCC), Securities and Exchange Commission (SEC), Civil Aeronautics Board (CAB), National Labor Relations Board (NLRB), and Federal Trade Commission (FTC). Typically, such agencies are headed by a group of bipartisan commissioners who hold their offices for fixed terms and cannot be removed by the president for policy reasons. (One Supreme Court decision has stated that the FTC, and by implication other regulatory agencies, occupies no place in the executive branch and consequently is not subject to presidential control through the dismissal of its leadership.[17]) The activities of the regulatory commissions have become highly controversial. One of the most serious complaints against them is that they tend to become "captives" of the very groups they were established to regulate.[18] In addition, the regulatory process is often painfully slow and the qualifications of commissioners are often questionable.[19]

There are other structural forms in the federal bureaucracy that have lesser importance in national politics. One is the federal corporation, such as the Tennessee Valley Authority (TVA) or the Federal Deposit Insurance Corporation (FDIC). The basic organizational notion behind them is that an agency which markets a product or service can be run by methods similar to those used in the private sector. Federal corporations can utilize private business techniques and may have a readily available yardstick (such as surplus revenue) for evaluating their output. Unlike other federal agencies, they can generate their own revenue and need not rely entirely upon an annual budget appropriation. However, corporate organization is no guarantee of success—as is shown most vividly by the Postal Service.[20] Other structural forms on the federal level include foundations, institutions, and institutes.

All this may seem confusing, but we have just begun to scratch the surface of organizational entities involved in federal bureaucratic politics. Political pluralism breeds organizational units. There are hundreds of interagency boards, councils, and committees. Some were founded by statute, others by executive order. Their purpose is to coordinate the activities of different departments and agencies, and they deal with most of the substantive policy areas of concern to the government. There are also statutory advisory bodies, made up primarily of citizens who can lend their expertise and perspectives to various policy areas. Federal bureaucratic organizations can also create advisory committees to supply them with the viewpoints of their clientele, and apparently they now have about a thousand of them. Furthermore, there are joint executive-congressional commissions, intergovernmental organizations, and what Harold Seidman refers to as the "twilight zone" of federal administration: semipublic, semiprivate organizations such as the Federal Reserve Banks.[21]

The legal, political, and administrative differences and nuances associated with these organizational forms require extensive study to be understood clearly. One lesson is that "the" bureaucracy, rather than being a coherent, well-coordinated branch of government, is pluralism incarnate. A dozen or more agencies may be involved in a single policy area such as education or health.[22] Different units are always pulling and tugging in different directions in response to different pressures. Rule by bureaucracy in this system need not be totalitarian; it might even be responsive to a multitude of competing interests. However, the very structure of the bureaucracy also hinders control and coordination by the political authorities at the top.

BUREAUCRATIC AUTONOMY

By its nature a bureaucracy has considerable autonomy. Expertise, specialization, information, discretion, and the established routines associated with bureaucracy reduce the potential for outside control and direction. As noted in Chapter 2, there is a "Law" of Countercontrol and a growing gap between formal authority and the actual ability to achieve desired results. And with respect to the federal bureaucracy, it happens that the Constitution itself ensures a high degree of autonomy.

Because the founders never envisioned a bureaucratic government, the place of the federal bureaucracy in the constitutional scheme is ambiguous. Indeed, there are only a few clauses in the entire document dealing with public administration. One of these allows the president to require the written opinion of the principal officers of the executive departments on subjects under their jurisdiction. Another is more complex: Article II, Section 2, reads in part that the president

> by and with the Advice and Consent of the Senate, shall appoint Ambassadors, other public Ministers and Consuls, Judges of the supreme Court, and all other Officers of the United States, whose Appointments are not herein otherwise provided for, and which shall be established by Law: but the Congress may by Law vest the Appointment of such inferior Officers, as they think proper, in the President alone, in the Courts of Law, or in the Heads of Departments.

This provision gives Congress a great deal of formal authority over the executive-branch bureaucracy. Since administrative positions must be established by law, the Constitution grants Congress the power to establish departments, agencies, and other institutional forms, to organize them as it deems appropriate, and to decide on the number of employees to staff them. In addition, it can establish their missions, or purposes. Because Congress can specify whether the president, the courts, or the department heads will appoint inferior officers, it has the authority to specify the qualifications and method of recruitment and selection of these appointments largely as it sees fit. Hence the Constitution gives Congress the opportunity to play the major role in federal personnel administration. The need for senatorial advice and consent in the appointment of department heads also gives that body a good deal of leverage over the top levels of the bureaucracy. In addition, Congress authorizes funding for bureaucratic agencies, personnel, and programs.

The founders' rationale for these provisions is clear: they feared executive power and sought to check it by placing limitations on the president's ability to control the executive branch or to turn it into a forceful administrative apparatus. In addition, at a relatively early date the Supreme Court declared:

> It would be an alarming doctrine that Congress cannot impose upon any executive officer any duty they may think proper, which is not repugnant to any rights secured and protected by the Constitution; and in such cases, the duty and responsibility grow out of and are subject to the control of law and not to the direction of the President.[23]

Under this line of reasoning, Congress can give direct orders to executive officers. In a legal sense, the bureaucracy is largely a creature of Congress.

Simultaneously, however, the Constitution places the bureaucracy under the direction of the president. Article II provides: "The executive Power shall be vested in a President of the United States of America," who "shall take Care that the Laws be faithfully executed." Congress and the courts have cleared up one constitutional ambiguity in favor of presidential control of administration by allowing the president to dismiss, without senatorial consent, any of his appointments in the executive branch who do not hold fixed terms. Nevertheless, in their effort to place a congressional check on the president and a presidential check on Congress, the founders allowed bureaucratic power largely to slip away.

THE PRESIDENT AND THE BUREAUCRACY

The constitutional ambiguity surrounding the bureaucracy requires presidential and congressional agreement and coordination to gain some control over administrative affairs. But given the competing interests of these governmental branches, agreement and coordination are not always possible. Congress and the president are elected by different constituencies and attuned to different sets of demands. The committee and seniority systems in the legislature exacerbate this situation. For even when the president and the majority of Congress are members of the same political party, committee chairmen may be at odds with the president. The bureaucrat who reaches a high level in an agency is likely to have the political savvy to exploit these differences. Congress, congressional committees, and the president can be played off against one another. And in the many cases where an agency has established strong ties with "its" congressional committee or subcommittee, it may be virtually immune to presidential interference.

Presidential outreach into the bureaucracy is limited. The Executive Office of the President (EOP) provides an institutional tool for grappling with the bureaucracy, but as discussed in Chapter 4, it is a tool with serious limitations. By its nature the EOP is limited because it is outside the mainstream of politics in the federal bureaucracy. Being superimposed upon the bureaucracy, the EOP is unable to become involved in its day-to-day work. Like the president, it tends to rely upon policy proposals from bureaucratic agencies. Moreover, since the presidential term is relatively short, top-level bureaucrats who may have taken twenty or twenty-five years to reach their positions tend to have time and organizational perspective on their side.[24] The EOP is far from inconsequential, but its influence is limited. This leaves the president's appointments to bureaucratic agencies as his major means of directing and controlling the bureaucracy.

The number of presidential appointments varies from agency to agency, but the total is approximately 3,800.[25] In the departments, appointees include the secretary, one or more undersecretaries, and the assistant secretaries. Many of these top jobs are obviously difficult if not impossible to perform well. For several reasons, the official's grasp on the agency is often tenuous. First, influencing people in a bureaucratic setting generally requires some degree of control over their jobs. But under the federal merit system, which in one way or another covers about 90 percent of all federal bureaucrats, dismissals become complex legal matters. So do demotions and other adverse actions. Even transfers may be difficult. Moreover, under judicial doctrines which first emerged during the 1960s, public employees have a good chance of winning a case where their dismissal somehow infringes upon their constitutional rights as citizens.[26] If a secretary wants to take an adverse action against a subordinate, chances are it can be done—but often only after large amounts of time and inordinate effort. In any event, once an official is removed, the merit system restricts the secretary's freedom to place his or her own personal choice in the position. Therefore little in the way of greater control may be gained.

The Civil Service Reform Act of 1978, which President Carter called the "centerpiece" of his reorganizational effort, may alleviate this situation to an extent. The act is complex and brings about many fundamental changes in federal personnel administration. Among its major features are the creation of a Senior Executive Service (SES) at the top of the general career service and providing agency heads with greater authority over these employees. For instance, while some checks exist, executives can be dismissed from the SES (but not the federal service) without a formal hearing. In addition, the act established a merit pay system in an effort to give political executives more leverage over employees in the three levels immediately below the SES.[27]

The second reason why even secretaries have little control over their departments is that virtually everyone who makes it to the top of the career system in an agency has a wide network of supporters. These supporters are found not only within the agency but also among client groups, other agencies, and often on congressional committees.[28] An executive who does battle with such people inspires fear and resistance, rarely obtains cooperation, and may provoke hostility in Congress.

Third, the secretary, whatever his or her area of expertise, will generally have only limited knowledge of departmental operations. In some political systems, such as Great Britain's, "shadow governments" exist to deal with this problem. There the political party out of power designates certain people to be minister or secretary of the various bureaucratic units, should the party gain power. From this position the shadow executives are able to study and keep track of departmental developments. They are therefore relatively well prepared for the jobs they may receive if their party wins the next election.[29] In the United States, however, department heads are generally brought into jobs with little preparation. While they may have expertise in a policy area, they are rarely familiar with their department or with all aspects of its mission. By conservative estimates it takes new department heads about six months to firmly grasp what is going on and about a year before they can begin to have a major impact. But from Roosevelt's New Deal to Kennedy's New Frontier, the median tenure of a department secretary was about forty months.[30] Under Nixon the median dropped to about eighteen months. This leaves very little time for an appointed official to accomplish anything.

Fourth, there is a built-in duality to a secretary's position. On the one hand, he or she is an arm of the president, and loyalty to him may be demanded. On the other, the department head is the leader of a bureaucratic organization and must do at least some of its bidding in order to win its cooperation. The individual thus becomes a kind of go-between for both the department and the president. But as such, the secretary does not have the full support and trust of either.[31] In departments such as Agriculture and Interior, which have strong, organized constituencies, the situation is complicated by the secretary's need to win their approval as well.

Finally, the secretary's ability to manage a department has been undercut by the EOP itself. As a former undersecretary of commerce put it,

"Although legally the appointee of and answerable to the President, it is now generally conceded that the typical cabinet officer's immediate supervisor is one or more members of the White House staff."[32] This reduces access of secretaries to the president and weakens their political effectiveness. It may also limit their ability to create the image of independence and forcefulness that is necessary to gain the support of their departments and clientele groups.

Undersecretaries and assistant secretaries face many of the same difficulties. Their loyalties are divided, their competence limited. Perhaps most important, their average tenure is even shorter than that of the secretary.[33] Moreover, they lack the aura of authority that surrounds their boss. The limitations of political executive positions are expressed in the words of those who have occupied them. A former undersecretary of commerce has written:

> In a real sense, delegation of authority to the operating manager of an entirely unfamiliar field means that the Secretary serves the bureau chiefs [career bureaucrats managing bureaus] rather than vice versa.
>
> The White House attitude is often bafflingly ambivalent. Thus, the staffer who is charged with relaying his own or the President's instructions to a cabinet officer usually expects unquestioning obedience. On the other hand, the President, when and if he has occasion to call on the Secretary to help, often expects him to enjoy at least the public image of independence.
>
> [The Secretary's] judgment on budget items is, of course, the most important decision he will make in his term in office and is the decision he is usually least well-equipped to make intelligently.
>
> The traditional answer of the busy executive to excessive workload—delegation of authority—is often a high-risk business in a political organization.[34]

Research on assistant secretaries has revealed many of the same difficulties and frustrations. Several have complained that the workloads required more than eighty hours a week and that "the responsibilities of that job were almost beyond human management."[35] Others found bureaucratic politics difficult: "Perhaps the hardest thing for a businessman accustomed to making decisions to adjust to in government life is the situation in which so many people have a *legitimate* right to be heard in making a decision. There are so many implications touching various departments. Representatives of all these sectors—both in government and out—demand, with right, to be heard."[36] Perhaps these words sum it up best: "An assistant secretary is all shot to pieces after two years and might as well get out."[37] From the White House perspective, on the other hand, one EOP staffer said: "After six to twelve months even the political appointees in the departments get captured and taken in by the agencies."[38]

It is important to stress that presidential appointees may become frustrated with the bureaucracy even when the bureaucrats and congressional committees are not trying to make things difficult. The pace of doing business is largely determined by the organization, not the individual who occupies its top position. Taking any action that is opposed by the career bureaucrats is difficult (or even impossible, as some case studies have shown), and setting the pace is often simply out of the question. Remember the Law of Increasing Conservatism from Chapter 2. Whether the Carter Civil Service Reform Act of 1978 will do much to alleviate this condition remains to be seen. Since it is based on the notion that bureaucrats' power comes from their protected tenure, it may underestimate the extent to which their authority is generated by their specialized expertise.[39]

CONGRESS AND THE BUREAUCRACY

The federal bureaucracy is relatively independent of presidential control. Traditionalists might argue that it is more subject to congressional influence through the process of "legislative oversight," that is, congressional supervision and investigation. The legal basis and general techniques of such oversight are clear, but Congress's legal authority is often confused with the actual relationship between the legislature and the bureaucracy.

Congress's formal authority for oversight has several bases. The Legislative Reorganization Act of 1946 provided that each committee should exercise "continuous watchfulness" over the activities of those units of the bureaucracy acting within its subject-matter jurisdiction. This was repeated in a similar act of 1970: "Each standing committee shall review and study, on a continuing basis, the application, administration, and execution of those laws, or parts of laws, the subject matter of which is within the jurisdiction of that committee."[40] Congress has also enacted several measures giving it a veto on administrative actions. Explicit or tacit committee approval, either in advance or shortly after the fact, is often required for administrative regulations and activities. Moreover, Congress has power over the budgets of various agencies (the appropriations and budget committees have been especially important in this respect), over the procedures by which agencies arrive at decisions, and over their organization. Congress can also investigate administrative operations. In addition, it has some influence in selecting the personnel who head administrative agencies, but as discussed above, this hardly gives Congress much control. Of course, the most effective way of ensuring congressional control over the bureaucracy would be to avoid vast delegations of power with vague standards such as "serving the public interest." It is the unwillingness or inability of Congress to provide statutory direction to bureaucrats that makes subsequent oversight so desirable.

In theory, congressional power over administrative agencies appears formidable. But unless congressmen see some compelling relationship between oversight and reelection, they may have little incentive to become involved in a forceful and systematic way. Time is limited, "case work" is heavy, and even routine oversight requires a vast amount of effort. Not surprisingly, oversight is a congressional function that has become heavily bureaucratized. Indeed, two congressional bureaucracies, the General Accounting Office and the Congressional Budget Office, exist largely for this purpose. In addition, the regular committee staff plays a substantial role in the oversight process. Thus even if Congress as an institution were able to control the bureaucracy through oversight, its power would be exercised largely through nonelected staffs.

But by almost all accounts, oversight suffers from worse problems than these. For example, studies suggest that congressional committee members tend to equate oversight with service for their own constituencies rather than for the public interest or on behalf of some constitutional mandate.[41] The technical nature of the work also limits their interest in oversight. But most important, congressmen have little incentive to supervise agencies where doing so might jeopardize their relationship with the agency and its clientele. Given the piecemeal nature of any oversight carried out by committees and subcommittees rather than by Congress as a whole,[42] it is likely that congressmen will sacrifice this aspect of the legislative process to the development of mutually supportive relationships. These are variously called "subgovernments" or "cozy triangles," which consist of a (sub) committee, an agency, and an interest group.[43]

The oversight by congressmen, the functioning of agencies, and the interests of client groups are often interrelated. These structures, and frequently the same individuals within them, interact over a period of years. Eventually they view problems and options from similar or identical perspectives. Having developed a vested interest in what has already taken place, they become mutually supportive in planning for the future. Differences may remain, but consensus becomes increasingly characteristic of their relationships. Perhaps the best-publicized example is the cozy triangle formed by the Department of Defense, the congressional armed services committees, and defense contractors. All want bigger expenditures on defense, new and bigger weapons systems. Similar arrangements can be found in areas as diverse as agriculture and federal personnel policy.

Although triangles exist, they are not necessarily equilateral. Often the relationship between congressional committee and agency is turned upside down and the committee ends by doing the bidding of the agency. An extreme example is the heavy criticism recently directed at congressional committees for failing to oversee forcefully the FBI and the CIA.[44] And for years far from the public limelight, the Civil Service Commission dominated the House Committee on Post Office and Civil Service.[45]

Perhaps the views of high-level administrators about the weaknesses of legislative oversight are a more telling indicator:

> The bureaucrat has a program to carry out that he believes in. The question of whether or not Congress has authorized it is not so important to him. . . . I never heard a respectful word spoken about Congress at one of [the department meetings].
>
> The real hard fact about life on the hill [Congress] is that very few times does Congress, acting together and well-informed, pass the laws. . . . You [an administrative official] go up there and explain to the subject-matter committee how these things work and why.
>
> They're a pretty dumb bunch. They have to voice an opinion about something they know nothing about. . . . I can't think of a more unhappy fate for me than to be put in the position of a congressman. . . . On the other hand, most people in administrative jobs are there because they are trained for the job; they are employed in the field they are qualified for.[46]

In essence, Congress has the potential tools, but generally neither the incentive nor the expertise to supervise the federal bureaucracy. By necessity, oversight tends to concentrate on details; it misses the broader perspective. A congressman's information about an agency is likely to come from the agency itself, as filtered through the congressional staff. Unless constituents' votes are at stake, the average member of Congress is not likely to be intensely interested in oversight. For those with long seniority on a subcommittee, the probability is that they have developed a mutually supportive relationship with the agency. Consequently, legislative oversight generally does not result in real control over agencies.

To be effective, oversight requires the following conditions:

1. The committee chairman must be devoted to "serving" other members of his committee, rather than imposing his own views upon it.
2. There must exist a relatively high level of subcommittee autonomy within the committee.
3. There must be a sufficient and aggressive committee staff.
4. The committee must consist of experienced and committed members.
5. The committee must be oriented toward oversight rather than new legislation.[47]

However, "Since few committees meet all of these conditions very often or for long periods of time the relative paucity of systematic oversight is easy to understand and explain."[48] Furthermore, Congress is highly dependent upon its staff and bureaucratic units to carry out oversight activities (see Chapter 5).[49]

THE JUDICIARY AND THE BUREAUCRACY

Another challenge to bureaucratic autonomy is the rulings of the judiciary. But whatever action the courts may have taken before the Second World War, since that time judicial impact upon the operation and decisions of federal administrative agencies has been minimal. Martin Shapiro, who conducted a definitive investigation of the matter, concluded: "At least during the last twenty years the federal court system has devoted the vast bulk of its energies to simply giving legal approval to agency decisions."[50] Courts typically provide agencies with wide discretion. They greatly defer to the judgment and expertise of administrators. Moreover, "Judicial review of administrative decision making is . . . marginal in the sense that, at least in the current Washington situation, policy differences are unlikely to arise in most of the instances in which review is theoretically possible."[51] Furthermore, when a court makes a policy decision, it faces the same set of actors, information, and arguments that the administrative agency has already faced. Shapiro observes:

> Thus in most instances where judicial review of administrative decisions is theoretically available, the Supreme Court will not review at all, for there is no general reason for a second government agency to make again a decision already made by another. Where special reasons do exist, the Court, having gone through the process of decision making again, is quite likely to arrive at roughly the same decision as the agency has. Even when it cannot agree with the agency, its difference of position is likely to be expressed in something other than a clear-cut no.[52]

The judiciary may set some of the outer boundaries of administrative power, especially in a procedural sense, but it hardly places a forceful constraint upon the formulation of public policy by public bureaucracies.

CLIENTELE GROUPS AND THE BUREAUCRACY

It has been forcefully argued that agencies become "captured" or heavily influenced by interest groups and so lose their autonomy to nongovernmental bodies.[53] To the extent that this is true, it is clear that bureaucratic agencies are not directed by elected public officials.

Certainly bureaucratic agencies are often influenced by their client groups. The same groups also have a powerful voice in the relevant congressional committees and subcommittees. They are the third side of the "cozy triangle." In cases where the participants are in harmony, the interest group may gain a de facto veto over the top political appointments to administrative agencies. This is characteristic of the regulatory commissions. When interest groups oppose appointments, they make it known to the president and members of the Senate whose approval is necessary. Just the thought of a long struggle over an appointment is sometimes enough to cause the president and the potential candidate to reconsider. In the extreme case, as has sometimes happened with the Interstate Commerce Commission, the agency becomes an adjunct of the economic interest it was originally established to regulate.

There are two major problems with the "capture" view of agencies: (1) Even those who are convinced that capture is widespread admit that it is impossible to say how extensive the process is.[54] (2) It tends to suggest that the agency is or should be resistant to takeover. But agencies seek survival, and if gaining the support of a powerful interest group is a way of guaranteeing it, then the inclination is not to resist. The same logic holds for members of Congress seeking electoral support. This is the crux of the development of subgovernments. While roles differ and interests may be somewhat divergent, the prevailing condition is one of consensus. Where interests are almost fully parallel, who captures whom is a moot point.

In summary, presidential control of the bureaucracy through the appointment power has been very limited. Secretaries, undersecretaries, and assistant secretaries simply do not have the political clout to dominate their agencies, although the 1978 Civil Service Reform Act may improve their position. Indeed, their agencies often dominate them. Even where political executives do have a degree of control, there is no guarantee that their loyalty will be to the president. Congressional oversight procedures are also seriously limited when it comes to exercising control over bureaucratic activities. There is often no incentive for oversight. Sufficient expertise is hard to come by. Oversight is often piecemeal and generally confined to details. Most important, the oversight power is now concentrated in congressional staffs rather than in congressmen. Nor does the politically appointed judiciary offer much of a check on the ordinary policymaking activities of administrative agencies. In combination, all three of these traditional mechanisms do place constraints upon bureaucratic power. Bureaucracies are not free to do whatever they please; there is recourse in the political system. However, the initiative and impetus are on the side of the agencies. Checking them requires concerted efforts elsewhere, and even these may be unsuccessful. The autonomy of the federal bureaucracy relative to the other branches of government is a fact.

BUREAUCRATIC POWER AND BUREAUCRATIC POLITICS

Bureaucratic autonomy was influenced but not created by the Constitution. It was not established from the outset, but developed as government penetrated more and more areas of society. Today the scope of bureaucratic power is truly astounding. Indeed, it is so pervasive that there is no fully satisfactory way of mapping it. Box 3–1 lists the major subject areas dealt with by the federal bureaucracy.

The power wielded by individual bureaucrats and even whole agencies may be modest or inconsequential. This is a paradox of bureaucracy, especailly one as fragmented as the federal service. As Balzac put it, bureaucracy is "giant power wielded by pigmies."[55] Collectively, the most influential set of actors in the bureaucratic realm were the "supergrades," who were largely converted into the new Senior Executive Service in 1979. These are the bureaucrats who sit at the top of the federal service career system. They are bureau chiefs, program managers, professionals, and staffers.[56] Many of them reach their high-ranking positions only after two decades in the federal service and almost as much time in the agency which they now serve. They know their way around the agency, the bureaucracy, Congress, and to a lesser extent, the White House. They are at the very heart of the federal service. Formally charged with implementing the policies established by the political executives who "oversee" them, these 8,000 or so bureaucrats actually play a very substantial role in formulating public policy. They develop policy proposals and promote them. They argue against proposals to which they are opposed. They may modify proposals in implementing them. They are recognized as legitimate participants in the policymaking process. Indeed, it has been argued that government would come to a "standstill" if these people did only what they were told.[57]

To the extent that bureaucratic power is concentrated in individuals, it has rested in the hands of the supergrades. However, a major characteristic of the federal bureaucracy is that power is fragmented. The politics of the bureaucracy operate on at least three levels.

The level to which most attention has been paid is that of *formulating* broad public policies.[58] Here the agency is viewed as one of several central actors. In formulating policy it seeks to mobilize political support among its constituency, Congress, the president, and elsewhere in the executive branch. If necessary, it may create a constituency or organize one. This was the case with the Office of Economic Opportunity and the "war on poverty," or in an earlier age, the Department of Agriculture and the American Farm Bureau Federation. Congress and/or the president are seen

BOX 3–1

The Reach of the Federal Bureaucracy

The *U.S. Governmental Manual* indicates that bureaucratic agencies deal with the following areas of American life: Abaca production and sale; adult education; the arts; consumer affairs; historic preservation; economic growth and stability; aeronautics; age discrimination and aging (there is an Office of Aging); agriculture, including the subsidization and regulation of the production of specific crops, marketing, and farmers in general; welfare; maintenance of an air force; various Alaskan projects; alcohol; drug abuse; mental health; tobacco; firearms; aliens; allergies and infectious diseases; battle monuments; Indians; Mexicans; the blind; transportation; technology; armed forces and defense, including the procurement of manpower and weaponry; astronomy; building of dams; reclamation of land; conservation of soil; arthritis; metabolism and digestive diseases; athletics; atomic energy; automobiles; Coast Guard; aviation; banks; standards and measures; biology; birds; bituminous coal; blood; boating safety; bonds; breakfast and school lunch programs; broadcasting; business; cable television; campaign financing; census; (Center for) Short-Lived Phenomena; chemistry; child development; children; environmental quality; cities; civil defense; civil rights; coins; colleges and community development; conservation; construction; corporations; cosmetics; cost of living; cotton; crime; dairy industry; day care; the deaf; Delaware River basin; disadvantaged persons; disaster assistance; discrimination; docks; earthquakes; economic development; the economy; education; electric power; emergencies; employment; unemployment; underemployment; the handicapped; energy; engineering; equal opportunity; exports; families; highways; radiation; railroads; fertilizer; fish, wildlife; fitness; fabrics; floods; food; gas; geographic names; patents; copyrights; grain; grazing; Great Lakes; hazardous substances; health; hospitals; housing; nutrition; hydroelectric power; icebreakers; immigration; imports; insects; intergovernmental relations; international affairs; irrigation; justice; juvenile delinquency; labeling; labor; land; law enforcement; libraries; livestock; loans; mail; manpower; maps; maritime activities; mediation; medical matters; minorities; Mississippi River; Missouri basin; motor vehicles; narcotics; outer space; national parks; water quality; national forests; naval matters; occupational health and safety; oceans; oil; minority business; outdoor recreation; passports; plants; police; pollution; postal service; power; prices; rat control; reading; refugees; rents; retirement; rivers; rubber; rural areas; safety; savings; scholarships; schools; science; screw threads; securities; small business; social security; subversive activities; sugar; tariffs and taxes; Tennessee Valley; textiles; trade; trademarks; veterans; visual disorders; vocational affairs; wages; war; water; waterways; weather; women; youth.

as playing a critical role by umpiring conflicts among agencies. No doubt this model does characterize some aspects of politics in the federal bureaucracy. However, issues at the policy level tend to be broad and generalized. They involve the articulation by elected political authorities of the aspirations and perspectives of the public. Moreover, it should be stressed that it is the agencies, or possibly their constituencies, that do much of the initiating even in these circumstances. More important, what is accepted at the level of broad policy pronouncement may be modified at another level of politics within the federal bureaucracy.

A second level involves matters primarily within the jurisdiction of one or a few agencies. Issues are likely to be relatively narrow, although their implications may be broad. They often involve the *application* of a policy or statute. For example, an issue at this level would not be whether to create an equal opportunity program, but how affirmative action is to be defined and applied. If only one agency is involved, it consults with interested parties (some of whom may be represented by advisory committees), congressional committees, and other agencies. It then formulates and circulates a written description of its intention or proposed rules. After receiving feedback, it may modify them. Then it issues its final directive, which may be published in the *Federal Register* (a compilation of executive branch regulations and related materials). Typically, consensus building of this type takes place over a long period of time. Notice that the agency itself is both initiator and judge of the matter under consideration. It is in control of the process.

Where other agencies also have jurisdiction, the process of deciding an issue involving policy application is similar but requires negotiation of an agreement among them. If this cannot be reached, the issue may be shifted upward to the broader level of bureaucratic politics and fought out before the legislature, presidency, or judiciary. On the other hand, if the issue is not perceived as critical, it may be dropped or handled in divergent ways by the agencies involved. It is at this level that the structural complexity of the bureaucracy becomes crucial. Advisory committees and interagency committees play major roles. While less glamorous than the level where broad national policies are formulated, the level of application can be even more important in terms of the government's nonsymbolic functions. It is also the heart of bureaucratic politics, for "touching base" and responding to other base touchers is the daily routine of the high-ranking bureaucrat. This is why consolidative, reactive agencies are nevertheless almost always in motion: the system is "chain-reacting."[59]

A third level of bureaucratic politics concerns the *implementation* of policy. Although it was once widely agreed that this is "administration," and that administration is by definition apolitical,[60] today it is generally accepted that politics can be involved in the implementation phase.[61] The aphorism "There's no Republican way to pave a street" ignores the patronage or general support that can be mustered by choosing one street or one way to pave it instead of another. Policies, legislative intent, presidential directives, and orders of the political executives are modified on a daily basis by the agencies engaged in implementing them. At times a policy may be somehow inappropriate to an agency's organization and culture. At other times the agency's decision makers find the policy threatening to their own interests or those of the agency. In such cases a strategy for implementation will be adopted not with the objective of maximizing the policy objectives, but rather of reducing the damage done to the agency. According to one study, for example, the Civil Service Commission's application of affirmative action in the federal service was an instance of an agency adopting an administrative strategy designed to ensure failure in attaining the policy's goals.[62]

At each of these levels of bureaucratic politics there are disparities of power among the various agencies. Elements which affect agencies' power include:[63]

- Autonomy within the Executive Branch Autonomy is particularly desirable for agencies engaged in distributive policy, such as building roads and dams.[64] This is because traditional "pork-barrel" politics are intense at the local level, to which Congress is most attuned. On the other hand, where the issue relates to the president's national constituency, which may include the relatively powerless segments of society, a close relationship to presidential power is desirable. This policy area often involves redistributive issues, in which "haves" confront "have nots."[65] Here it is useful for the agency to claim that it is carrying out the "people's mandate" to the president.
- Relationship with Congress The most powerful agencies have a close working relationship with "their" congressional committees. If the agency can make Congress its constituency, as the Army Corps of Engineers has done, it will be extremely powerful.[66] A hostile relationship with Congress will weaken an agency unless it has strong support from its clientele or the presidential establishment. It is especially important for agencies administering distributive policies to avoid congressional wrath.
- Constituencies Agencies with organized and influential constituencies tend to be powerful. Those that cannot mobilize their clientele are more vulnerable to legislative power.
- Economic Interests Served Powerful agencies tend to serve a number of strong economic interests, even within one sector such as agriculture. This provides them with a wide base of support at the same time

that it enables them to play one group off against another and so retain freedom of action.

- CENTRALIZATION/DECENTRALIZATION Decentralization—geographic dispersal of agency authority—increases the power of an agency whose relationships with its clientele are of major importance.
- EXPERTISE This is crucial to any agency's effort to achieve a powerful position. In general, technical expertise insulates agencies from political authorities who attempt to control them.
- ORGANIZATIONAL INTANGIBLES Less concrete determinants of an agency's power include the quality of its leadership and the nature of its ideology, morale, staff, and mission. Factors like these can be vital in the world of bureaucratic politics.

In short, although the bureaucracy is largely autonomous, each agency is not equally so. This is because the major check on federal bureaucratic power in the United States comes from the bureaucracy's fragmentation. Bureaucratic politics places a premium on consensus within the bureaucracy, but agreement requires compromise, and the need for compromise is an important limitation on the power of individual agencies. This structural check on bureaucratic power is a direct outgrowth of the organization of the bureaucracy itself. James Madison's argument in *Federalist Paper No. 10* that faction could be pitted against faction has considerable validity in federal bureaucratic politics. Moreover, another structural check on the bureaucracy comes from the nature of its personnel.

A REPRESENTATIVE BUREAUCRACY

In terms of structures and missions, the federal bureaucracy obviously reflects most major, and a good many minor, economic and social interests in the United States. The very names of some units—departments of Labor, Agriculture, Commerce, and Health, Education, and Welfare—exhibit the country's concerns. Given the nature of bureaucratic politics, many of these interests are actually also represented in a policy sense as well.[67] Despite the protests of businesses and others against "government intervention and interference," many economic interests have actually sought representation in the bureaucracy. In fact, some could not possibly survive as currently constituted without it.

The major shortcomings in this representational scheme are that (1) not every interest is represented, (2) differences in agency (and constituency) power deprive some groups of equal representation, and (3) there is no guarantee that the wider public interest can be served by parceling it up into small segments to be represented by individual agencies.[68] The first two limitations, while important, are not as fundamental as the third. They are also far more subject to change through structural tinkering.

The third limitation—that fragmentation may not serve the general public interest—raises the broader question of the values and attitudes of bureaucrats. Bureaucracy is an impersonal structure, and the activity of individual bureaucrats is constrained by its hierarchy, formalism, and specialization. Yet several studies have shown that dehumanization is not complete,[69] and it has been argued that collectively, the social and attitudinal representation provided by a public bureaucracy is of crucial importance. As Samuel Krislov put it, "Who writes the [bureaucratic] directive—his or her style, values, concept of role—is as significant as who gets to be president, congressman, senator, member of parliament, or cabinet member."[70] Although some have contested the possibility of a link between one's social background and *attitudes* after attaining high rank and accruing long seniority in a public bureaucracy, the existence of such a connection with regard to issues of high salience to a social group is now established.[71]

Socially, as Table 3–4 suggests, the federal bureaucracy *as a whole* is

TABLE 3–4

Social Representativeness of the Federal Service

GROUP	YEAR	PERCENTAGE IN U.S. POPULATION	PERCENTAGE IN FEDERAL SERVICE*
Blacks	1975	11.1	12.6
Hispanics	1975	4.5	2.5
American Indians	1975	0.4	1.1
Orientals	1975	0.5	0.9
Women	1974	35.0†	41.8
Middle class	1959	60.0	81.0

SOURCE: David H. Rosenbloom, *Federal Equal Employment Opportunity* (New York: Praeger, 1977), pp. 7, 17; V. Subramaniam, "Representative Bureaucracy: A Reassessment," *American Political Science Review*, 61 (December 1967), 1010–1019.

* Figures are for General Schedule and equivalent grades.

† Percent in workforce.

representative of our middle-class society and of women, blacks, American Indians, and Orientals.[72] It is underrepresentative of the Hispanic population. Its representation of other ethnic groups or religious groups is unknown. However, this picture changes as one goes

TABLE 3–5

Attitudes of General Electorate and Federal Bureaucrats* Compared

ATTITUDES	PERCENTAGE WHO AGREE	
	General Electorate	Bureaucrat
1. There are times when it almost seems better for the people to take the law into their own hands rather than wait for the machinery of Government to act.	26.9	31.9
2. We might as well make up our minds that in order to make the world free, a lot of innocent people will have to suffer.	41.6	31.0
3. If congressional committees stuck strictly to the rules and gave every witness his rights, they would never succeed in exposing the many dangerous subversives they have turned up.	47.4	28.0
4. To bring about great changes for the benefit of mankind often requires cruelty and even ruthlessness.	31.3	27.0
5. The true American way of life is disappearing so fast that we may have to use force to save it.	34.6	18.6
6. A person who hides behind the laws when he is questioned about his actions doesn't deserve much consideration.	75.7	24.8
7. When the country is in great danger, we may have to force people to testify against themselves even if it violates their rights.	36.3	24.6
8. Vote for Nixon 1972	64.6	61.0
9. Republican Party identification	34.6	32.3
10. Withdraw from Vietnam	43.7	47.6
11. Trade with Communists	64.1	83.3
12. Increase taxes on high incomes	52.8	60.0
13. Legalize marijuana	23.7	31.9
14. Protect rights of the accused	43.1	50.7
15. Government should help minorities	44.1	51.4

SOURCES: James R. Beck, Jr., "Communication," *Public Administration Review,* 34 (July/August 1974), 416; K. Meier, "Representative Bureaucracy," *American Political Science Review,* 69 (June 1975), 541. Reprinted from *The Public Administration Review* © 1974 by The American Society for Public Administration, 1225 Connecticut Avenue, N.W., Washington, D.C. All rights reserved.

*Items 1–7 are for upper-level bureaucrats only.

up the hierarchy, and it is drastically different in the supergrade and SES positions. There some 96 percent of all employees are nonminority, and an even higher percentage are males.

From the perspectives of attitudes and values, however, the bureaucracy both as a whole and in its top positions appears to roughly parallel the populations'. Moreover, where there are differences, the bureaucrats appear to be more committed to the democratic principle of the rule of law than the general public is. This is evident from Table 3–5. They also appear to be somewhat more supportive of liberal policies. A major structural influence on bureaucrats' attitudes tends to be the type of agency in which they are employed. Those in defense-related units are less committed to democracy and equality than those in social welfare and other agencies.[73] In addition, it has been shown that older, more senior bureaucrats have a weaker commitment to democratic values. But research has failed to distinguish the relative importance of each of these factors.[74] Finally, it has been found that despite their nonrepresentational social character, the supergrades were a representative group in an attitudinal sense.[75] That is, they reflected the political attitudes of the general population.

These findings suggest that despite our electoral rhetoric, which rings with denunciations of public bureaucrats for their dictatorial and authoritarian outlooks, upper-level federal bureaucrats have more faith in democracy and equality, and their attitudes are more politically and socially tolerant than those of the average citizen. On policy issues federal bureaucrats tend to be somewhat more liberal than the population, but the congruence between their views and those of the average citizen is more striking than this difference. If bureaucracy is to be politically feared, then, it is for the impact of its structural characteristics upon the behavior of its personnel, not for their attitudes.

Conclusion Our Bureaucratic Future

The discussion in this chapter points in two directions. First, it shows that bureaucratic autonomy and power are pronounced. Bureaucracy has proliferated in terms of both the number of structural units and the number of personnel. It is here to stay, although its organizational characteristics may be modified. Not only has our society opted for bureaucracy as a tool for the resolution of economic, social, and political problems, but the other branches of government have relinquished much of their potential control over it. Moreover, attempts by Congress and the presidency to control the bureaucracy almost invariably lead to their own further bureaucratization.

Second, the chapter's discussion should allay some traditional fears about bureaucracy. The federal bureaucracy is characterized by fragmentation, and federal bureaucrats tend to adhere to democratic attitudes and values. Although bureaucrats are not elected, they are broadly representative of the nation's population, and so is the bureaucracy in a structural sense. In the United States, there is no federal "administrative elite" in the European tradition.

But even a politically and socially representative bureaucracy has serious shortcomings from the perspectives of humanistic and democratic values. Bureaucracy is by nature hierarchical, and this has an impact on bureaucrats and citizens alike. Bureaucratic autonomy negates accountability to elective and appointive political authorities and to the citizenry at large. A bureaucratic government may be representative, but at best it can only be democratic in spirit, never in form.

NOTES

1. See Herbert Kaufman, *Are Government Organizations Immortal?* (Washington: Brookings, 1976); and Herbert Kaufman, *Red Tape* (Washington: Brookings, 1977). For a historical analysis, see Ernest Barker, *The Development of Public Services in Western Europe* (Hamden, Conn.: Archon Books, 1966).

2. For a brief history of the federal bureaucracy, see Paul P. Van Riper, *History of the United States Civil Service* (Evanston, Ill.: Row, Peterson, 1958). A more elaborate account is presented by Leonard White in his four-volume series issued in paperback by the Free Press in 1965: *The Federalists; The Jeffersonians; The Jacksonians; The Republican Era.*

3. D. Rosenbloom, *Federal Service and the Constitution* (Ithaca, N.Y.: Cornell University Press, 1971), chap. 2.

4. See ibid., chaps. 1 and 2; and White, *Federalists* and *Jeffersonians,* for a discussion.

5. See Rosenbloom, *Federal Service,* p. 2.

6. Ibid., chap. 3.

7. See David A. Shannon, *Twentieth Century America* (Chicago:Rand McNally, 1963), part I.

8. Rosenbloom, *Federal Service,* p. 103. "Wagner's Law" holds that government bureaucracies expand in times of crisis and that subsequent retraction will not reach precrisis levels. See L. Wade and R. Curry, eds., *A Logic of Public Policy* (Belmont, Calif.: Wadsworth, 1970), pp. 75–83.

9. See Stephen Hess, *Organizing the Presidency* (Washington: Brookings, 1976), chap. 2.

10. See Harold Seidman, *Politics, Position, and Power,* 2nd ed. (New York: Oxford University Press, 1975), for a discussion (esp. chap. 1).

11. D. H. Rosenbloom and F. Bryan, "The Size of State Bureaucracies: an Exploratory Analysis," *Midwest Political Science Association Convention,* Chicago, April 1979.

12. *New York Times,* April 7, 1977, p. A17.

13. Ibid.

14. Ibid.

15. Kaufman, *Are Government Organizations Immortal*?

16. Seidman, *Politics, Position, and Power,* p. 142.

17. *Humphrey's Executor v. U.S.*, 295 U.S. 602 (1935).

18. Grant McConnell, *Private Power and American Democracy* (New York: Knopf, 1966), esp. pp. 157–165; Marver Bernstein, *Regulating Business by Independent Commission* (Princeton, N.J.: Princeton University Press, 1955); and Seidman, *Politics, Position, and Power*, pp. 248–253.

19. See *Wall Street Journal*, 184: Nos. 83, 88, 95. *New York Times*, Aug. 1, 1976, p. 1, sect. 3.

20. For a discussion of government corporations, see Seidman, *Politics, Position, and Power*, pp. 253–263.

21. Ibid., pp. 279-286. See this source generally for a description of the various structural units in the federal bureaucracy.

22. President Nixon complained bitterly of this tendency. See Richard Nathan, *The Plot that Failed* (New York: Wiley, 1975), p. 137.

23. *Kendall v. U.S..*, 12 Peters 524 (1838).

24. See Eugene B. McGregor, Jr., "Politics and the Career Mobility of Bureaucrats," *American Political Science Review*, 68 (March 1974), 18–26; and J. Corson and R. Paul, *Men Near the Top* (Baltimore: Johns Hopkins Press, 1966).

25. Hugh Heclo, *A Government of Strangers* (Washington: Brookings, 1977), p. 38.

26. Rosenbloom, *Federal Service*, and Rosenbloom, "The Public Employee in Court," in Charles Levine, ed., *Managing Human Resources: Urban Affairs Annual*, 13 (Beverly Hills, Calif.: Sage Publications, 1977), pp. 357–382.

27. Civil Service Reform Act, Public Law 95–454, 95th Congress, 47 *Law Week* 45 (November 28, 1978). See also *New York Times*, March 3, 1978, p. 1; May 10, 1978, p. A13; May 17, 1978, p. A21, for a summary of the content and politics surrounding Carter's proposals.

28. See Francis Rourke, *Bureaucracy, Politics, and Public Policy*, 2nd ed. (Boston: Little, Brown, 1976), for an extended discussion.

29. Ex-President Ford has suggested the development of a "shadow cabinet" in the United States. See *New York Times*, Jan. 16, 1977.

30. Thomas Cronin, *The State of the Presidency* (Boston: Little, Brown, 1975), p. 180. See chap. 7 for a discussion of the politics of the cabinet.

31. This problem is well described in ibid. See also J. Bartlett and D. Jones, "Managing a Cabinet Agency," *Public Administration Review*, 34 (January/February 1974), 62–70.

32. Bartlett and Jones, *Public Administration Review*, 34:63.

33. See David T. Stanley, Dean E. Mann, and Jameson W. Doig, *Men Who Govern* (Washington: Brookings Institution, 1967), esp. chap. 4. See also Dean E. Mann, *The Assistant Secretaries* (Washington: Brookings, 1965).

34. Bartlett and Jones, *Public Administration Review*, 34:63, 63, 64, 63.

35. Mann, *The Assistant Secretaries*, p. 205.

36. Ibid., p. 209.

37. Ibid., p. 210.

38. Cronin, *State of the Presidency*, p. 168.

39. See Frederick Thayer, "The President's Management 'Reforms': Theory X Triumphant," *Public Administration Review*, 38 (July/August 1978), 309–314, for a related critique.

40. Quoted in William Keefe and Morris Ogul, *The American Legislative Process*, 4th ed. (Englewood Cliffs, N.J.: Prentice-Hall, 1977), p. 391.

41. Ibid., chap. 12; Randall Ripley and Grace Franklin, *Congress, the Bureaucracy, and Public Policy* (Homewood, Ill: The Dorsey Press, 1976), esp. pp. 173–178.

42. Ibid. See also R. K. Huitt, "Congress, the Durable Partner," in E. Frank, ed., *Law Makers in a Changing World* (Englewood Cliffs, N.J.: Prentice-Hall, 1966), p. 20.

43. Ripley and Franklin, *Congress, Bureaucracy, and Policy*, esp. pp. 166–170.

44. See *New York Times*, Feb. 12, 1978, p. E3.

45. Part of the reason for this is the committee's low prestige. See Morris S. Ogul, "Congressional Oversight: Structures and Incentives," in L. Dodd and B. Oppenheimer, eds., *Congress Reconsidered* (New York: Praeger, 1977), pp. 217–218.

46. James Burnham, "Some Administrators' Unkindly View of Congress," in R. T. Golembiewski et al., eds., *Public Administration* (Chicago: Rand McNally, 1976), pp. 127–134.

47. Ripley and Franklin, *Congress, Bureaucracy, and Policy*, p. 175.

48. Ibid.

49. Keefe and Ogul, *American Legislative Process*, 4th ed., chap. 12. See also *Newsweek*, Jan. 17, 1977, p. 20, in which a knowledgeable observer claims that 99 percent of oversight is done by the staff.

50. Martin Shapiro, *The Supreme Court and Administrative Agencies* (New York: The Free Press, 1968), p. 264.

51. Ibid., p. 268.

52. Ibid., pp. 270–271.

53. McConnell, *Private Power;* Ripley and Franklin, *Congress, Bureaucracy, and Policy,* esp. pp. 119–120, and chap. 4.

54. McConnell, *Private Power*, p. 162.

55. Quoted in Martin Albrow, *Bureaucracy* (New York: Praeger, 1970), p. 18.

56. See J. Corson and R. Paul, *Men Near the Top*. Under the Civil Service Reform Act of 1978, only 10 percent of these appointments can be political.

57. Herbert J. Storing, "Political Parties and the Bureaucracy," in Robert A. Goldwin, ed., *Political Parties, U.S.A.* (Chicago: Rand McNally, 1964), p. 152.

58. Francis E. Rourke, *Bureaucracy, Politics, and Public Policy*, 3rd ed. (Boston: Little, Brown, 1969), is very much in this vein.

59. For a case study in this mold, see D. Rosenbloom, *Federal Equal Employment Opportunity* (New York: Praeger, 1977), esp. chaps. 4 and 6.

60. For example, see Frank Goodnow, *Politics and Administration* (New York: Macmillan, 1900).

61. Storing, "Political Parties and the Bureaucracy," in Goldwin, ed., *Political Parties, U.S.A.*, provides a thoughtful statement on the matter.

62. Rosenbloom, *Federal Equal Employment Opportunity*.

63. See Rourke, *Bureaucracy, Politics, and Public Policy,* 2nd ed., chap. 4, for a more extensive discussion.

64. See Ripley and Franklin, *Congress, Bureaucracy, and Policy,* chap. 4.

65. Ibid., chap. 6.

66. Ibid., pp. 79–81.

67. Norton Long, "Power and Administration," *Public Administration Review*, 9 (Autumn 1949), 257–264, provides a classic statement.

68. See McConnell, *Private Power and American Democracy*, chap. 4, for a forceful statement of the problem.

69. Seymour M. Lipset, "Bureaucracy and Social Change," in R. Merton et al., eds., *Reader in Bureaucracy* (New York: The Free Press, 1952), pp. 221–232; D. Nachmias and D. Rosenbloom, "Bureaucracy and Ethnicity," *American Journal of Sociology*, 83 (January 1978), 967–974; D. Rosenbloom and J. Featherstonhaugh, "Passive and Active Representation in the Federal Service," *Social Science Quarterly* (March 1977), pp. 873–882.

70. Samuel Krislov, *Representative Bureaucracy* (Englewood Cliffs, N.J.: Prentice-Hall, 1974), pp. 7–8.

71. See sources cited in note 69.

72. See Rosenbloom, *Federal Equal Employment Opportunity,* chap. 1, for an analysis.

73. Bob Wynia, "Federal Bureaucrats' Attitudes toward A Democratic Ideology," *Public Administration Review*, 34 (March/April 1974), 156–162.

74. Ibid.

75. K. Meier and L. Nigro, "Representative Bureaucracy and Policy Preferences," *Public Administration Review,* 36 (July/August 1976), 458–469.

4

The Bureaucratic Presidency

According to classical bureaucratic theory, the last place we would expect to find bureaucratization is in the presidency—an office occupied by one person selected at least partly on the basis of charismatic qualities. Yet this is precisely what we find happening in the United States today. A major cause of the increasing bureaucratization of the presidency is that presidential power is not commensurate with the public's expectations of the president. This is not to say that the president is powerless; rather, the presidency is becoming a structured bureaucratic organization largely in response to public demands for presidential performance.* The key to understanding the problem of the presidency is to contrast the imaginary powers of the president with the actual authority of the office.

IMAGINARY POWERS: THE IMAGE OF THE PRESIDENCY

The powers, status, importance, and capabilities attributed to the president by popular belief are truly astounding. Like Atlas, we are told, the world, or at least the *good* world, rests on his shoulders. As Daniel Patrick Moynihan once put it, "America is the hope of the world, and for that time given him, the president is the hope of America."[1] Not only does this view hold that "the President of the United States of America is, without question, the most powerful elected executive in the world," but also that his powers are increasing primarily because "the President is the literal embodiment of American mass democracy and . . . the symbol of the pervasive egalitarianism which from the beginning has characterized the emergent forces of the American democratic ideal."[2] Moreover, in this view, "There is virtually no limit to what the President can do if he does

*It may help clarify matters to suggest at the outset that those who feel the presidency is too strong and should be constrained often implicitly refer to its bureaucratic component, while those who believe it should be strengthened tend to be concerned with the constitutional and legal powers of the presidential office itself.

it for democratic ends and by democratic means."[3] Although somewhat extreme, this outlook nevertheless represents a central strand of American thought concerning the presidency.

When they are asked to name the best presidents, most people, including social scientists, select Lincoln, Washington, Franklin D. Roosevelt, Wilson, Jefferson, and Jackson. These men transformed our political system, taking action for the general welfare against forces that favored the status quo. They strengthened the office of the presidency. Furthermore, all of them were associated with wars of one kind or another. In addition, Lincoln was martyred, Roosevelt died before the victory was complete, and Wilson was destroyed by his struggle for a better world. Even social scientists who take a psychobiographical approach have lent some support to this model. They stress the desirability of a president who feels positive "affect" (positive emotions) toward himself and the office, and who takes an activist role.[4]

Thomas Cronin, a forceful critic of traditional concepts concerning the presidency, has distilled four central propositions from the wealth of literature which constitutes the "textbook" presidency.

1. The president is *the* strategic catalyst for progress in the American political system and the central figure in the international system as well.
2. Only the president can be the genuine architect of U.S. public policy, and only he, by attacking problems frontally and aggressively and by interpreting his power expansively, can slay the dragons of crisis and be the engine of change to move this nation forward.
3. The president must be the nation's personal and moral leader; by symbolizing the past and future greatness of America and radiating inspirational confidence, a president can pull the nation together while directing its people toward fulfillment of the American Dream.
4. If, and only if, the right person is placed in the White House, all will be well; and, somehow, whoever is in the White House is the best person for the job—at least for a year or so.[5]

In short, the president is the moral and political savior of the nation, its people, and ultimately the world. He can right wrongs, keep the country strong, reduce crime, increase employment, reduce inflation, manage urban, energy, and social problems, and serve as a role model for the citizenry. Indeed, at an early age children develop a positive affect toward the president as a "benevolent leader."[6]

From the perspective of the late 1970s, the "textbook" model is somewhat tarnished. Presidents Johnson, Nixon, and Ford lost the support of the people, and even the optimistic Carter has found the office full of frustrations. Yet the "textbook" presidency should not be counted out, for it has important structural props which will not go away as quickly as unpopular presidents do. Moreover, there is a self-fulfilling dynamic to the textbook presidency.

One of the structural sources of the textbook presidency is constitutional in nature.[7] The founding fathers had few clear expectations when they designed the constitutional aspects of the presidency. James Wilson, generally considered the moving force behind Article II (executive power), called the presidency the most difficult part of the constitutional system to create. Some of the founders' basic notions were clear, but beyond them the presidency was a set of compromises. The founders greatly feared executive power, but they favored an independent executive who would be forceful enough to resist the legislature. Accordingly they rejected both popular election and legislative appointment of the president. Eventually they settled upon the electoral college system which, although modified, is still in use. Some of the founders wanted a plural executive, but others felt that only a single person could supply the energy, speed, and responsibility necessary for effective action. Another controversial question was the length of the president's term in office.

The founders' perplexity over the executive office is indicated by the many votes they took on it and their delay in arriving at final decisions. There were twelve votes on how to choose the president and five on the term of office. A number of the important provisions were not adopted until the final weeks of the Philadelphia Convention. Perhaps Alexander Hamilton described the problem of the presidency best, for both his time and ours, when he said, "As to the Executive, it seemed to be admitted that no good one could be established on Republican principles."[8]

The founders' incoherent approach to the presidency led to several structural ambiguities. These in turn contribute to the great expectations Americans have of their presidents, but also to the presidents' inability to fulfill them. One way of looking at the presidency is to consider it as a set of specialized roles, some of which are only partially compatible. For example, the president must act as chief of state, commander-in-chief of the armed forces, chief legislator, chief diplomat, manager of the economy, head of the government, and party leader. Later in the chapter we will look at some of the president's powers connected with these roles. The main point here is that being chief of state, head of the government, and party leader creates inevitable role conflicts. Party leaders are partisan actors; chiefs of state must be above party politics. The head of the government has the responsibility for developing and implementing policy, but the chief of state is supposed to be an ideal representative of the nation who is not associated with transitory policy matters. (The relationship of these two roles is not unlike that between the Constitution and the laws.

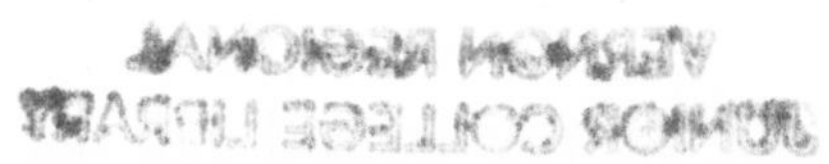

One is a lasting framework, while the other adapts the system to the needs of the times.) Where distinctions become blurred, one or another of the president's roles suffers. Moreover, the limitations inherent in different roles are often not appreciated by the public. People tend to ask why, if the president is the most powerful person in the world as commander-in-chief, he can't solve economic problems at home. Or why, if he is the leader of his political party, he can't deal more effectively with Congress when it is dominated by his party. The founders' lack of a clear idea of the presidency left the nation with an ever-changing, ambiguous office at the center of its political life.

The ambiguity of presidential roles contributes to the textbook presidency by suggesting that the president has more responsibility and therefore more power than is actually the case. The "cult" of the presidency exacerbates this problem. The presidency has become *personalized*, that is, the media and the public tend to view the office and the men who occupy it as a single entity. Cronin quotes one of the post-New Deal textbooks that have helped to create the personalized textbook presidency:

> The President's values, his qualities of character and intellect, his capacity for leadership, his political skills, his definition of his own role, and the way he performs it—*these are fundamental determinants* of the working of the American government and of American politics.[9]

A wealth of literature produced in recent years dwells on presidents' personalities, public decisions, and personal lives. Whether the story deals with missile crises or the presidents' daughters' love lives and lemonade sales, the consequence is to put the spotlight on the president as public celebrity number one. These accounts are often written by those who are a part of the presidency or the "presidential press." More often than not, at least during the early days of a presidency, such people have far more to gain than lose by being more than sympathetic to the president. As occurred during the Nixon presidency, they may even come to feel that the well-being of the president and a favorable public image of him are an all-important aspect of national security.

The personalization of the presidency creates a gap between the president's public image and the man himself. While the press may make the image worse than the reality, generally the process works the other way around, at least in the early stages of an administration. Presidents are portrayed as heroic figures. Again, however, expectations rise to such a height that they are inevitably disappointed. The resulting disillusionment is more of a problem for the nation and the president than for those who bask in his image and contribute to it.

The textbook president and the cult of the president are not simply

grist for the media; they create a dynamic of their own. The gap between expectations and capabilities places barriers in the way of rational politics. At the broadest level, "What the nation has been beguiled into believing ever since 1960 is surely the politics of evangelism: the faith that individual men are cast to be messiahs, the conviction that Presidential incantations can be substituted for concrete programs, the belief that what matters is not so much the state of the nation as the inspiration-quotient of its people."[10] This is the essence of style over substance, with which every American should now be familiar. Style is the primary characteristic of presidential campaigns, but it does not stop there. Since popularity is an ingredient in presidential power, imagery moves into the White House. As actual performance falls short of expectations, presidents inevitably claim more credit for their deeds, try to cast them in the best light, begin to avoid the press, and attempt to manage the news.

A good example of this tendency occurred in 1978. With his popularity declining precipitously, President Carter appointed Gerald Rafshoon, the advertising executive and public relations expert who had been a key figure in Carter's election campaign, to the White House staff. Rafshoon saw his role as "developing the themes of the Presidency and getting them out."[11] But in commenting on the appointment, Tom Wicker of the *New York Times* sensibly observed that Carter's "political deficiencies, errors and failures are a far more fundamental kind of politics than the imagery and media politics Mr. Carter and Mr. Rafshoon produced so successfully in [the election campaign of] 1976."[12]

In the worst instances of "media politics," a president who is mired in unsolvable problems describes himself as seeing "light at the end of the tunnel" and speaks of a national military defeat as "peace with honor." When failure becomes too obvious to deny, the typical presidential response is to redouble efforts at creating the right kind of image. The net result may be that the public does not trust the personalized president and he becomes a national albatross. As Wicker put it with reference to Carter, the "record so far suggests the danger inherent in the era of media politics. Candidates who get elected primarily by their successful use of television and imagery may not have, or may gain too slowly, the skill and experience necessary to manage the political offices they have won. And the danger is doubled when such candidates arouse expectations that cannot be met by political performance."[13]

Imagery is one way of trying to cope with the problem of the presidency. Another is to create a large and forceful presidential organization to deal not only with style but also with substance. Thus the gap between expectations and performance is a major cause of the bureaucratization of the presidency. This point will be discussed shortly, but first, what are the fundamental limitations of the presidential office?

REAL POWERS

Although presidents themselves have contributed to the cult of the presidency, in more candid moments many have spoken of the frustrations and limitations of their office. None of them compares with Truman for graphic clarity: "They talk about the power of the President, they talk about how I can just push a button to get things done. Why, I spend most of my time kissing somebody's ass."[14] Indeed, many observers—even while embracing the textbook model—have argued that the president's powers are too limited.

The constitutional grant of authority to the president can be divided into several areas. First there is the realm of executive power, where the founders' ambiguity has created perplexing problems. The basic debate has been over whether the Constitution grants inherent and implied powers (sometimes called "prerogative") to the president, or whether the president can exercise only those powers specifically enumerated by the Constitution. Much of the argument over inherent powers turns on Article II, Section 1: "The executive Power shall be vested in a President of the United States of America." The critical question has been whether this is a simple statement that there is to be one chief executive who will be called the president, or whether it grants something called "executive power" to the president. And if it grants executive power, what does that power consist of? The answer generally given is that the president has power to act in crisis situations.

Obviously the question of *inherent* powers is a crucial one, for if they do exist, their constitutional limits are unspecified. Consequently presidents would be entitled to do whatever they feel is necessary, as long as it is not specifically prohibited by the Constitution. In Theodore Roosevelt's words, "It was not only [the president's] right but his duty to do anything that the needs of the Nation demanded unless such action was forbidden by the Constitution or by the laws."[15] This might include the purchase of the Louisiana Territory, the invasion of foreign countries at presidential direction, the seizure of steel mills, or the commission of crimes under the pretense of national security. The great problem here is that some flexibility in executive power is clearly necessary—indeed, without it the United States might have stopped expanding at the Mississippi River—but equally important, there must be some limits.

Closely allied, and equally perplexing, is the question of *implied* powers. Article II, Section 3, states that the president "shall take Care that the Laws be faithfully executed." The issue here is whether this allows the president to exercise powers or establish mechanisms necessary or desirable for the implementation of various laws. An early example was a dispute over whether the president could, in the absence of congressional authorization, supply federal protection against bodily attack to Supreme Court justices. In the case of *In re Neagle* (1889), the Supreme Court, not surprisingly, ruled that the president is entitled to do so as part of his power to see that the laws are faithfully executed.[16]

In other cases the question of limitations on executive power has presented great constitutional problems. In general the courts have provided more forceful checks on the president's reliance on inherent or implied powers in domestic matters than in foreign affairs. Thus in *Youngstown Sheet and Tube v. Sawyer* (1952), the Supreme Court struck down President Truman's executive order directing the secretary of commerce to take possession of the nation's steel mills a few hours before a nationwide strike was scheduled to begin.[17] While several justices accepted the notions of inherent and implied executive power, a majority found its use unconstitutional in that instance. In deciding the case, however, the court did not establish a body of principles which could serve to clarify the proper use of executive power in the future.

A similar situation grew out of *United States v. Nixon* (1974), the case involving President Nixon's tapes and which ultimately resulted in his resignation.[18] The facts and the decision are interesting because they indicate that there are mechanisms, short of impeachment, for legally compelling the president to do something he refuses to do. On April 16, 1974, Special "Watergate" Prosecutor Leon Jaworski requested that some sixty-four tapes be made available in connection with the trial of former Nixon administration officials, including White House aides H. R. Haldeman and John D. Ehrlichman and former Attorney General John Mitchell. The presiding trial judge, John Sirica, set May 1 as the deadline for delivery of the tapes to him for inspection. Earlier, on March 1, a grand jury had named Nixon as an unindicted coconspirator in the case. Among the desired tapes was one made on June 23, 1972, which turned out to be the "smoking gun" for which so many members of Congress were waiting. The tape indicated that Nixon and Haldeman had fabricated a story about CIA activity in Mexico. They hoped to force the CIA to tell the FBI that for "national security" reasons, the FBI would have to discontinue an investigation which threatened to trace money found in the rooms of the Watergate burglars back to Mexico where it was "laundered." (The money was actually derived from campaign contributions.)

Understandably, Nixon did not want to give up the tapes. His lawyer argued before the Supreme Court that executive privilege was an inherent executive power. This would mean that the president could not be forced to yield materials under subpoena or be compelled to testify in court. Executive privilege has long been accepted practice in the president's dealings with Congress; it has even been extended to presidential aides in that context. The court denied the existence of an absolute executive privilege with regard to the judiciary. Nevertheless, it suggested that such a claim might be upheld if it were based on a need to protect military, diplomatic, or sensitive national security secrets. Nixon had not specifically made such a claim, and the president was forced to submit the tapes for inspection by Judge Sirica in private to determine their admissibility in the criminal proceedings before his court. Thus in *United States v. Nixon* as in earlier cases, the Supreme Court ruled against the plea of inherent powers but at the same time the court indicated that such powers could exist in some circumstances.

Judicial decisions on the president's power in foreign affairs are far less ambiguous. In *United States v. Curtiss-Wright Export Corporation* (1936),[19] the Supreme Court reasoned that the president has "very delicate, plenary and exclusive power . . . as the sole organ of the federal government in the field of international relations."[20] In what afterwards became a familiar refrain, the court noted that the president has a better opportunity than Congress to learn about conditions in foreign countries. He is informed by his agents in the diplomatic corps and has confidential sources of information, and he must operate on the basis of secrecy. In subsequent cases the president's authority to conclude executive agreements was upheld, as was his power to grant recognition to foreign nations, even when these acts have domestic consequences.[21] Executive agreements, which are agreements between the heads of state, have become an important means of bypassing the treaty-making process and thereby excluding the Senate from its constitutional role in foreign affairs. While originally intended for matters too minor to justify a treaty, such as postal conventions, executive agreements have been used for acts of major diplomatic importance. For instance, executive agreements set the stage for post–World War II political arrangements in Europe and the Far East. Recognition is an outgrowth of the president's constitutional authority to receive ambassadors. Its importance has been demonstrated recently in presidential policy toward China.

If the courts are somewhat ambivalent toward inherent and implied executive powers, so are presidents themselves. Some, such as Lincoln and the two Roosevelts, championed the "stewardship" conception of the presidency. Their idea was that the president has inherent power to do whatever is necessary for the good of the nation, at least in times of crisis or of great opportunity. Lincoln, who violated both the law and the Constitution on occasion, said that the question was whether to save the Constitution and lose the union, or save the union and then repair the constitutional scheme of government. "Stewardship" presidents are "strong" presidents and have been assigned an honored place in standard histories.

However, as the Lyndon Johnson and Nixon administrations indicate, presidents who intend to be stewards can be misguided in the forceful, and even unconstitutional or illegal, activities they pursue in the name of the common good. The United States war in Southeast Asia and Watergate were the fruits of such "stewardship." Other presidents who are usually labeled "weak," such as Taft and Eisenhower, followed a more "literalist" conception of executive power. According to this outlook, Article II grants the president no inherent or implied powers. Literalist presidents tend to agree with those founding fathers who favored a weaker executive. They regard the executive as little more than an institution for carrying out the will of the legislature. However, a literalist president is no longer likely to fulfill popular expectations of the office.

Less ambiguity surrounds the specific powers granted by the Constitution to the president. These can be categorized as legislative, administrative, and military-foreign powers. Among the president's legislative powers are those concerning the State of the Union address, the proposal of legislation, the adjourning of Congress, the convening of one or both houses for special sessions, and the vetoing of legislation. In theory these legislative powers are quite limited. The president's State of the Union speech and proposals for legislation require little congressional action. Congress is free to totally disregard them if it sees fit. The president's power to adjourn Congress is limited to situations where the two houses cannot themselves agree on a date for adjournment. And although he can convene both houses, he cannot compel action from them, and they can adjourn without his consent. This leaves the veto as the president's most important legislative power granted by the Constitution.

The traditional view, supported by the observation that only about 3 percent of all vetoes (amounting to about 3,000) have been overridden since the days of George Washington, is that the veto is a major strength of the presidency. But other analysts tend to dismiss it. For example, Cronin argues, "The veto power, which is almost always cited as a major source of presidential strength, is often a clumsy instrument." He argues that in practice the threat of a veto is rarely successful in blocking legislation to which the president really objects.[22] And he points out that perhaps 90 percent of all vetoed bills are unimportant nationally; they are private bills directed at the relief of individuals from specific problems such as flood damage. Nonetheless, the veto can be an important negative instrument in the domestic field, depending upon the composition of Congress.

Since the president's constitutional powers over the legislature are so unimpressive, how has the president come to be considered the chief legislator? It is because much of the initiative for legislation, which once rested with the legislature, has now shifted to the executive. Congress expects the president to submit a legislative package. As one irate member of the House told an official in the Eisenhower administration, "Don't expect us to start from scratch on what you people want. That's not the way we do things here. You draft the bills and we work them over."[23] Furthermore, the legislature has tended to delegate power to the president subject to a "legislative veto." As is discussed later in the chapter, the roles of initiator and reactor have been almost entirely reversed. And as the scope of federal participation in the society has grown, presidents have been increasingly able to use executive orders as a substitute for legislation. This is not to say that Congress never writes a major bill on its own, but only to indicate that for the most part it now spends a great deal of its legislative time dealing with presidential bills. Aside from its negative power (the power of refusing to legislate), perhaps Congress's most important legislative role lies, as Gary Orfield suggests, in "the accumulation of year by year alterations [that] can ultimately be more important than the initial legislative process."[24]

The president's administrative powers are similarly unimpressive. The Constitution gives him the authority to make major appointments, subject to the advice and consent of the Senate. As we have seen, he is also charged with the faithful execution of the laws. And he may require the opinions in writing of the heads of departments. These formal powers, however, hardly make the president the nation's administrative chief. In fact, Congress has far more *formal* authority over national administration. It can create agencies, positions, programs, and missions, establish personnel procedures, set salaries, and allocate funds to administrative agencies. But again, the initiative has been shifted to the president in terms of budgets, personnel, spending, and administrative organization.

It is in the realm of foreign affairs and military matters that the president's constitutional powers are most formidable. As commander-in-chief he formally heads what may be the most powerful military force in the world. Presidents have dispatched troops to many lands. Korea and Vietnam were presidential wars; Cambodia was bombed and invaded without congressional knowledge or consent. The founders specified that wars must be declared by Congress, and they did not expect the nation to maintain a standing army. The development of a regular army and world events have made the founders' intentions obsolete. To some extent Congress has recognized this by formally authorizing the president to commit troops to combat for a limited period before obtaining legislative consent. Thus here again, the initiative has shifted to the executive.

Summing up the relationship between imaginary and real powers, we can see that although the president's formal constitutional powers are rather limited, they have been expanded in extraconstitutional fashion.

Certainly the president is now far stronger than the founders intended; but he is still far too weak to fulfill the nation's expectations of the textbook presidency. The expansion of presidential power has come about through both events and men. The emergence of the United States as a major international power, the standing army, and the development of the national and world economies are some of the events involved. Equally important, however, have been presidents, such as Franklin D. Roosevelt, who expanded the powers of the presidency and adapted it more to contemporary life. They did so through the subtle mechanisms of persuasive politics, as well as the garish techniques of image management. For a time it appeared that the net result would be an "Imperial Presidency"[25] or a "Presidential Nation,"[26] in which the real powers of the office would actually match the imaginary ones. Today, however, many observers believe that the gap between presidential power and public expectations should be closed by curtailing the expectations, not increasing the power.

DELEGATION AND SUBDELEGATION

Ironically, efforts both to grant the president more authority and to curtail his authority have involved delegating power to him. Sometimes these are coupled with legislative vetoes—that is, Congress's opportunity to block the president's specific use of a delegated power by a vote of disapproval or by failure to approve of its use within a legally specified period of time. Congressional delegations of power to the president in his role as manager of the economy are examples of the delegating process. Under the Constitution Congress has authority over interstate and foreign commerce. But Congress is an inertia-ridden institution with a system of hurdles that can slow bills down or kill them outright. It is not well suited for action where flexibility is desired (see Chapter 5). Therefore Congress often delegates its power to the president or to various administrative organizations. A typical delegation of power states only the broad ends that Congress hopes to see achieved, such as the furtherance of the "public interest" or "national security." This leaves the president or administrators with vast discretionary authority. Recent examples have been delegations authorizing the president to institute wage and price controls to combat inflation and giving him the authority to use price controls to manage the energy situation.

Congressional delegations of this sort can be found in almost every area of federal activity, from education to civil rights to agriculture to establishing martial law. They are one way of coping with federal penetration of the nation's social and economic life—something never fully foreseen by the founders. However, delegations of power are filled with problems and support the tendency toward the bureaucratization of government. Put simply, the president must make decisions on many of the matters delegated to him, but he cannot personally master all the relevant information and skills. Consequently he must depend upon his aides and upon career bureaucrats. Whatever the formalities, in practice, delegations turn into subdelegations to career bureaucrats, the president's staff, or political executives. The president is left with important decisions to make, but in reality he is largely reacting to the policy proposals of his aides and career bureaucrats rather than actually formulating new policies of his own. In the words of one observer, the president ends up "retailing" policy.[27] The scope of delegations demands too much of one individual, and this has been a major reason for the growth in the number and specialization of presidential aides and offices.

Delegations coupled with legislative vetoes are sometimes used in an effort to constrain presidential power, but the end results only indicate how much the initiative has shifted away from Congress and into the executive branch. Three examples will make this clear. First, ever since the 1930s (with a brief lapse during the second Nixon administration), Congress has authorized the president to reorganize the federal bureaucracy as he sees fit, subject to congressional veto. This authorization has done as much as anything else to make the president the head of the executive branch in fact, if not by constitutional authorization. For instance, legislation passed in 1977 enables the president to abolish, transfer, consolidate, or modify existing agencies and units within departments, subject to a rejection of these plans by either house of Congress within sixty days of their submission. The president cannot, however, create a cabinet department in this fashion. But under earlier legislation, the Department of Health, Education, and Welfare was created in 1953 by a presidential reorganization plan. During his 1976 campaign, candidate Jimmy Carter pledged to use reorganization authority to drastically reduce the number of federal agencies.[28] Since taking office the major achievements in this area have been the creation of the Department of Energy and the reorganization of federal personnel administration. Presidential activity involving reorganization plans is presented in Table 4–1, which indicates that Congress has rejected only about 22 percent of all proposals from 1939 to 1973.

A somewhat more complex example is the War Powers Resolution of 1973. This was passed by Congress over President Nixon's veto, in reaction to the decade of presidential war in Southeast Asia. It authorizes the president to commit U.S. troops to combat. He must notify Congress of such action, and unless it approves within sixty days, the troops must be withdrawn. The president has an additional 30 days to accomplish the

TABLE 4–1
Reorganization Plans, 1939–1973

PRESIDENT	PLANS PROPOSED	PLANS ENACTED	PLANS REJECTED
Roosevelt	5	5	0
Truman	48	32	16
Eisenhower	17	14	3
Kennedy	10	6	4
Johnson	17	17	0
Nixon	8	8	0
Total	105	82	23

SOURCE: Stephen J. Wayne, *The Legislative Presidency* (New York: Harper & Row, 1978), p. 197.

withdrawal. Although touted in the press as a restraint on the "imperial" presidency, from a legal perspective the War Powers Resolution is best understood as a delegation. For according to the Constitution, sending troops into combat, as opposed to allowing them to respond when attacked, requires a congressional declaration of war. Since the Constitution does not authorize the president to place U.S. troops in combat without such a declaration, Congress's War Powers Resolution actually increased presidential power by authorizing "sixty- to ninety-day wars." But in another way, since presidents have long committed troops to combat without congressional authorization, the resolution also places something of a check on the president's practical authority. Whether it is a check that can withstand constitutional challenge remains to be seen.[29]

A third example concerns impoundments. Congress often passes omnibus bills and riders. (Omnibus bills are bills that treat several distinct subjects or policy areas. Riders are clauses attached to a bill that deals with subjects totally unrelated to the clauses.) The president does not have constitutional authority to exercise an "item veto," which would allow him to accept or reject parts of bills sent to him for approval. He must accept or veto any bill in its entirety. Given the nation's expectations of the president and the diversity of presidential roles and interests, this is a source of frustration. One way of dealing with it has been for a president to refuse to spend money allocated by Congress for purposes of which he does not approve. This practice can be traced back almost to the beginning of the republic, but did not become an important political issue until the Nixon administration. Halfway through his first term, Nixon had already impounded some $12.8 billion, much of which was earmarked for low-rent housing, model cities, highways, and other transportation projects. In this way Nixon intended not only to eliminate programs he did not favor, but also to reduce government spending, which he thought was feeding inflation. The latter is a constant problem, because the electoral interests of congressmen often tend to support spending, while in times of economic difficulty it is the president, not Congress, who is generally blamed for the state of the economy.[30]

In order to control impoundments, Congress passed the Budget and Impoundment Control Act of 1974. It requires the president to notify Congress of impoundments and gives either house the power to have the funds released by passing a timely resolution disapproving of the action. As in the case of the War Powers Resolution, since it is not clear whether the impoundment process was constitutionally permissible in the first place, the act can be seen as expanding the president's legal power, even though its real purpose is to constrain his power.

THE EXECUTIVE OFFICE OF THE PRESIDENT (EOP)

The Executive Office of the President was established in 1939. The rationale was to give the modern presidency, as developed under Franklin D. Roosevelt, an organizational tool for regulating the sprawling and rapidly growing federal bureaucracy and dealing with the increasing number of matters requiring presidential attention. The days when a president could fight a Civil War with only four presidential aides, or answer the White House telephone himself, were long gone. Indeed, the President's Committee on Administrative Management (known as the Brownlow Committee) concluded that the presidency was inadequately structured and staffed to cope with the bureaucratic "headless fourth branch of government."[31] Over sixty new agencies had been created by the end of F.D.R.'s first term. The Brownlow report recommended that the president have a few aides with a "passion for anonymity" and some organizational units to help him manage the executive branch. Roosevelt appointed a handful of assistants and had the Bureau of the Budget moved from the Treasury to the newly created EOP. A National Resources Planning Board, Liaison Office for Personnel Management, and Office of Government Reports rounded out the early EOP.

The EOP had a pattern of relatively steady growth until the Nixon administration, when its size and budget more than doubled. Table 4–2 shows the growth of the White House staff. The Ford EOP included a White House staff of some 550 presidential aides of one sort or another,

TABLE 4–2

FULL-TIME WHITE HOUSE EMPLOYEES 1934–1976

PRESIDENT	FISCAL YEAR	TOTAL SALARIED AND SPECIAL PROJECTS EMPLOYEES	DETAILED EMPLOYEES*	GRAND TOTAL
Roosevelt	1939	45	112	157
	1940	63	114	177
	1941	62	117	179
	1942	47	137	184
	1943	46	148	194
	1944	47	145	192
	1945	48	167	215
Truman	1946	51	162	213
	1947	190	27	217
	1948	245	23	268
	1949	220	26	246
	1950	223	25	248
	1951	257	40	297
	1952	252	31	283
	1953	262	28	290
Eisenhower	1954	250	23	273
	1955	272	28	300
	1956	351	41	392
	1957	364	59	423
	1958	352	51	403
	1959	354	31	385
	1960	355	33	388
	1961	342	134	476
Kennedy	1962	309	123	432
	1963	318	111	429
Johnson	1964	306	125	431
	1965	294	154	448
	1966	256	219	475
	1967	251	246	497
	1968	250	206	456
	1969	314	232	546
Nixon	1970	345	287	632
	1971	555	17	572
	1972	550	34	584
	1973	496	24	520
	1974	505	47	552
Ford	1975	500	23	523
	1976	471	26	497

SOURCE: Adapted from Stephen J. Wayne, *The Legislative Presidency* (New York: Harper & Row, 1978), appendix A, pp. 220–221.

*Federal employees assigned to White House duty for a temporary period.

some 5,000 other EOP employees, and an annual budget of about $20 million.

The contemporary EOP has four central units:

- THE OFFICE OF MANAGEMENT AND BUDGET (OMB) This office replaced the Bureau of the Budget in 1970. Its primary tasks are to help prepare the budget and to suggest ways of improving federal management. Agency proposals for legislation or executive orders must be submitted to it for approval before they go to Congress or the president. OMB also makes recommendations to the president concerning the desirability of vetoing congressional enactments. OMB's policy coordination and budget functions have placed it in an adversary relationship with federal agencies outside the EOP. It remains a strong and controversial office, whose leadership has sometimes been criticized for being too powerful. Its director is now appointed by the president with the advice and consent of the Senate. An organizational chart of OMB is presented in Figure 4–1.

- THE DOMESTIC COUNCIL/DOMESTIC POLICY STAFF The Domestic Council was created at the same time as OMB. Its purpose was to coordinate domestic policy and develop integrated sets of policy choices, thereby enabling the president to play a greater role in the actual formulation of domestic policy. Its membership consisted of the heads of the domestic departments. Under Nixon the Domestic Council was directed by John Ehrlichman and was used as a "superagency" to control regular domestic agencies. As one observer has written: "It was immediately clear that Nixon relied considerably more on Ehrlichman and the Domestic Council staff than on his Cabinet for the initiation and implementation of domestic policy. The Domestic Council's Cabinet members seldom met as a body. Task-force committees that included Cabinet officers were run mostly by a Domestic Council staff aide. And there was little doubt that Ehrlichman was Nixon's lead man in domestic affairs."[32] President Carter phased out the Domestic Council in favor of a Domestic Policy Staff. However, aside from the name change, early indications were that it remained substantially the same in terms of size, form, functional responsibilities, internal divisions, and hierarchy. Its organization is presented in Figure 4–2 on page 86.

- THE NATIONAL SECURITY COUNCIL (NSC) This unit was established in 1947. Its primary function is to advise the president on the integration of domestic, foreign, and military policies as they relate to national security. The council is composed of the president, vice president, and secretaries of State and Defense. The chairman of the Joint Chiefs of Staff and the director of the CIA serve as advisors to the council. The

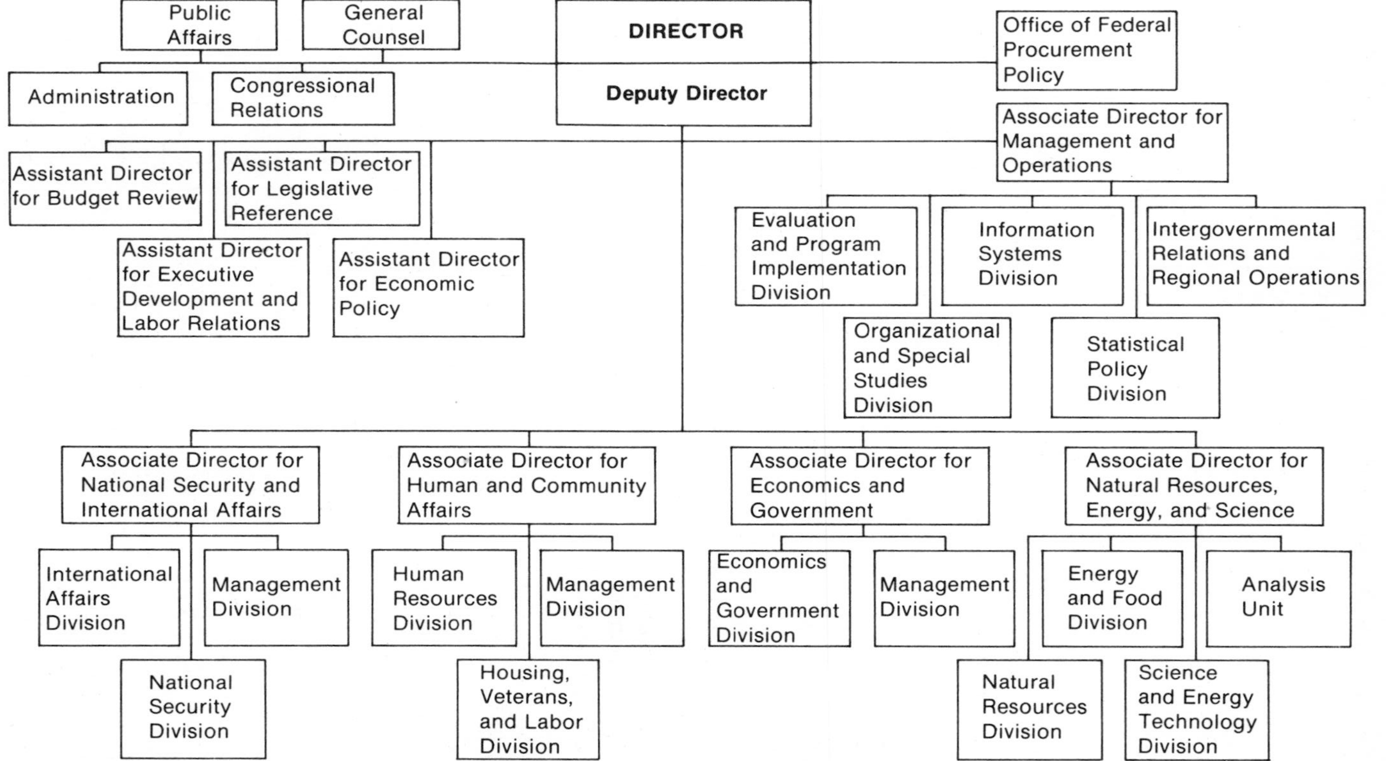

Figure 4–1 **The Office of Management and Budget, 1973–1976**

SOURCE: Stephen J. Wayne. *The Legislative Presidency* (New York: Harper & Row, 1978), p. 88. Copyright © 1978 by Stephen J. Wayne. Reprinted with permission.

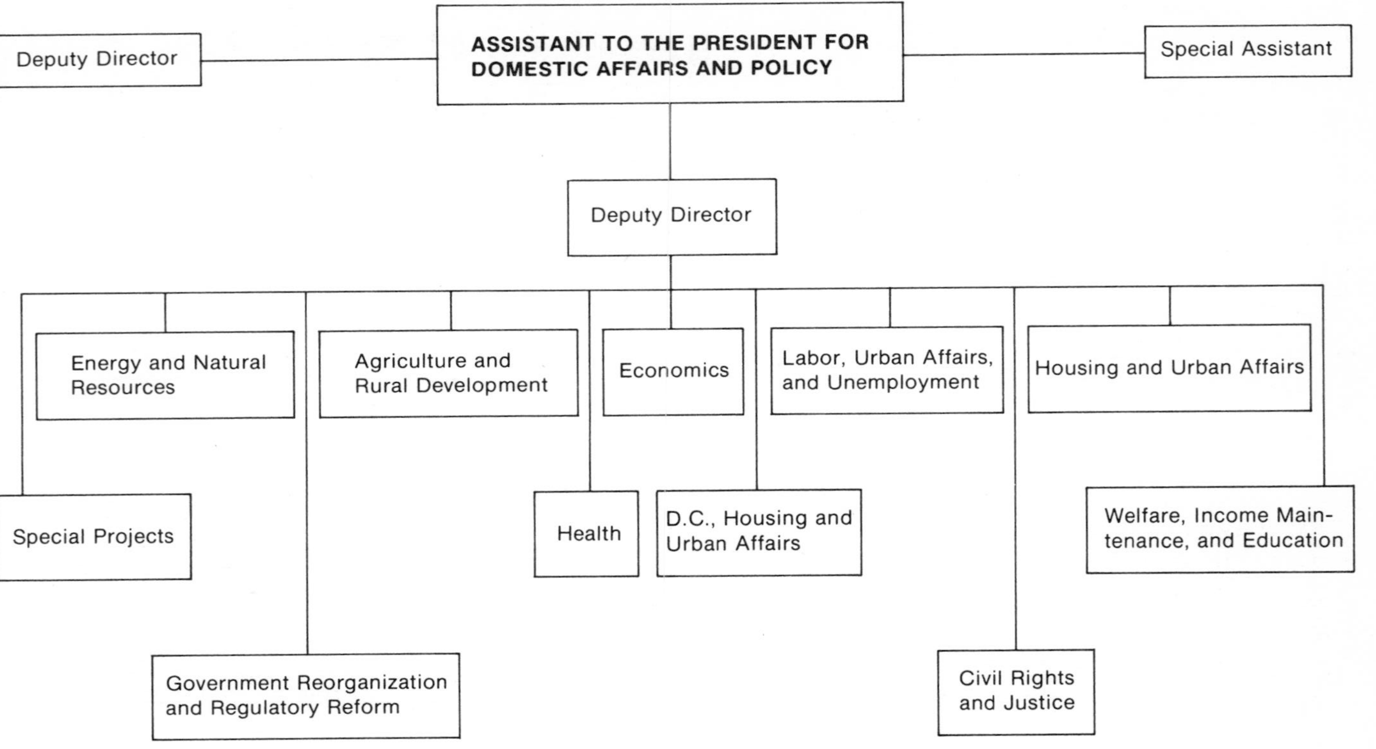

Figure 4–2 **Carter's Domestic Policy Staff Structure, 1977**

SOURCE: Stephen J. Wayne, *The Legislative Presidency* (New York: Harper & Row, 1978), p. 208.

NSC has been used in different ways by various presidents. Whereas Eisenhower and Nixon often relied on the NSC, Kennedy and Johnson tended to avoid it.

- The White House Office (WHO) This is a catchall organization consisting of the president's personal assistants. It is structured as the president sees fit and has emerged as his "alter ego." Although some positions are now standard, such as press secretary, appointments secretary, and various advisors for domestic, international, and legislative affairs, others are arranged on a flexible basis. The president has great freedom in making appointments to the WHO—they are not subject to senatorial confirmation—and theoretically he can use them as he sees fit. The WHO has emerged as an extremely powerful organization which in many respects has superseded the cabinet. In personnel it reached 632 appointees during the Nixon administration—far more than anticipated when the EOP was established. It has taken on a hierarchical structure of its own and is not necessarily under the full control of the president, despite his potential authority over it. The WHO, more than any other office, typifies the bureaucratization of the presidency. Its organizational elements of hierarchy, specialization, formalization, and secrecy have intervened in the relationship between the president and what were intended to be his closest aides. Although this bureaucratic behavior has been more pronounced under some presidents than others, it has been noticeable in the WHO since the middle 1950s.[33] The overall organization of the Carter WHO is presented in Figure 4–3 on the next page.
- Other Units At any given time there are several other units in the EOP. These are generally of less importance and tend to wax and wane with the political tenor of the period. They have included the Council of Economic Advisors, Office of Economic Opportunity, Special Action Office for Drug Abuse Prevention, Council on Environmental Quality, Council on Economic Policy, and Council on International Economic Policy. Table 4-3 (page 89) is a list of offices, special assistants, and assignments typically included in the modern EOP. Figure 4–4 (page 90) provides a sketch of the entire EOP early in President Carter's term of office. The Carter administration, knowing the difficulties inherent in the bureaucratized presidency, has planned to reduce the number of EOP units from seventeen to ten. Even the lower figure, however, is much greater than that anticipated by the Brownlow Committee when it developed the rationale for an EOP.

The growth of the EOP in size and importance has been a major development in the evolution of the presidency. Its emergence as a prime locus of power can be attributed to several factors. First, the fragmented

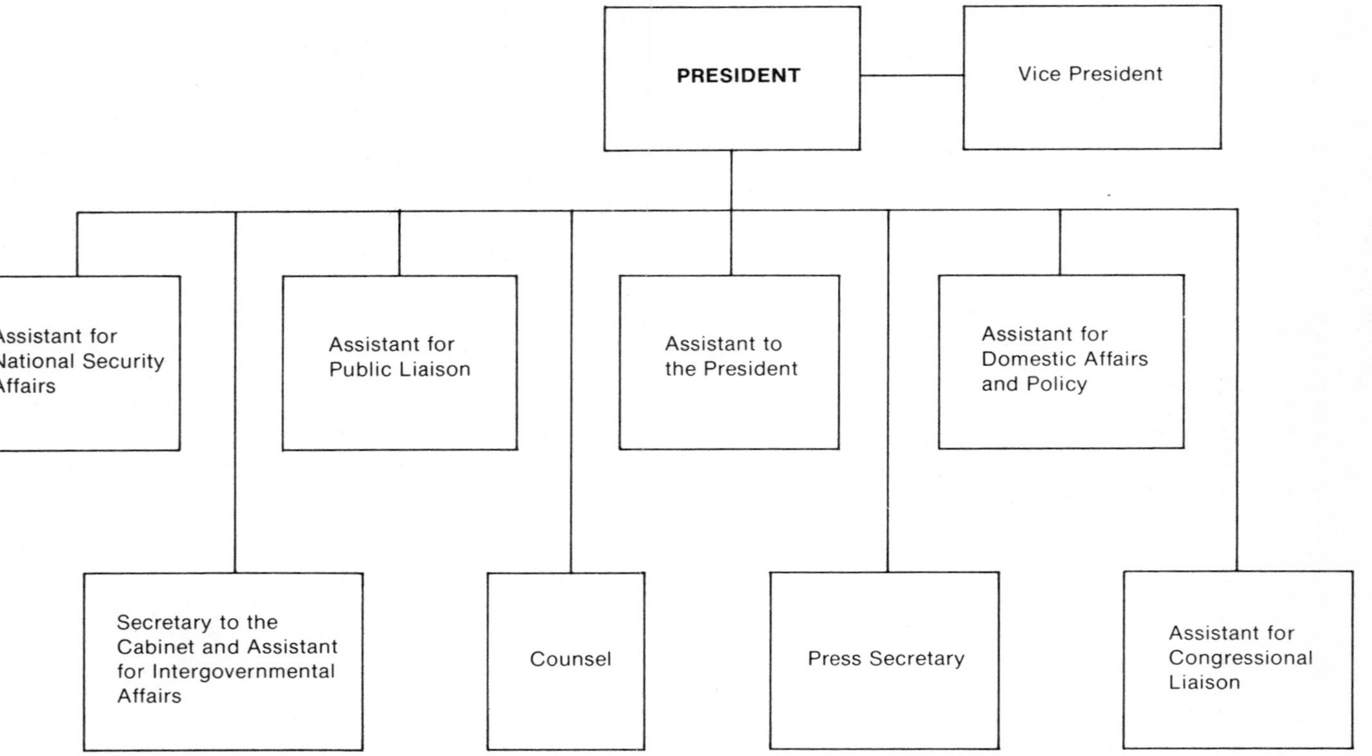

Figure 4–3 **The Carter White House, 1977: Senior Staff**

SOURCE: Stephen J. Wayne, *The Legislative Presidency* (New York: Harper & Row, 1978), p. 204. Copyright © Stephen J. Wayne. Reprinted with permission.

TABLE 4–3
The Modern Presidential Establishment

OFFICES		
National security	National goals	Intergovernmental relations
International economics	Domestic policy	Management and budget
Congressional matters	Economics	Energy
Science and technology	Telecommunications	Environment
Consumers	Drug-abuse prevention	
SPECIAL ASSISTANTS		
Military affairs	Disarmament	Foreign trade and tariffs
Energy policy	District of Columbia	Civil rights
Labor relations	Cultural affairs	Education
The aged	Health and nutrition	Physical fitness
Volunteerism		
AD HOC PORTFOLIOS		
Regulatory agencies and related industries	Wall Street	State party chairmen
Governors	Mayors	Intellectuals
Women	Blacks	Latinos
Ethnics	Jews	Youth

SOURCE: Adapted from Thomas Cronin, *The State of the Presidency* (Boston: Little, Brown, 1975), p. 123.

nature of the federal bureaucracy outside the EOP has made the coordination of federal policy difficult. The EOP has been organized and reorganized in an effort to provide this coordination. To a considerable extent the EOP—especially the Office of Management and Budget, the National Security Council, and for a time, the Domestic Council—emerged as "superagencies" for economic, foreign, and domestic policy.

Second, the EOP has been the result of increased complexity and uncertainty in foreign affairs and economic matters. The president's roles as chief protector of the nation and manager of the economy require that he be equipped with the organizational apparatus to act effectively in these spheres. But some observers, including Jimmy Carter in 1976, have suggested that the EOP has turned into an unmanageable bureaucracy instead.

Third, the EOP has come to reflect partisan and electoral concerns. Presidents have brought in representatives of various groups and interests

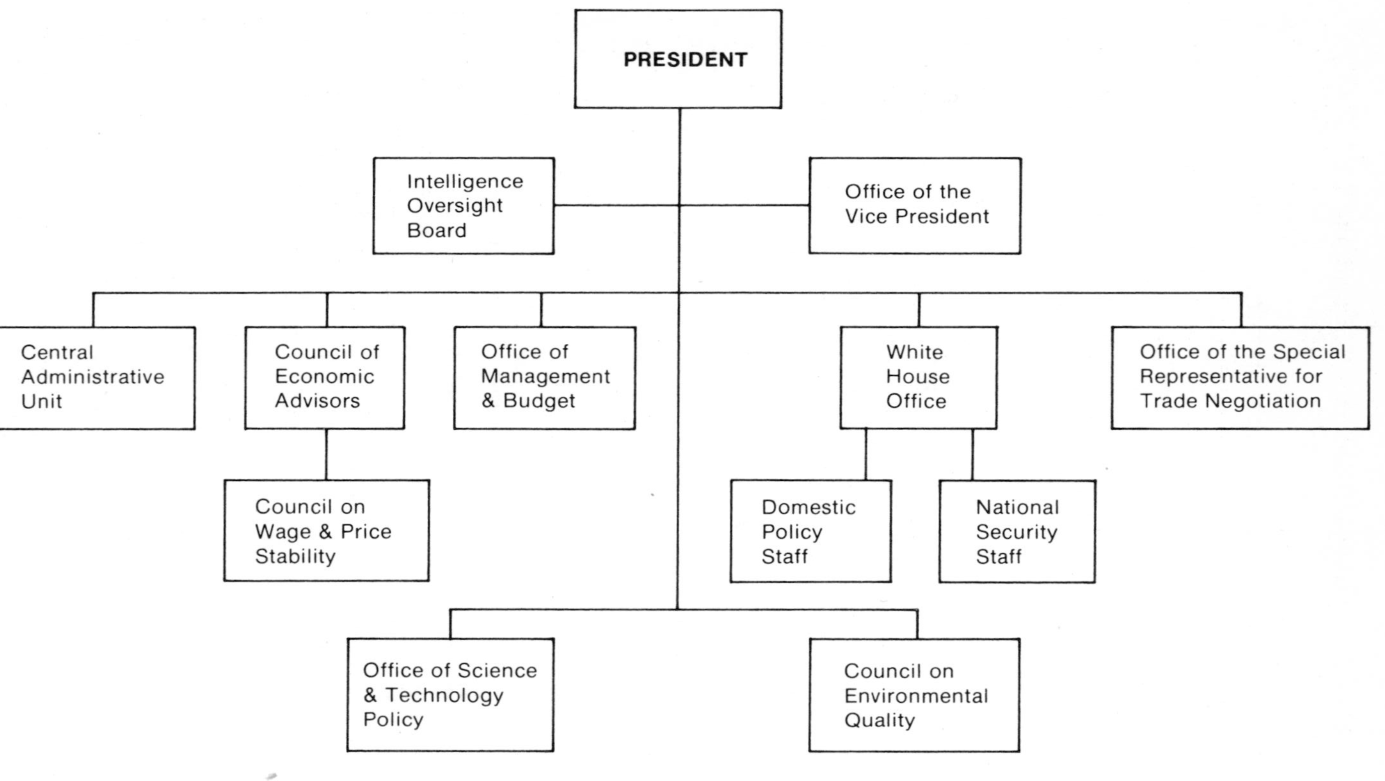

Figure 4–4 **The Carter EOP**

SOURCE: Stephen J. Wayne, *The Legislative Presidency* (New York: Harper & Row, 1978), p. 227. Copyright © 1978 by Stephen J. Wayne. Reprinted with permission.

in order to stress their importance and gain their support. To an extent this was the reason for establishing the Office of Economic Opportunity, the Council on Environmental Quality, and the Special Action Office for Drug Abuse Prevention. Although such units can be effective in addressing social, economic, and environmental problems, often they stress style and imagery over substance. While they call attention to the high priority being given their policy areas, they may be doing little else besides generating publicity.

Fourth, obviously the EOP has become involved in public relations. Many presidential aides work on press relations, speech writing, and arranging political trips:

> One of the more disquieting aspects of the recent enlargement of the presidential establishment is the emergence of a huge public relations apparatus. Under Nixon more than one hundred presidential aides were engaged in various forms of packaging and selling the president and, at the same time, projecting imperial images of the office. This presidential press-agentry has not only expanded public expectations of the presidency but also distorted the self-perceptions of persons within the presidential establishment.[34]

By its very nature public relations is concerned with image making, not necessarily with truth or substance. The packaging of policies for public consumption may become more important than the policies themselves. For example, it sometimes seemed as though the Ford EOP thought that putting on a "WIN" (Whip Inflation Now) button could really solve complex economic problems. Moreover, the EOP's growth, like that of other organizations, tends to encourage more growth. So despite presidential statements and efforts to the contrary, the EOP is likely to become even larger, more structured, and more hierarchical in the future. Indeed, President Ford's WHO staff was as large as that of his predecessor, even though the Watergate experience had strongly suggested that it was already too big. Despite President Carter's plan to reduce the size of the WHO to 351 positions, initially his WHO was larger than Ford's.[35] Even at 351 it will be larger than that of most of his predecessors prior to 1971. (See Table 4–2, page 83). Perhaps the most intriguing statistic of all is that in 1978, First Lady Rosalynn Carter's White House staff was half as large as Franklin D. Roosevelt's during World War II.[36]

Different presidents organize the WHO and the rest of the EOP along different lines. Some have favored an open, flexible kind of organization giving the staff easy access to the president. Others have preferred a more rigid hierarchical structure under which the president's top confidants regulate access to him and actually run the EOP. F.D.R. relied on the flexible style, Eisenhower and Nixon on the rigid one. Other presidents have been somewhere in between, although the looseness of the Roosevelt format now seems to be prohibited by the overall size of the EOP. The president's success in coordinating and controlling the EOP is of great importance for American democracy.

Under our form of government, the people elect only two of the federal branches. One, Congress, is elected by states and districts. Consequently its members do not have a genuine national constituency. The other, the president, while formally elected through the mechanism of the electoral college, does have a national constituency and is in practice elected by it. Power in the last half century has shifted away from Congress, with its overburdening structure and local constituencies, to the president. This transition is one reason for the expansion of the presidency in image, real powers, and structure. Today few people would seriously dispute the statement that the presidency has grown too large for one person to fill it. The EOP is a necessary management organization. But unless it is controlled by the president, a major link between the electorate and the government is weakened. When the EOP acts independently or influences the president too strongly, the result is government by unelected managers. Yet there is much to suggest that this outcome may be inevitable.

There are at least two reasons why the EOP tends to develop great power of its own. One is that the president must rely substantially upon it for policy advice, owing to the unsatisfactory character of the cabinet. Virtually every president appoints his first cabinet with great fanfare. He stresses how closely he will work with the cabinet, and how talented and well-qualified his appointees are. However, it has been at least half a century since executive power was concentrated in the cabinet as a group. Moreover, a powerful cabinet is not necessarily desirable per se; President Warren Harding's, for example, was one of the most corrupt in United States history. The cabinet is inherently a difficult body to work with. Presidents may not have free choice in selecting all the cabinet members. Partisan and electoral choices play a role, as does the necessity of senatorial confirmation. Moreover, the cabinet officers may have obligations to people other than the president, such as to their senior-level administrators and departmental clientele groups. They are also in close contact with Congress and congressional committees and may feel accountable to them. In addition, they may seek to represent nongovernmental constituencies, such as farmers, organized labor, business interests, or mining and timber interests. Another disadvantage of the cabinet is that its members are not covered by the executive privilege that generally protects the EOP staff. Thus the cabinet member *must* testify before Congress when summoned. What has been called the "outer cabinet"—the heads of departments that have strong ties to congressional committees and interest groups—is inevitably isolated from the president. Among these departments are Agriculture, Transportation, Commerce, and Housing and Urban Development. The loyalty of outer-cabinet members to the chief executive generally decreases over time.

As Theodore Sorenson, President Kennedy's principal domestic aide, put it:

> Each department has its own clientele and point of view, its own experts and bureaucratic interests, its own relations with the Congress and certain subcommittees, its own statutory authority, objectives, and standards of success. No cabinet member is free to ignore all this without impairing the morale and efficiency of his department, his standing therein, and his relations with the powerful interest groups and Congressmen who consider it partly their own.[37]

John Ehrlichman, Nixon's chief domestic advisor, expressed it with less elegance: "We only see them [cabinet members] at the annual White House Christmas party: they go off and marry the natives."[38] Indeed, even in the early stages of the Carter administration when relations between the president and several cabinet members were excellent, the WHO began a personnel review by announcing that in the future, "there will be a fuller realization of the priority of Administration goals over agency goals."[39] The statement was taken as a criticism of parts of the cabinet, especially Secretary of the Treasury Blumenthal, who, along with several other cabinet members, resigned as part of a shake-up of the Carter administration in 1979.

Since the cabinet has only limited utility for developing and coordinating policy, a strong president assigns these functions to the EOP. This was the idea behind the Domestic Council. In several policy areas the EOP intercedes between the president and the cabinet, with the cabinet members being in fact under the direction of one or more members of the WHO or some other unit in the EOP. This places EOP staff on top of policy development and coordination, but by the same token it gives them an advantage vis-à-vis the president. He relies on them for advice on general and specific policy matters. Moreover, an adversary relationship tends to develop between EOP staffers and cabinet members, since the former see themselves as the loyal "protectors" of the president, whereas the latter expect and need easy access to the president. This conflict contributes to the insecurity inherent in the nature of EOP positions. One organizational theorist has argued:

> The staff people have no job and every job. They have the fullness of their chief's power, yet are not accountable. They are totally insecure, having no grounds of support except the boss' favor. And so, in the end, they always act irresponsibly, immorally, and with at least a touch of paranoia. For their basic position is irresponsibility and in the last analysis immoral—as power without responsibility always becomes.[40]

EOP staffers speak in the name of the White House, they are largely unprepared for their jobs, they may move into specialized policy areas without adequate knowledge, they may assume that there is hostility where none exists, they try to please the president, and they seek to protect themselves from his displeasure. In short, they are independent actors whose jobs require that they make political judgments. While they may try to serve the president's interests and communicate adequately with him, their discretionary area is large and their clout outside the EOP is formidable. Their interests and judgment are not necessarily identical with those of the president. And given the nature of their tasks, they are not easily controlled by him. Remember the Law of Imperfect Control!

While one is tempted to go back to the days of Watergate to illustrate these tendencies, it is equally possible to recognize them in the Carter administration. The inexperience of Carter's White House aides quickly became legendary. As one congressman put it, "Every night is amateur night at the White House."[41] The bureaucratic pathology of "goal displacement" was also evident. Jody Powell, the White House press secretary, admitted: "We have been so preoccupied in getting our own house in order that we may have failed to develop relationships outside the White House with the major cogs that move this country so they can and will speak out for us."[42] Although the Carter White House was far more open than Nixon's, aides who disagreed with Carter on important issues either found it desirable to resign their White House jobs voluntarily or were demoted.[43]

The EOP staffer's immersion in policy areas and in the day-to-day implementation of public policy places him or her in the position of an expert when interacting with the president. This calls for considerable independence. But independence also flows from another source—the control of information. No single individual can process all the necessary information to carry out the functions of the presidency effectively. Information must be screened and organized. A president may require that no memo submitted to him be more than one page long. Even these are screened by subordinates in the EOP. They may also select his newspapers and other sources of information, and they regulate personal access to him. To the extent that a president is dependent upon the EOP for information, he becomes subject to the influence and sometimes the control of its staff.

Coupled with the pomp, circumstance, and security surrounding the president, the control exercised by his aides contributes to a situation in which he becomes isolated. The more isolated he is, the more power the White House Office has in government, politics, and national policy. For instance, Nixon's earliest White House appointments were of men largely devoid of government experience who had worked for him during the campaign or earlier. Many came from the world of advertising and public relations. H. R. Haldeman, whose official designation was "assistant to the president," was in fact Nixon's chief of staff and an "assistant president." He was variously described as "by far the second most important man in the government" and "*the* isolation of the President."[44] Haldeman saw his job as being the president's "s.o.b." He regulated access to Nixon, handled firings, and was the all-purpose strongman of the "palace guard." Organizationally, the EOP took on a pyramidal shape with Haldeman at the top. Beneath him were John Ehrlichman, with responsibility for domestic matters, and Henry Kissinger, who was in charge of foreign affairs and national security. Together these three appointees, unconfirmed by Congress, became the most influential advisors to the president. They had independent power of their own.

> Nixon seldom made a major decision without consulting Haldeman, whose influence was truly enormous, albeit more passive than active, more custodial than creative, and more private than public. He guarded the portals of the Oval Office with the ferocity of a wounded bull, and to paint him as a glorified usher is to distort vastly his real role as White House major-domo and confidant of the President.[45]

As for Ehrlichman, "The key . . . was his contact and rapport with the president. . . . Substantive policy papers from departmental secretaries or the [Domestic] council staff normally had to filter through him before they reached the president. Ehrlichman enjoyed complete discretion in the kinds of matters he brought to Nixon's attention."[46]

The "administrative" presidency, with its hierarchical structure and staff of close confidants, has an appealing rationale. It enables the president to concentrate on matters of major importance and to bypass the details in which he would otherwise be inundated. But as Richard Neustadt points out, "A staff system that liberates the President to think frees staff men from his watchful eye. The price he pays for liberty comes in the coin of power."[47] In Nixon's case the price was very high indeed. Arthur Schlesinger, Jr., writes:

> Nixon, in short, created the Nixon White House. "There was no independent sense of morality there," said Hugh Sloan, who served in the Nixon White House for two years. "If you worked for someone, he was God, and whatever the orders were, you did it. . . . It was all so narrow, so closed. . . . There emerged some kind of separate morality about things." "Because of a certain atmosphere that had developed in my working at the White House," said Jeb Stuart Magruder, "I was not as concerned about its illegality as I should have

> been." "The White House is another world," said John Dean, "expediency is everything."[48]

Nor were these problems confined to the White House Office. The Office of Management and Budget and the Domestic Council were among units of the EOP that quickly won a reputation for arrogance and authoritarianism within the federal bureaucracy and, to a lesser extent, in Congress. What was particularly disconcerting about the Nixon administration was that "the White House staff fell under the control of senior aides so lacking in propriety."[49] Indeed, the Nixon presidency was extreme; yet tendencies for power to accrue to the WHO and EOP staffs are likely to be found in almost any administration.[50]

In the past, the question of structuring the WHO and the EOP was to some extent a partisan one. Democrats favored the free-floating Roosevelt style, Republicans the hierarchy created by Eisenhower. However, both Kennedy and Johnson placed far more emphasis on structure than F.D.R. did, and consequently the evolution of the EOP shows increasing formalization. President Carter has suggested a number of reforms, including greater access to the president, the downgrading of some EOP units, and more autonomy for members of the cabinet. But as one observer notes, "Most, if not all, of these proposals have been made by other presidents, without ringing success. There is little guarantee that Carter will fare much better, mainly because the White House, like the federal bureaucracy, has become an institutionalized giant, impervious to presidential demands."[51] Indeed, in 1979 Carter restructured his WHO by centralizing authority within it.

In sum, the EOP has enhanced the growth in power of the nonelective component of government. Its inner sanctum tends to consist of nonpoliticians, often lacking in Washington experience, who were associated with the president's election campaign and who come from private management and academic life. They may, as in the Nixon administration, be more interested in power as an end in itself than in the public good. As such they are in some ways more characteristic of the managerial approach to government than the political approach. For the most part, such political experience as they possess has focused on electoral as opposed to policy politics, and they have little independent political base of their own. In general this stands in substantial contrast to members of the cabinet. The entire WHO and several of the top officials in the EOP are appointed without benefit of congressional consent. In short:

> The presidential establishment had become over the years a powerful inner sanctum of government isolated from the traditional constitutional checks and balances. Little-known, unelected, and unratified aides on occasion negotiate

sensitive international commitments by means of executive agreements that are free from congressional oversight. With no semblance of public scrutiny other aides wield fiscal authority over billions of dollars.[52]

Even if the president keeps these aides under control, their power raises a serious question about the loss of traditional checks and balances and the rise of "presidential government." Observers have noted that the WHO and EOP's growth in size and complexity was accompanied by their bureaucratization, as well as by some pathologies associated with bureaucracy. Stephen Hess, a former White House staffer, writes, "With the bureaucratizing of the presidency, it is hardly surprising that the White House fell heir to all the problems of a bureaucracy."[53] In addition, "The President's time increasingly is allotted on the basis of internal bureaucratic politicking and trade-offs between staff members that do not necessarily reflect the relative importance of issues."[54] Moreover, these conditions have led to "the distorting of information as it passes up the chain of command and frustrating delays in decisionmaking."[55] Indeed, there appears to be no immediate limit on these developments: "The presidential bureaucracy is becoming a miniaturization not only of important departments and agencies but also of politically important pressure groups and professions."[56] It now presents the president with a new and serious constraint and problem of control. Stephen Wayne sums up this dilemma:

> The growth of presidential policy making has encouraged the development of a large, specialized and highly structured White House, one that has become capable of assisting the president in more of his duties, but one that also has become less amenable to his direct, personal control. . . . In the process of expansion, the White House aggregated considerable power. By the 1970s, it had clearly become more than the president's personal office.[57]

This is the problem posited by the Law of Countercontrol discussed in Chapter 2.

COPING WITH THE EXECUTIVE BRANCH

Seventy years ago Woodrow Wilson wrote, "Men of ordinary physique and discretion cannot be Presidents and live, if the strain be not somehow relieved."[58] The EOP was created precisely for this reason, but it does not necessarily serve the purpose. Indeed, it may even exacerbate the difficulties of the presidency. This is especially evident in the wake of Watergate, but few administrations are likely to escape the strain of ill-advised EOP appointments and problems in coordinating and controlling the EOP. Yet the EOP might be worth the price if it effectively served to coordinate and direct the federal bureaucracy with some semblance of responsibility to the president. Even if it is an organizational tool that cannot be completely mastered, it might still give the president more leverage over the federal bureaucracy than he would otherwise have.

The power of the president and the EOP over what is often called the "permanent government" varies with a host of factors. The organization and talent of the EOP is important, as is the president's popularity. But it is always difficult for presidents to manage the rest of the executive branch effectively. President Carter expressed his frustration with this aspect of the presidency: "I think I underestimated the inertia and the momentum of the Federal bureaucracy . . . it is difficult to change."[59] The autonomy of the bureaucracy is discussed in Chapter 3; only its relationship to the EOP need be considered here.

The permanent government consists of the federal bureaucracy and the committee and subcommittee structures in Congress. Especially important are the high-ranking career bureaucrats who manage the bureaus or offices found within the executive branch. This is where public policy is implemented—and often made. The relationships that develop between bureau chiefs and congressional committees are not readily subject to presidential interference. Despite efforts to use the EOP to coordinate policy and screen policy proposals emanating from the bureaucracy, the task of maintaining effective control is always formidable. Bureaucrats possess a great deal of expertise, time, information, and job security. The lack of presidential control can lead to bizarre and even dangerous situations:

> The bureaucracy, sometimes with Congress but often by itself, has frequently been able to resist and ignore Presidential commands. Whether the President is FDR or Richard M. Nixon, bureaucratic frustration of White House policies is a fact of life. Furthermore, the bureaucracy often carries out its own policies which are at times the exact opposite of White House directives. A classic case occurred during the India-Pakistan war in 1971 when the State Department supported India while the White House backed Pakistan.[60]

Bureaucratic agencies, like presidents, have their own sources of political strength and support.

The fragmentation, lack of coordination, and power of the bureaucracy inevitably place it in an adversary position vis-à-vis the presidency. The first victims of the struggle for control over the executive branch are likely to be cabinet members and other political executives. Originally appointed as the president's "team" for managing the bureaucracy, cabinet members are likely to be "captured" by their departments or agencies. From the White House perspective this creates difficulties. Firing a cabinet officer may be politically inappropriate, in which case that executive must be bypassed. But as the White House staff and other EOP personnel become involved in departmental and agency matters, the bureaucracy resists them. White House policy aides find that "mostly, the bureaucrats are unresponsive; they view themselves as the 'professionals' and see your [White House] impact as purely political. They don't fight you openly, but they don't cooperate if they can help it!"[61] This situation is exacerbated by the presidential tendency to develop a host of new programs and neglect those which are ongoing.[62] To a large extent conflict inevitably results from the tendency of different structures to develop different loyalties, and sometimes different substantive views on policy matters. The EOP is supposed to be loyal to the president. On the other hand, the agencies and departments are chiefly concerned with their constituencies and ongoing organizational activities. As the bureaucracy and the president's own political appointments at its head become more suspect within the EOP, more matters of substance and detail are shifted upward toward the White House, and bureaucratic resistance to the presidency is bound to increase. As Hess observes, the president "begins to feel that if he wants action he will have to initiate it himself—meaning through his own staff. The White House grows bigger, despite his early promises to reduce its size. Types of decisions that used to be made in the departments now need White House clearance. . . . Programs that the President wishes to give high priority are placed directly within the Executive office."[63] Eventually a wide gap can develop between formal policy pronouncement by the EOP and its implementation by bureaucratic agencies. Perhaps the overall problem was best seen by Neustadt:

> Agencies need decisions, delegations, and support, along with bargaining arenas and a court of last resort, so organized as to assure that their advice is always heard and often taken. A president needs timely information, early warning, close surveillance, organized to yield him the controlling judgment, with his options open, his intent enforced. In practice these two sets of needs have proved quite incompatible; presidential organizations rarely serve one well without disservice to the other.[64]

The outcome, in the judgment of a former secretary of the Department of Housing and Urban Development, is that despite what might be billed as "heroic" efforts by EOP staffers, and despite bureau shuffling, juggling, reorganization, and other changes aimed at allowing more decisions to be presidential, "in the end, after thirty years, the effort to help the president in making government work has not succeeded."[65]

SOME LESSONS OF WATERGATE

The Watergate scandals of the early 1970s have been used to illustrate many difficulties of American politics. For some observers, they are a sign of serious shortcomings in our society.[66] For others, Watergate has come to symbolize a fundamental paradox of contemporary politics. In Aaron Wildavsky's words: "We demand more of government but we trust it less. Angered and annoyed by evident failures, our reaction is not to reduce our expectations of what government can accomplish but to decrease its ability to meet them. This is how a society becomes ungovernable."[67] For the authors, Watergate epitomizes the consequences of the bureaucratization of the presidency and illustrates the perplexing nature of the shift of power into the hands of the nonelective component of government.

The Nixon White House illustrates several specific difficulties with the bureaucratization of politics. The EOP, and especially the White House Office, were staffed with political outsiders. Many of them came from the world of public relations and advertising. Their behavior was unchecked by a moral acceptance of the constitutional rules of American politics. In general they were not imbued with the respect for political institutions and for the separation of powers that often comes with long service, say, in the legislature. For them the White House was an end in itself; it could take on and ultimately even attempt to subsume the larger bureaucracy. The Nixon White House distrusted the Supreme Court and disliked Congress. It was suspicious of newspapers and the media and regarded them as objects for manipulation. Critics of the administration were considered "enemies" to be dealt with by the IRS, FBI, or special units such as the "plumbers." The White House staff's loyalty was to the EOP and the president. A siege mentality served to protect the world of the White House from the outside world. The more isolated and inner-oriented the president and the EOP grew, the greater became the sanctity of internal considerations. This was nowhere better shown than in the absurdity of White House language. A military attack became a "protective reaction strike"; the purported truth became "inoperable." And all the while, every conceivable symbol and media approach was employed to gain or maintain the support of the American people. Bureaucracy in this case created an artificial world that came to supersede reality. In the end, Nixon may very well have convinced himself that nothing unusual had happened, that he was not culpable, that he was the victim of his enemies.

One is tempted to take refuge in the belief that the Nixon White House was an aberration, an extreme manifestation of the dangers inherent in the bureaucratization of the presidency. To a considerable degree there is truth in such a notion. However, the same tendencies—especially the internal and procedural orientations—are found in bureaucracies everywhere. As politics becomes bureaucratized, democracy inevitably suffers.

Conclusion The Presidential Problem

The presidency, caught in a gap between rising popular expectations and the increasing complexity and difficulty of achieving national objectives, has become bureaucratized. Bureaucratization, however, has not served the office well. It has not enabled the president to control the larger federal bureaucracy beyond the White House, and it has presented severe difficulties of its own. Some of them have been stated by Herman Finer:

1. In our time, the qualities demanded in the presidential office, with no foreseeable easing of responsibilities, are those of a genius. . . .
2. . . . The weight of the office is impossible; the intellectual demands are unfulfillable; the charge on the conscience is too exacting for one man alone.
3. The selection and election of the President is a gamble. . . .
4. The President's responsibility is demagogic rather than democratic. . . .
5. . . . The presidency becomes a "privileged sanctuary," in part because the President is a symbol of the nation, however inept a Chief Executive he may be.
6. The speeches and reported actions attributed to the President are too frequently public deception.[68]

Barbara Tuchman sums it up: "The office has become too complex and its reach too extended to be trusted to the fallible judgment of any one individual."[69]

What can be done? Several possibilities have been proposed and debated inconclusively. Some authorities have advocated debureaucratization. Certainly a smaller, less formalized EOP might be helpful, but the president *does* need assistance. It has been suggested that help could be provided by additional vice presidents or by a council of some sort. Other analysts maintain, however, that such approaches are ill suited to our constitutional framework of government. Perhaps, as many have suggested, a single six-year term would be most satisfactory. This would relieve the president of the opportunity to be reelected and therefore might take some of the imagery and partisanship out of the office and put some more substance into it. But by the same token, "lame duck" presidents have not been noted for their effectiveness. Moreover, some better mechanism than impeachment would be necessary as a check upon poor performance.

Many observers have argued that because presidential responsibilities are too heavy, either the responsibilities should be shifted elsewhere, or more authority should be granted to the office. Those who say that the responsibilities should be shifted generally believe that more of the duties of government should be assigned to the legislature,[70] as the founders originally intended and as actually occurred for much of the nineteenth century. Chapter 5 will discuss the potential of this approach. Granting more authority to the president, an idea much in vogue among political scientists in the 1960s, has obvious flaws.

In the end there may be no solution to the problem of the bureaucratic presidency. When the founders met almost two hundred years ago, they were unable to develop a strong rationale for the executive they created. Today we may be even further away from knowing what to do with the presidency. Perhaps as citizens all we can do is to follow Wildavsky's line of reasoning and simply reduce our expectations.

NOTES

1. Thomas E. Cronin, *The State of the Presidency* (Boston: Little, Brown, 1975), p. 23.
2. Ibid., p. 27.
3. Ibid., p. 28.
4. James D. Barber, *The Presidential Character* (Englewood Cliffs, N.J.: Prentice-Hall, 1972). See also Alexander George, "Assessing Presidential Character," in Aaron Wildavsky, ed., *Perspectives on the Presidency* (Boston: Little, Brown, 1975), pp. 91–134.
5. Cronin, *The State of the Presidency*, p. 33.
6. See Fred I. Greenstein, "The Benevolent Leader Revisited," *American Political Science Review*, 69 (December 1975), 1371–1398.
7. See Richard Pious, *The American Presidency* (New York: Basic Books, 1979), and Edward Corwin, *The President: Office and Powers, 1787–1957*, 4th rev. ed. (New York: New York University Press, 1957).
8. Winton U. Solberg, ed., *The Federal Convention and the Formation of the Union of the American States* (Indianapolis: Bobbs-Merrill, 1958), pp. 145–146.
9. Cronin, *State of the Presidency*, p. 30. The quote is from Burton P. Sapin, *The Making of United States Foreign Policy* (Washington, D.C.: Brookings Institution, 1966), p. 90. Emphasis added by Cronin.
10. Anthony Howard, "No Time for Heroes," *Harper's*, February 1969, pp. 91–92; as quoted in Cronin, *State of the Presidency*, p. 42.
11. *New York Times*, May 19, 1978, p. A11.
12. Ibid., May 21, 1978, p. 29.

13. Ibid.

14. Robert Sherrill, *Why They Call It Politics,* 2nd ed. (New York: Harcourt Brace Jovanovich, 1974), p. 8.

15. Corwin, *The President,* p. 153. Quoted in Martin Diamond et al., *The Democratic Republic* (Chicago: Rand McNally, 1970), p. 220.

16. 135 U.S. 1 (1889).

17. 343 U.S. 579 (1952).

18. 418 U.S. 683 (1974). See also Frank Mankiewicz, *U.S. v. Richard M. Nixon* (New York: Ballantine Books, 1975).

19. 299 U.S. 304 (1936).

20. Ibid., p. 320.

21. See *U.S. v. Belmont,* 301 U.S. 324 (1937), and *U.S. v. Pink,* 315 U.S. 203 (1942).

22. Cronin, *State of the Presidency,* pp. 76–77.

23. Stephen J. Wayne, *The Legislative Presidency* (New York: Harper & Row, 1978), p. 19.

24. Gary Orfield, *Congressional Power* (New York: Harcourt Brace Jovanovich, 1975), p. 54. Quoted in Wayne, *Legislative Presidency,* p. 21.

25. Arthur Schlesinger, Jr., *The Imperial Presidency* (Boston: Houghton Mifflin, 1973).

26. Joseph A. Califano, Jr., *A Presidential Nation* (New York: W. W. Norton, 1975).

27. William D. Carey, "Presidential Staffing in the Sixties and Seventies," *Public Administration Review,* 29 (September/October 1969), 450–458.

28. See *New York Times,* April 7, 1977, p. A17.

29. See *New York Times,* May 18, 1975, sec. 4, p. 2.

30. For instance, when confronted with pressures of this kind, President Carter stated, "But somebody has to hold the line on spending and I am willing to do it even if it means I have to take the political consequences." *New York Times,* June 25, 1978, sec. 1, p. 18.

31. U.S., President's Committee on Administrative Management, *Administrative Management in the Government of the United States* (Washington, D.C.: Government Printing Office, 1937).

32. Dom Bonafede, "White House Staffing: The Nixon-Ford Era," in Thomas E. Cronin and Rexford G. Tugwell, eds., *The Presidency Reappraised,* 2nd ed. (New York: Praeger, 1977), p. 161.

33. See, among others, Stephen Hess, *Organizing the Presidency* (Washington, D.C.: Brookings Institution, 1976).

34. Cronin, *State of the Presidency,* p. 137.

35. Wayne, *Legislative Presidency,* p. 203.

36. *New York Times,* July 7, 1977, p. 1 and following. According to Senator Daniel Moynihan, "Imperial Government," *Commentary,* 65 (June 1978), 30, Carter also sought to add an additional 100 "super-grade" and executive-level positions to the White House.

37. Richard Nathan, *The Plot that Failed* (New York: Wiley, 1975), p. 42; quoting Theodore Sorenson, *Decision-Making in the White House* (New York: Columbia University Press, 1963), pp. 68–69.

38. Nathan, *Plot that Failed,* p. 40; Wayne, *Legislative Presidency,* p. 49.

39. *New York Times,* March 12, 1978, p. 25.

40. Cronin, *State of the Presidency,* p. 124, quoting Peter Drucker. These tendencies were most evident in the Nixon White House. Indeed, there the staff sought to protect the president from extreme ideas, as well as from inordinate drains upon his time. See Sherrill, *Why They Call It Politics,* pp. 95–97. See also Donald W. Harwood, ed., *Crisis in Confidence* (Boston: Little, Brown, 1974), p. 150.

41. *New York Times,* Oct. 23, 1977, p. 36.

42. Ibid.

43. The former happened to Mark Siegel, Carter liaison with the Jewish-American community, the latter to Margaret Costanza. See *New York Times,* March 9, 1978, p. A9. See also ibid., Feb. 13, 1979, p. A15, describing Carter's effort to limit his staff's access to the press.

44. Christoper Wren, "Nixon's Haldeman: Power Is Proximity," *Look,* 35 (Aug. 24, 1971), 15–19. Reprinted in A. Scott and E. Wallace, eds., *Politics, USA* (New York: Macmillan, 1974), pp. 343–350. The quoted material can be found on pp. 343 and 346.

45. Bonafede, "White House Staffing," in Cronin and Tugwell, *The Presidency Reappraised*, p. 162.

46. Wayne, *Legislative Presidency*, p. 46.

47. Richard E. Neustadt, "The Constraining of the President," in Ronald E. Pynn, ed., *Watergate and the American Political Process* (New York: Praeger, 1975), p. 127.

48. Arthur M. Schlesinger, Jr., "The Runaway Presidency," in Pynn, *Watergate*, p. 136.

49. Neustadt, "Constraining of the President," ibid., p. 128.

50. See Bonafede, "White House Staffing," in Cronin and Tugwell, *The Presidency Reappraised*.

51. Ibid., p. 171. Moreover, as noted earlier, by mid-1978, the Carter administration was becoming less open and more critical of dissent.

52. Cronin, *State of the Presidency*, p. 138.

53. Stephen Hess, *Organizing the Presidency*, p. 9.

54. Ibid., p. 160.

55. Ibid., p. 9.

56. Cronin, *State of the Presidency*, p. 139.

57. Wayne, *Legislative Presidency*, pp. 59–60.

58. Schlesinger, "Runaway Presidency," in Pynn, *Watergate*, p. 137.

59. *New York Times*, Oct. 23, 1977, p. 36.

60. Peter Woll and Rochelle Jones, "Bureaucratic Defense in Depth," in Pynn, *Watergate*, pp. 216–217.

61. Cronin, *State of the Presidency*, p. 167.

62. For the Carter case, see *New York Times*, Oct. 23, 1977, p. 36.

63. Hess, *Organizing the Presidency*, p. 21.

64. Quoted in Cronin, *State of the Presidency*, p. 160.

65. Quoted ibid., p. 159.

66. See Henry Steele Commager, "The Shame of the Republic," in Pynn, *Watergate*, pp. 5–21.

67. Aaron Wildavsky, "Government and the People," ibid., p. 24.

68. Herman Finer, "The Indispensible Solution," in Stanley Bach and George T. Sulzner, eds., *Perspectives on the Presidency* (Lexington, Mass.: D. C. Heath, 1974), p. 282.

69. Quoted in Schlesinger, "Runaway Presidency," in Pynn, *Watergate*, p. 137.

70. This group includes Cronin, *State of the Presidency*, and Hess, *Organizing the Presidency*.

5

The Bureaucratization of Congress

The United States Congress is often considered the most powerful legislative body in the world. Yet there is also widespread public and scholarly agreement that its effectiveness and responsiveness leave much to be desired.[1] Ironically, in large part both of these characteristics are a result of the fact that Congress has taken on many of the attributes of a bureaucracy. In the process it has developed many forms of bureaucratic behavior which are inappropriate for a representative legislative assembly. Even more important, as the organization of Congress becomes more bureaucratized, power is increasingly exercised by the unelected professional staffs of committees, subcommittees, congressional agencies, and individual congressmen. Thus the bureaucratization of Congress not only has prevented it from effectively fulfilling its constitutional roles but has also led to the expansion of the power of the unelected component of government.

POWERS AND FUNCTIONS

When the founding fathers met at the Philadelphia Convention in 1787, they had many differences of opinion. Nevertheless, there was almost universal agreement that the legislative branch, however constituted, would be the most powerful institution of the new government. Congress is the subject of Article I of the Constitution, and it is often called the "first branch" of government. And at various times in the last century it lived up to the founders' expectations by functioning in fact as the center of the federal government.

Article I places immense powers in the legislature. Indeed, the powers enumerated in Section 8 are virtually synonymous with those of the national government. They include the power to levy taxes and customs duties; to borrow money; to regulate commerce with foreign nations and among the states; to coin money and regulate its value; to provide for naturalization, bankruptcies, and standard weights and measures; to establish post offices and post roads; to set up a system of copyrights; to declare war; to raise and support an army and navy; "to provide for calling forth the Militia to execute the Laws of the Union, suppress Insurrections and repel Invasions"; and "to make all Laws which shall be necessary and proper for carrying into Execution the foregoing Powers, and all other Powers vested by this Constitution in the Government of the United States, or in any Department or Officer thereof." The last clause shows most clearly that because the founders wanted a government of laws rather than of personalities, the legislature would necessarily have the greatest authority. Indeed, the establishment of executive agencies, all executive positions other than the presidency and vice presidency, and all courts other than the Supreme Court rests squarely within the Constitution's grant of authority to Congress.

So identical with government itself did the founders consider Congress that Article I also contains limits on Congress's, and therefore the government's, powers. Section 9 can be seen as a partial precursor of the Bill of Rights. Among other things, it protects citizens against the suspension of the writ of habeas corpus and the application of bills of attainder and ex post facto laws. Even the First Amendment, ratified in 1791, which is often considered a hallmark of American democracy, was based on the assumption that Congress and the government were largely synonymous. It reads, "Congress shall make no law respecting an establishment of religion, or prohibiting the free exercise thereof; or abridging the freedom of speech, or of the press; or the right of the people peaceably to assemble, and to petition the Government for a redress of grievances." The amendment says nothing about executive actions designed to abridge these rights because they were considered to lie outside the potential scope of executive power.

Significantly, the Constitution also gives Congress vast authority over its own organization: "Each House may determine the Rules of its Proceedings," and "Each House shall be the Judge of the Elections, Returns and Qualifications of its own Members."[2] The Constitution also authorizes each House to choose its own officers and to discipline its members.

Within the framework of these constitutional powers, Congress has three main functions. First and foremost is its responsibility for legislation. Second, it has authority for oversight, that is, checking the executive branch. Third, and overlapping these two functions, is Congress's role of representing the population. (Originally the Senate was considered a representative of the states, though today that view is less prevalent.) But as a result of its bureaucratic organization, the fulfillment of each function has become increasingly difficult.

ORGANIZATION: THE CONGRESSIONAL BUREAUCRACY

COMMITTEES

The Constitution authorizes each house of Congress to organize itself as it sees fit. Aside from mentioning a few officers, including the speaker of the House and the president pro tempore of the Senate, that document does not specify what form the organization shall take. Congress has elected to follow the bureaucratic principles of specialization and hierarchy, although this choice is based partly on politics as well as on the more traditional bureaucratic effort to rationally manage workloads. Specialization is built into the committee system; hierarchy is seen in the nature of congressional leadership. Both of these organizational features militate against Congress's ability to effectively legislate, oversee the executive branch, or even represent the nation's population.

At the heart of congressional organization are the standing committees and subcommittees. These units deal with legislative proposals and oversee matters falling within specific jurisdictional spheres. They include such areas as agriculture, the armed services, banking, education and labor, human resources, foreign relations, commerce, finance, and appropriations. Within any one standing committee there are likely to be several subcommittees. For example, at one time (the 92nd Congress, 1971–1972) the Senate Committee on Agriculture and Forestry contained the following subcommittees: Agricultural Credit and Rural Electrification, Agricultural Exports, Agricultural Production, Marketing and Stabilization of Prices, Agricultural Research and General Legislation, Environment, Soil Conservation and Forestry, and Rural Development. For the most part the committee and subcommittee structure is congruent with the subject-matter organization of the executive branch bureaucratic agencies. In 1975 there were 18 standing committees with 140 subcommittees in the Senate,[3] and 22 standing committees with 139 subcommittees in the House of Representatives.[4] In addition, there were a number of joint committees and temporary select committees.

The committee system obviously encourages a high degree of specialization; there are many units with limited jurisdictions. It is important to recognize that this arrangement is not dictated by any tenet of politics or political science. Legislatures in other democratic nations do not carry specialization by standing committee and subcommittee as far as Congress does.[5] Nor was Congress as specialized during the nineteenth century, the heyday of its power relative to the executive branch. The number of committees and subcommittees depends exclusively upon the discretion of Congress itself and can be altered at will. In recent years the tendency has been toward greater specialization by subcommittees.

To a very large extent congressional activity takes place within committees and subcommittees. It is here that legislative proposals, once introduced, are first considered, amended, rewritten, or rejected. Because so many admittedly unwise bills are introduced by congressmen anxious to please groups in their constituencies back home, the vast majority of the thousands of bills introduced in any one legislative session simply die in committee or subcommittee. Generally they are not even considered seriously, and often their congressional sponsors are glad to see them die. Although mechanisms exist to force a bill out of a recalcitrant committee, they are complex, require a concerted effort, and are seldom successful. Therefore committees and subcommittees play an important gate-keeping function. To a considerable extent, their actions form the basis of the legislature's agenda. When a subcommittee reports a bill out negatively, its parent committee is likely to do the same or not report it out at all. Under most circumstances this spells doom for the bill—whatever its merits as judged by those beyond the bounds of the committee. On the other hand, a favorable report by a committee improves a bill's chances but certainly does not guarantee passage. Similarly, since the overwhelming bulk of oversight takes place within committees, they determine the competence and forcefulness with which Congress checks the executive branch.

The committee framework, like specialization in bureaucratic organizations generally, creates a system of vetoes. Most bills die of inaction at the subcommittee or committee level; others are rejected as a result of negative committee reports. Like any system of vetoes, it favors inaction and resists change. To be accepted by the entire legislature, a proposal must pass successfully through many veto points, that is, units and procedures which make its rejection possible. If it fails to cross any one of these barriers, it is likely to fail altogether. This form of organization creates such inertia that it is difficult for Congress to legislate in a coherent and timely fashion. Indeed, when Congress delegates its power to the executive branch, it often does so subject to a legislative vote of *disapproval* of executive actions. (That is the case with presidentially proposed reorganizations and impoundments, as discussed in Chapter 4.) Congress is aware that if it had to actively approve, it might often fail, owing to the constraints of inertia and particularistic vetoes. Organization by committees and subcommittees also makes it difficult for Congress to be an assembly that truly represents the electorate. Since the congressmen occupying the most important veto points are more powerful in the legislative process than other members of Congress, the legislature is more hierarchical than collegial. But once some representatives are "more equal" than others, some congressional districts have potentially stronger representation than others, and a fundamental requirement for a truly representative body is violated. The Supreme Court's "one man, one vote" mandate with regard to the apportionment of legislative seats cannot turn a stratified body into an assembly providing equal representation for its constituents.[6]

How are positions on committees allocated? The committees and subcommittees in Congress are not equal in scope of jurisdiction or prestige. Some are more attractive to members of Congress because they are far more important than others. Table 5–1 lists the most attractive and the least attractive committees in the Senate and House in recent years. The procedures for allocating seats on committees in both houses are extremely complex. Ostensibly the process is democratic, but in practice, with a few exceptions which should not be mistaken for the rule, it depends on two factors: partisan affiliation and seniority in the legislative chamber. Essentially it works like this: in the Senate, Democratic assignments to committees are handled by a moderate-sized Democratic Party Steering Committee, which is chaired by the majority leader (assuming that the Democrats are a majority in the Senate). Republicans use a Committee on Committees. These committees primarily use the criterion of seniority in making their assignments. However, under the "Johnson rule" adopted during the 1950s when Lyndon Johnson was Senate majority leader, all

Table 5–1

Relative Attractiveness of Congressional Committees

SENATE		HOUSE	
Most Attractive	**Least Attractive**	**Most Attractive**	**Least Attractive**
Foreign Relations	District of Columbia	Rules	Veterans' Affairs
Finance	Post Office and Civil Service	Ways and Means	Post Office and Civil Service
Appropriations	Government Operations	Appropriations	Merchant Marine and Fisheries
Judiciary	Rules and Administration	International Relations	Banking, Currency and Housing
Armed Services	Public Works	Armed Services	Interior and Insular Affairs

SOURCE: Reprinted from *The Little Legislatures: Committees of Congress* by George Goodwin, copyright © 1971 by the University of Massachusetts Press, pp. 114–115.

Democrats, regardless of seniority, are supposed to be given at least one major committee assignment. Moreover, even freshman senators may chair subcommittees. The composition of each committee broadly reflects the partisan composition of the Senate as a whole, with whatever adjustments are agreed upon by the party leaders. The number of committee assignments per senator has been increasing over the last decades, and by the end of 1975 a senator served on an average of four committees and fifteen subcommittees.[7] As senators spread themselves thinner in terms of committee specialization, the professional staff of committees increased. The process of committee assignment in the House of Representatives is similar. But each member of the House has only one committee assignment and an average of 3.5 subcommittee assignments.[8]

The nature of assignment to committees is crucial in terms of Congress's legislative and oversight activities. Yet the seniority criterion is hardly neutral. The most senior members of Congress are those who have been elected most often (consecutively to the Senate and with some adjustment for missed terms in the House).* Congressmen who have the longest service are likely to come from districts or states where there is relatively little political competition. These localities also turn out to be more homogeneous in terms of economic and social factors, whether they are urban neighborhoods, single-crop or single-industry areas, or whole states. Although their representatives achieve positions of substantial power in Congress, such districts, even taken collectively, are not representative of the political perspectives of the American population. In general, the more homogeneous the constituency, the more fixated it is on a single political objective or viewpoint.[9] The "safest" districts simply do not do justice to the diversity of social, economic, and political interests found in the society at large. Yet the representatives from these districts gravitate toward the most important committees in Congress. This is likely to remain true despite the exceptional turnover of congressional membership during the 1970s, which resulted from a wave of retirements, primary defeats, and other causes.

Therefore Congress is not simply bureaucratic in its reliance on specialization; it also uses the bureaucratic principle of seniority in allocating positions on its specialized units. A hierarchy of power is also manifested in this system, as some committees have more important jurisdictions

*Seniority in this sense differs somewhat from bureaucratic seniority in general because it has a presumptive political base: members of Congress must be elected to gain it. However, as will be discussed at a later point in this chapter, the reelection of incumbents is frequently pro forma and even apolitical in a very real sense. Moreover, the application of seniority has become relatively rulebound, as in bureaucratic organizations generally, and members of Congress have been stripped of seniority at times as a punishment for various transgressions.

than others. Again, the similarities between congressional organization and bureaucracy are striking. Even more important, the principles of hierarchy, specialization, and seniority are combined in the creation and selection of committee chairmen.

This discussion should not be taken to imply that all members of a given committee have an equal voice in legislation and oversight, or that committees are run on the basis of equality among their members. Committee chairmen often play veto and gate-keeping roles on their own. Basically the chairman of a committee, sometimes alone, sometimes in consultation with other committee members, determines the committee's agenda. The chairman largely decides if and when a committee will meet, what it will consider, which of its subcommittees will be assigned which bills, what kind of hearings should be held, and who should be asked to testify. In short, "Chairmanships mean influence; the ability to hold hearings, investigate problems, oversee executive branch activities, and report legislation is highly significant in the policy process."[10] Although committees have on occasion revolted against their chairmen, influence generally runs from the top down, and it is usually the chairman who has the edge when internal disagreements arise. To a lesser extent the chairmen of subcommittees exercise similar authority at their level.

The primary criteria for the selection of committee chairmen, like the criteria for assignment to committees, have been partisanship and seniority. As long as a single party holds a majority of the seats in the House or the Senate—which has been the usual situation for about a century—all the committee chairmen of that chamber will be members of that party. Within this partisan framework, *seniority on the committee* all but dictates the appointment of the chairman. Although seniority is not formally binding, and although there are now mechanisms by which the Democratic members of either house can prevent assignments to the chairs of committees, in practice seniority is still close to an inviolable rule.[11] The appointment of subcommittee chairmanships also tends to follow seniority, although there is some effort to distribute these positions more widely among the members of the majority party.[12] Again, the use of seniority is not politically neutral. Indeed, since even more seniority is required for a choice chairmanship than for a desired committee assignment, the use of seniority further exacerbates the conflict between the allocation of power and the requirements of a representative assembly.

LEADERSHIP ROLES

In addition to the hierarchy of committees, Congress has a hierarchy of partisan leadership positions. The House is more complex in this regard. The Constitution specifies that there shall be a speaker of the

House. This official is elected strictly along partisan lines by the whole House. Seniority is not followed, although the speaker is certain to be a congressman with long service. The powers of speakers have fluctuated greatly over the years. In broadest terms, they are supposed to be at once partisan and nonpartisan: they are representatives of the entire House in their interaction with outsiders such as the president, but they also hold their position as a result of a partisan decision.

In recent years the formal powers of the speaker have not been nearly as great as those held by this office at various times in the past, especially during the late nineteenth century and at the beginning of the twentieth. Today the speaker's most important powers include:

1. Selecting the chairman of the Committee of the Whole. This committee is a procedural device that allows the entire House of Representatives to sit as a committee, thereby releasing it from the rigidity of the rules that govern debate on the floor.
2. Appointing members to select committees, special committees,* and conference committees.
3. Assigning bills to committees. This power includes the authority to parcel them out in piecemeal fashion.

In addition, the speaker determines the existence of a quorum, makes rulings on parliamentary procedure, and votes in case of a tie. A Democratic speaker, as all speakers have been since early 1955, can nominate Democratic members for positions on the Rules Committee. He also chairs the Democratic Steering and Policy Committee, which directs the party's legislative strategy.

The speakership has thus emerged as an important bureaucratic office, designed to use hierarchical authority to overcome the fragmentation brought about by committee and subcommittee specialization. Indeed, the effort to strengthen the speakership in recent years has been part of the same movement that has increased the number of subcommittees. Placing the speakership in historical perspective, two noted analysts of Congress write:

> The development of the office of Speaker . . . provides good evidence of the growing "institutionalization" of that chamber. In earlier times, it was not uncommon for men who had served only one or two terms in the House to rise to the speakership. Henry Clay, for example, was elected Speaker at the age of 34, a mere eight months after he was first elected to the House. . . . A typical

* Select committees and special committees are temporary bodies created to undertake relatively specific tasks such as investigations. Select committees are empaneled for the length of a Congress, special committees generally for a shorter duration.

> Speaker during the nineteenth century would have served six years in the House before his election to the speakership; by contrast, during the twentieth century he would have served a remarkable twenty-six years prior to his election.[13]

The strengthening of the speakership is a sign of the transformation of the House from a collegial body not bound by rigid rules, jurisdictional specializations, or seniority into an organization far more akin to a bureaucracy.

The power of the House Rules Committee, like that of the speaker, has fluctuated over the years. Today the committee is important, but far less so than it was even a few years ago. The Rules Committee is commonly described as the "traffic cop" of the House. Nearly all important and controversial measures must pass through the Rules Committee prior to reaching the House floor for debate. The committee determines the conditions ("rules") under which such debate will take place, and to a considerable extent it can even decide whether a given bill will actually come before the whole House for discussion. Among the conditions under its control are how much time will be available for general debate, how the time will be divided and who will manage it for the opposing sides, how and what kind of amendments may be offered, and whether a motion to recommit the bill to committee will be allowed. The committee may also adopt a rule waiving the use of points of order against provisions of a bill. In addition, it may establish the conditions for House participation in a conference with the Senate when both have passed different versions of the same bill.[14] Obviously the rules handed down by the Rules Committee have a lot to do with whether a given bill meets with favorable action on the House floor. If it is controversial, for example, unlimited debate and an open amendment procedure are almost certain to spell defeat. On the other hand, limiting debate and prohibiting the amendment of a bill on the floor may increase its chances for success.

But the power of the Rules Committee is not limited to rules of this kind. It may also prevent a bill from ever reaching the floor. This can be accomplished in two ways. First, when other committees request hearings before the Rules Committee, it may deny them. Second, after holding hearings, the Rules Committee may fail to grant rules, which has the effect of bottling up the bill. Although there are procedures for bringing legislation to the floor of the House despite efforts of the Rules Committee to block it, these are cumbersome and the committee is not easily circumvented. The Rules Committee's power is not limited to saying "Yes" or "No." It can also say "Yes, if . . ." and "No, unless . . ." and thereby induce other committees to make changes in bills that they want to reach the floor.

In the past the Rules Committee (particularly its chairman) was a major stumbling block to much legislation, especially bills concerning civil rights. The bias of the seniority system was pronounced in this context. It gave a few individuals, who had been elected time in and time out from homogeneous, generally conservative districts, great power in the nation's legislative process. Indeed, the committee was described as a "legislative cemetery."[15] Now that a Democratic speaker can nominate the Democrats on the committee, it is closer to an arm of the leadership. Its role stresses coordination and control. Hence today, in the view of some commentators, the Rules Committee is as much a "field commander" as it is a "traffic cop."

Leadership in both houses involves majority and minority leaders, whips, and their assistants. These are strictly partisan posts. The leaders are chosen by the party members (the party caucus). The majority leader plans the work of the chamber. In the House the leader is the number two party functionary, following the speaker; in the Senate he is number one. In both houses he plays a role in committee assignments and has some control over the legislative schedule. He is the major spokesman for his party through the media and the press. The majority leader is also in a position to help members with various special projects, and when he is successful, he acquires great influence in his legislative chamber. The minority leader plays similar roles in his party, but since it is a minority, his impact on matters affecting the chamber as a whole is inevitably weaker. Of course, when his party's votes are crucial on a particular issue or matter, the minority leader's importance is accentuated. The majority and minority leaders in the Senate have a somewhat wider role than their House counterparts: they fulfill functions similar to those of the speaker and the Rules Committee in the lower chamber.

Whips are chosen by the party caucus or the floor leader in each house. Their chief role involves communication with and coordination of party members. A whip is supposed to keep in touch with the rank and file and find out what they would like to see done by the chamber, how they intend to vote, when they intend to be absent, and the like. The whips inform members about the leadership's position on various issues and announce when votes are coming up on specific bills. As members file onto the chamber floor from their committee rooms or offices, the whips tell them how the party leaders want them to vote on the issue at hand.

Finally, conference committees enhance the hierarchy of power in Congress. Conference committees are convened when both houses pass different versions of the same legislation. Typically the chairmen of the committees which had jurisdiction over the bill are members of the conference committee. Here again the effects of seniority are strong. They are exaggerated even more by the fact that if the House and Senate members of a conference committee can reach agreement, their report must be either accepted in full or rejected in full by the membership of their chambers. For this reason conference committees are sometimes called the "third house" of Congress.[16] The modifications of a bill by a conference committee can be major and controversial. Indeed, a bill coming out of conference committee may differ significantly from either of the versions passed by the House or the Senate.

IMPACT ON FUNCTIONS

The organization of Congress greatly influences its general operation and the nature of its policymaking. Hierarchy is ill suited to representation. Specialization tends to turn oversight into collusion. Combined, hierarchy and specialization result in a complex legislative process with many veto points.

Representation. The hierarchical nature of Congress means that the representatives of some districts are more influential than those of others. Seniority rather than ability is the chief determinant of this greater influence. While the most able legislator may also become the most senior, seniority is also enhanced by safe, homogeneous districts. A forceful chairman of a powerful committee may emerge as a central political figure in the nation (as in the case of Wilbur Mills, chairman of the House Ways and Means Committee before his downfall). But should a majority of voters in a "safe" district be able to have such an impact on the rest of the nation? More important, why should the House as a whole be so heavily influenced by some twenty or so individuals whose districts have returned them to office longer than anyone else in the majority party? Even if the districts from which these legislators come were more representative of the nation's population, there would still be cause for concern since those elected from other districts would still have less influence vis-à-vis the federal bureaucracy and would be less able to bring federal funding and projects to their districts. In the Senate the problem, while less pronounced because of the larger size of constituencies, is similar. The principle of representation demands an equal distribution of formal authority among the representatives, but the hierarchical organization of Congress makes this impossible.

Oversight. Chapter 3 discussed congressional oversight of federal agencies and the "cozy triangles" that develop. In theory, the specialization of committees and subcommittees should lead to forceful oversight of the executive branch. After years of concentrating on a policy field, congressmen should be able to match the knowledge and expertise of senior bureaucrats. However, specialization produces the effect of coziness as well. Rather than representing different and competing perspectives, congressmen and bureaucrats may arrive at a harmonious accommodation with each other and with clientele groups. The committee or subcommittee, the bureaucratic agency, and the interest group may blend into a single policy "complex," such as the military-industrial complex. Checking does take place, but at least as often the committee, the agency, and the interest group are spokesmen for each other and the same policies. Perhaps sensing the inevitability of such "cozy triangles," congressmen generally see little political glamor in oversight and leave most of it to their staffs.

Legislation. Figure 5–1 maps the structure of the legislative process. It is evident that passing a law is complex and formalistic, and that the organization of Congress creates many points at which a bill may fail. It can die in House and Senate subcommittees and committees, in the Rules Committee of the House, on the floor of either house, or in conference committee, if any. Or the partisan leadership can act in various ways to reduce the likelihood that the bill will be passed. Again, it is important to emphasize that in reality the organization of Congress and its legislative procedure give some forty to fifty members of Congress a great deal of control over the content of bills and the action that the rank-and-file members will take on them. From an institutional perspective, it is equally important that congressional organization favors inaction, largely because of the proliferation of veto points. Moreover, specialization in Congress may create a situation in which bills are parceled up among committees in such a way that virtually no one has a firm grasp of the content of a legislative proposal, even after it is passed or defeated on the floor. The incompatibility between congressional organization and fulfillment of legislative tasks is most evident during the last weeks of a session, when Congress is compelled to deal very rapidly with a host of major bills. Nor will the argument that specialization allows the weeding out of poor proposals absolve the legislature, since it also eliminates good proposals.*

Given the relationship between the organization of the legislature and the nature of its major functions, it is not surprising that Congress has come under great criticism. Although it has adopted several reforms, these tend toward increased bureaucratization. They strengthen both specialization, as shown by the proliferation of subcommittees, and hierarchy, as seen in the enlargement of the powers of the speaker. Perhaps even more telling is Congress's lapse into another bureaucratic response: increasing its staff.

* In any event, if congressmen thought that they would be held responsible for all of the poor legislative proposals they introduce, the number of particularistic and publicity-oriented bills introduced would surely decline.

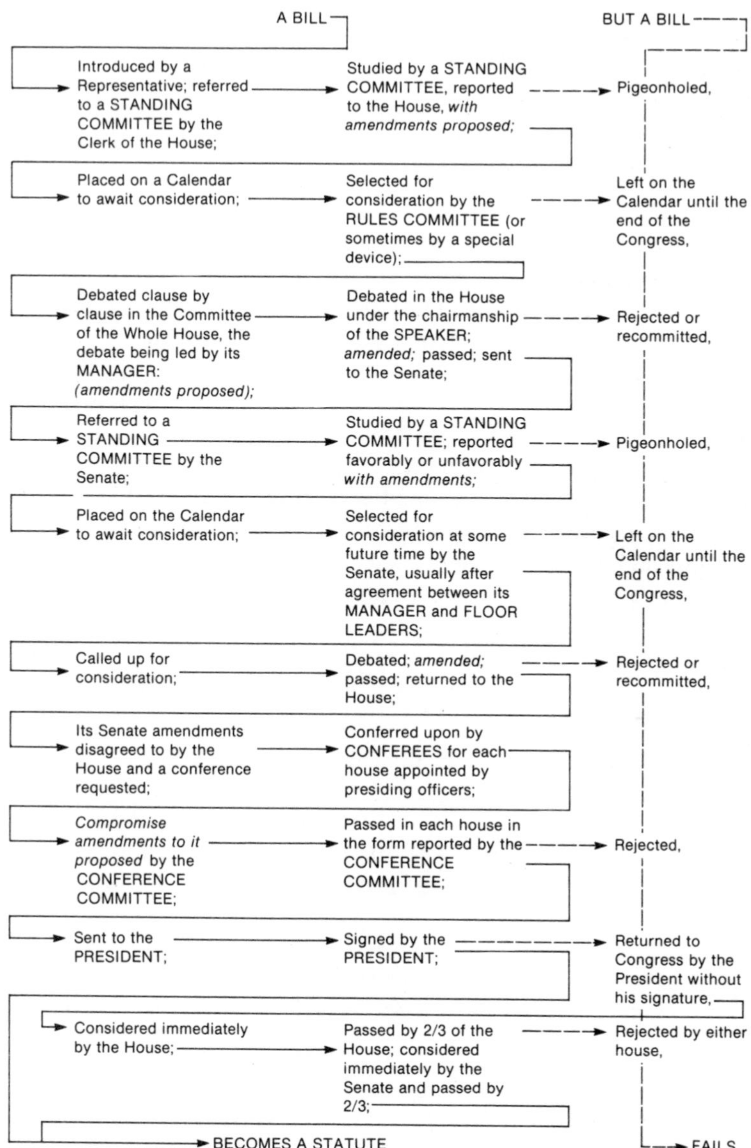

Figure 5–1 **How a Bill Becomes a Law**

SOURCE: Reprinted with permission of Macmillan Publishing Co., Inc., from, *Democracy in the United States*, 2nd ed., by William H. Riker. Copyright © 1965 by William H. Riker.

THE STAFFS OF CONGRESS

PERSONAL AND COMMITTEE STAFFS

The bureaucratization of Congress does not end with the organization of its membership. Indeed, that is scarcely the beginning. In addition to the elected, there are the unelected. The unelected include the personal and committee staffs of Congress and the employees of its administrative units: for example, the Congressional Budget Office, the General Accounting Office, the Office of Technology Assessment, and the Congressional Reference Service, to name four of the more prominent. In the past decade the growth of the unelected in numbers and power has been truly phenomenal. In 1976 Senator Robert Morgan announced on the floor of the Senate: "This country is basically run by the legislative staffs of the Members of the Senate and Members of the House of Representatives. We ought to have the best staffs available that we can find anywhere, because they are the ones who give us advice as to how to vote, and then we vote on their recommendations."[17] While the senator may have overstated the power of Congress, his assessment of the influence of the staff on members of Congress is indisputable.

Perhaps nowhere else in the government has the subtle growth of the influence of the unelected been more interesting. The process began with the expansion of personal and committee staffs. Until the 1840s, committee matters were handled by the members themselves. Then Congress au-

Table 5–2

House and Senate Standing Committee and Subcommittee Staffs (Selected Years)

Year	NO. EMPLOYED House	NO. EMPLOYED Senate
1947	182	222
1957	348	371
1962	466	472
1965	506	448
1972	727	814
1975	952	1,120

SOURCE: Reprinted with permission from the *Proceedings of the Academy of Political Science*, vol. 32, no. 1 (1975): 115; edited by Harvey Mansfield.

Table 5–3

Personal Staff Employees of Members of Congress (Selected Years)

YEAR	SENATE	HOUSE
1891	39	—
1914	72	(No limit on number of staff; staff allowance of $1,500 a year per representative)
1930	280	870
1935	424	870
1947	590	1,449
1957	1,115	2,441
1967	1,749	4,055
1972	2,426	5,280
1975	2,600	6,114

SOURCE: Reprinted with permission from the *Proceedings of the Academy of Political Science*, vol. 32, no. 1 (1975): 115; edited by Harvey Mansfield.

thorized committees to hire first part-time, and subsequently full-time, assistance. For about a century the growth of committee staffs was gradual. However, the Legislative Reorganization Act of 1946 placed the committee staffs on a more formal basis by providing each committee with a permanent authorization for funds to cover professional and clerical help. Appropriations for this purpose a year later signaled the beginning of rapid expansion in the size, specialization, and power of legislative staffs. The growth of committee staffs from 1947 to 1975 is reported in Table 5–2.

The personal staffs of representatives and senators have grown in similar fashion. In 1885 the Senate arranged to provide its members with an allocation of six dollars a day while in session for the purpose of obtaining clerical assistance. Eight years later the employment of clerks on an annual basis was authorized for both houses of the legislature. As in the case of committee staffs, growth in personal staffs was gradual until the 1940s, when it began to accelerate as shown in Table 5–3. By 1975 there were more than fourteen times as many personal staff employees in the House as there were representatives; the ratio in the Senate was twenty-six to one. In 1978 the combined total of personal and committee staffs was 13,276.[18]

Committee staffs are divided into two groups: those for the members of the majority party and those for the minority. Under the Legislative Reorganization Act of 1970, the minority party was supposed to have at least one-third of the allocation of the majority party for staff purposes. In 1971, however, the Democrats changed this standard to one of "fair consideration" for the minority members on a committee. The Republicans have not been able to recoup their loss, and it is often alleged that the minority party members of committees are relatively understaffed.

The chief majority and chief minority counsels head their party staffs on a committee. Their power, especially that of the majority counsel, is seen in virtually all the committee's activities. Indeed, so important have the counsels become that they may view the committee as their own and thus come into conflict with its chairman. In two House committees during the 1970s—one investigating the assassinations of John F. Kennedy and Martin Luther King, Jr., and the other exploring the "Koreagate" scandal—the chief counsels for the majority publicly denounced the political leadership of the committees they were serving.[19] In essence they accused the committee chairmen of interfering with *their* investigations and hearings. Predictably, both staffers left their posts, but the lesson was clear: the staff of committees, and especially its leadership, is increasingly willing to assert its influence publicly. It is significant that the "Koreagate" investigation was turned over to Leon Jaworski, former Watergate special prosecutor. The committee sorely needed to reestablish its ethical credibility.

It should not be surprising if the staff is stealing the show on committees, for to some extent they *are* the show. Indeed, Harrison Fox, a chief counsel to a Senate committee studying the committee system, says, "All research is done by staff and perhaps 90 per cent of all legislative ideas are generated by staff."[20] One Senate staffer described the functions of committee staff as follows:

1. The staff organizes all hearings on specific pieces of legislation, as well as the more general "investigative" hearings. Witnesses are frequently selected by the staff, subject to the approval of the Members. Staff aides brief Senators on the subject matters of hearings, and *supply questions to be asked of witnesses*. [Italics added.]
2. The drafts of committee bills are written by the staff in "staff mark-up" sessions in which aides present the views of their Senators. These staff drafts are then amended by Senators in a "committee markup."
3. A staff-written "committee report" accompanies every bill that reaches the floor. Although they are often partisan, these reports serve as the major channel of information between the committee and other Senators and staffs. On emergency bills, or late in a session, they must be written in haste. Despite the fact that they are almost exclusively staff-produced and rarely receive more than cursory Senatorial attention, they are the major guideposts for judicial and agency interpretations of Congressional intent.[21]

Committee staffs in the House perform virtually identical functions. Generally, the staffs of counterpart committees in each chamber communicate with one another in an effort to integrate the activities of their committees. Committee staffs, like personal staffs, are also in frequent contact with middle- and upper-level executive branch bureaucrats. Indeed, a knowledgeable observer has said, "In oversight—that is, checking that the laws are being properly carried out by executive agencies—. . . 99 percent [of the work] is done by staff."[22]

Personal staffs are attached to individual representatives and senators. They can be organized and assigned to functions as the member sees fit. In fact, congressmen have had more freedom in this regard than the average employer because they have exempted themselves from many restrictive labor and civil rights laws.[23] Nevertheless, several organizational patterns and types of staff activities are common. Members of both houses generally assign administrative matters to an administrative assistant (AA), although an office manager is not uncommon in the Senate. These individuals are responsible for such matters as supervising the office personnel, coordinating and assigning work, overseeing hiring, and handling the payroll. The AA is usually the member's spokesman to the press, constituents, and interest groups. The more routine administrative matters are commonly handled by an executive secretary. Legislative affairs fall under the jurisdiction of the legislative assistant (LA). This employee generally works with the member in committee, performs research, drafts bills, analyzes legislative proposals, and writes speeches to be delivered on the floor by the member and articles to be published under his or her name. LAs of the same party as the president are often in frequent contact with the Executive Office of the President. They may also accompany a senator to the floor of that chamber. In addition, most congressmen have press aides who "advertise their member's work through any available media."[24]

Virtually all staffers, professional or clerical, share the work in dealing with the huge volume of mail that flows into any congressman's office. In many cases no more than a standardized reply is called for. In others, however, the appropriate response involves "casework," that is, an effort to help a particular constituent with some problem he or she is having. Often this requires nothing more than an inquiry to a federal agency to find out why a social security check or other benefit appears to have gone astray. But in other instances it may mean helping a constituent draft an application for a federal grant or find a job. Casework has become a pervasive feature of the congressman's job, because it is viewed as highly relevant to reelection. Consequently it takes up a substantial amount of staff time. As the importance of casework increased, "the percent of staff assigned to the home districts has more than doubled, from 14 percent of all listed staff members in 1960 to 34 percent in 1974."[25] Casework inevitably distracts the congressman from matters of more general importance and forces him or her to concentrate on situations of individual or parochial concern. Such an "ombudsman" function may be desirable, but obtaining it through the members of Congress has important costs.

The organization of a member's office reflects his or her own biases, but the largest group of congressmen organize their staffs hierarchically. Thus almost all communication and coordination between the senator or representative and the staff are channeled through the administrative assistant.[26] Republicans and congressmen with long seniority seem especially prone to this form of organization. Since these hierarchies are complemented by specialization, such staffs tend to behave in a bureaucratic fashion. In contrast, other staffs are organized to allow direct access of all personnel to the congressman. Still others follow a modified hierarchical form, allowing access to the member through two senior staffers. The overall climate of many offices is bureaucratic, often involving set routines and form replies for various matters. Whatever the relationships among staff members, bureaucratic impersonality prevails in the sense that the casework they do for constituents and the speeches and bills they write will be attributed to the congressman. Perhaps one indicator of the growing institutionalization of personal staffs is that after the election of 1978, seventeen members of the staff of a defeated congressman sought to "sell their services as a team to a Congressional newcomer."[27]

Given the proliferation of committee and personal staffs and the nature of their functions, it is not surprising that their political influence has become great—sometimes greater than that of their congressmen. A number of observers have noted this development.

> Committee staffs exercise substantial influence. The extreme, but common example of this occurs when committee or subcommittee chairmen defer to the judgments of senior staff members whether to accept or reject floor amendments to major and detailed bills.[28]

> More impressive are the kinds of tasks Members of Congress have become willing to delegate to their staffs. This has reached the point where some Members publicly ask whether they or their staffs are in charge.[29]

> As demands on congressmen have become more intense and frequent, congressional staff members have had to assume a greater role in policy making and oversight. . . . For instance, the Congressional Budget and Impoundment Control Act of 1974, surely one of the most important bills enacted by Congress in the last twenty-five years, was largely formulated by staff in a long series of "markup" sessions. . . . It was finally redrafted by a conference of a few select staff members from the major committees and joint committees that were concerned with the bill. Senators, indeed, are functioning more and

more like directors or trustees of a large organization, giving direction to policy but not working out the details.[30]

> I feel [said a staff member of the House Armed Services Committee] that the staff has an enormous impact on the policy output of the committee. It works under the general guidance of the chairman, but has a pretty wide berth. Further, the advice of the staff is very often sought by [executive] agency staff people, and given regularly without consulting the members of the committee; and, it usually is taken.[31]

> The staff tends to frame the options, and if you frame the options you can often frame the outcome.[32]

The influence of an individual staff member depends largely on three sets of factors. First, *circumstances* can enhance a staffer's power. In one documented case, a senator told a top aide to "take care of" matters pertaining to a bill concerning the establishment of a Federal Elections Commission (FEC). Later the aide advised the senator to vote against an amendment to the bill, and the senator unhesitatingly did so. After the amendment lost by one vote, the aide reflected: "If I had told him to vote the other way, the FEC would be out of existence now. . . . I had the power—me, an appointed staff member, elected by nobody and responsible to nobody—to overturn a major law in this country. It's scary."[33]

Second, a staff member's *long service, specialization, and expertise* generate influence. It has been said that the staff director of the Joint Committee on Internal Revenue Taxation "has probably had a greater impact on the nation's tax laws than any member of Congress."[34] As one staffer described it, this director "simply knows more about his subject than any member. . . . As a result, he writes proposals as he sees fit."[35]

Finally, the *personal qualities* of a staffer are an important element in his or her influence. One staffer, held in great respect by the Democratic membership of the Senate, said, "I've had a greater input to the national policy than I ever could have had in any other job. It's very satisfying to translate your own ideas into national policy."[36] In recent years aides to Senators Edward Kennedy and Henry Jackson have been among those who became prominent in policymaking and received national attention,[37] though this should not be taken to imply that these senators are overpowered by their staffs.

In sum, a great share of Congress's power now rests in the hands of its appointive component. Several pitfalls are inherent in this development. The major difficulty presented by the staff can be summarized as follows: "The new staff bureaucracy and the 'legislative explosion' it has helped create threaten to bury Congress under its own paperwork, just as surely as if the staff had never existed. Congress has become just as incapable of evaluating the biases in the information from its own staffs as it has from sources outside Congress."[38]

This observation can be broken down into two parts. First, there is a problem presented by the "staff mentality." As noted in Chapter 4 on the presidency, staff positions have something basically irresponsible about them. Staffers exercise public power without accountability to the public, or even to the officials elected by it. Although they are termed "professional," neutrality and objectivity are not the hallmark of committee or personal staffs. Partisanship is built into staffing, which is intended to reflect broadly the thinking of either Democrats or Republicans on committees, and the ideological shade of the individual member in his or her office. Moreover, many staff members are lawyers, trained in the adversary style. They consider it their job to make the most forceful presentation of their client's case, not to discover truth or promote the public interest.[39] This approach has advantages where disputes are played out before the public or juries, but distortions can occur in the legislature, where neither the minority party nor all concerned individuals and groups have an equal right, opportunity, or ability to present their cases. Congressmen depend on information presented by their staffs, but their staffs tend to color the information. When the chairman and ranking minority member of a committee or subcommittee favor a bill, the staff will present highly supportive information in its report to the rest of the chamber. If there are facts on the other side of the issue, they may never become available to Congress as a whole.

The second problem is that the increased staff, rather than reducing Congress's work load, has contributed to its expansion. Many committee and personal staffs are encouraged to play an entrepreneurial role, that is, members of Congress want them to identify problem areas and develop legislation intended to help solve the problems. While such activities could be very desirable for the public good, their cumulative effect is to flood the legislative system with bills to consider and work to perform. While the whole legislative overload cannot be attributed to this problem, the number of bills now introduced per session is enormous, surpassing 22,000 in the 95th Congress (1977–1978).[40] Moreover, there is a circular tendency in the process. The more bills introduced, the greater the committee specialization that is desired; the more committees and subcommittees created, the more staff that is hired; the more staff, the more bills.

In addition, there is no evidence that the growing number of staffers has actually made Congress less dependent on the executive branch and interest groups for information. Indeed, staff research often consists of assembling facts already known and supplied by these sources. Yet despite all these pitfalls, it may well be the case that increasing staff power is desirable. After all, congressional staffs are typically well educated, bright, energetic, and relatively expert in their areas of activity. Being unelected, like bureaucrats and judges, they do not have to worry about being reelected. While there have been some scandals involving staffs, on the whole corruption involving them seems limited. In all these respects, the staffs add valuable characteristics to the legislature. Perhaps their contribution is even more evident in the "other staff," the employees of Congress's leading administrative agencies.

ADMINISTRATIVE STAFFS

An organizational chart of Congress (Figure 5–2) indicates that the legislative branch has developed a substantial number of administrative agencies. Except for their placement in Congress, some of these, including the Government Printing Office, are virtually indistinguishable from executive branch bureaucracies in their organization and operation. Others, such as the office of Architect of the Capitol, the Library of Congress, and the United States Botanic Gardens, have unique and mostly apolitical roles. By contrast, still others are politically powerful and provide further evidence of the bureaucratization of the legislature. Two of these, the General Accounting Office (GAO) and the Congressional Budget Office (CBO), deserve special attention.

General Accounting Office. The GAO was established in 1921 as an independent agency within the legislative branch.[41] It is headed by a comptroller general and a deputy comptroller general, both appointed by the president with the advice and consent of the Senate for a term of fifteen years. Although originally created to assist Congress in providing legislative control over the use of federal funds, in recent years the agency has often been involved in broader and sometimes more controversial matters. For example, it is now commonly concerned with not just the costs, but also the quality of the decisions and general management practices of the executive branch. While its overall mission is to improve the economy and efficiency of government and the effectiveness of federal programs, the GAO has on occasion been thrust into the very heart of partisan politics. Thus during the 1976 presidential campaign, it issued a report that was highly critical of President Ford's use of military force to free the *Mayaguez* from Cambodia.[42] In addition, the GAO may be directed by Congress to investigate the feasibility of presidentially sponsored programs. In September 1977, after investigating some of the assumptions of the Carter energy program, the GAO issued a report concluding that several of its crucial premises were untenable.

In recent years, as budgets have grown and public policy and governmental operations have become more technical and specialized in content,

UNITED STATES SENATE

THE VICE PRESIDENT
PRESIDENT PRO TEMPORE
DEPUTY PRESIDENT PRO TEMPORE

Secretary of the Senate

Assistant Secretary

Parliamentarian
Assistant Parliamentarians
Journal Clerk
Legislative Clerk
Assistant Legislative Clerk
2d Assistant Legislative Clerk
Executive Clerk
Legislative Information Clerk

Printing Clerk
Bill Clerk
Enrolling Clerk
Clerk of Enrolled Units
Special Assistant
Deputy Assistant Clerks

Official Reporters of Debates

Senate Daily Digest

Office of Public Records

Disbursing Office

Library

Document Room

Stationery Room

Curator of Art and Antiquities

Senate Historian

Administrative Director
Technical Advisor

Secretary for the Majority
Assistant Secretary

Secretary for the Minority
Assistant Secretary

Chaplain

Legislative Counsel

Elected Officers of the Senate:
President Pro Tempore
Deputy President Pro Tempore
The Secretary
The Sergeant at Arms
The Chaplain
Secretary for the Majority
Secretary for the Minority

Sergeant at Arms of The Senate

Administrative Assistant To Sergeant At Arms

Deputy Sergeant At Arms

Special Assistant To Sergeant At Arms

Executive Secretary to Sergeant At Arms

Senate Post Office

Service Department (Office machines, supplies, repairs; warehouse, duplicating; speech folding; heavy documents)

Computer Center

Custodial Service (Senate side of Capitol)

Communications (Telepone and Telegraph)

Barber Shops

Beauty Shop

Elevator Operators

Press
Press gallery, Radio-TV Periodical, and Press Photogs gallery

Senate Chamber (Order in; furnishings; Pages, Doorkeepers)

Capitol Police Board (Member of; Chairman, odd years)

Capitol Police-Senate Side (Appointive authority for Senate detail)

Radio-TV recording studio (Radio tapes, video tape and TV films)

Capitol Guide Board (Member of; Chairman, in odd years)

Capitol Guides (Appointive and supervisory authority)

Cabinet Shop

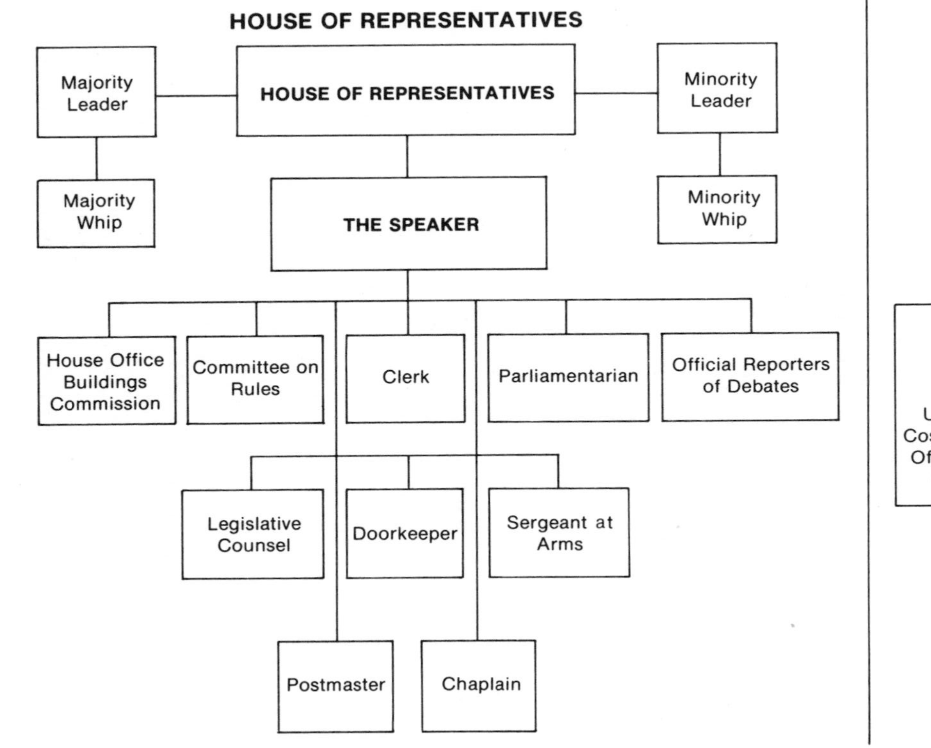

Figure 5–2 **Administrative Organization of Congress**

SOURCE: *U.S. Government Manual*, 1977–1978 (Washington, D.C.: Government Printing Office), pp. 28, 32, 33.

Congress has turned increasingly to the GAO for direction. In the words of Elmer Staats, comptroller general, "The direct assistance provided by this office in the form of special studies to the Congress as a whole and to committees and to individual members has increased from approximately 8 per cent of a professional staff of 2,400 in 1966 to 34 per cent of a professional staff of approximately 3,700 currently [1975]."[43] Again we find Congress increasingly relying on its unelected component and being increasingly influenced by it. And again we find that component expanding in size. GAO conclusions, of course, can be ignored or rejected. Nevertheless, it is evident that here, as in the case of personal and committee staffs, the choices before Congress may be structured by the alternatives, advice, and information presented by the legislature's unelected component. The tendency in this direction is even more obvious with regard to budgeting.

Congressional Budget Office. It is hornbook wisdom that the "power of the purse" is the hallmark of legislative authority. Executive power, or so the founding fathers thought, can be easily curtailed by a legislature that refuses to pay for it. In recent years, though, Congress has lost a good deal of control over the budgeting process. Executive initiative in the creation and structuring of the budget, as well as various mechanisms that leave billions of dollars outside the immediate reach of legislative control, have placed Congress's power of the purse in precarious circumstances.[44] Realizing this, Congress turned to bureaucratization and to the unelected for assistance—this time in the form of the Congressional Budget Office (CBO), created by the Budget and Impoundment Control Act of 1974. The act provided for new House and Senate budget committees. The House committee has an interesting feature in that its membership must be rotated. No representative may remain on it for more than four years in any ten of his or her legislative service. Both committees have large staffs—about forty professionals and twenty-five support personnel on the House side, and fifty-five and thirty respectively in the Senate.[45] Given the rotational requirement in the House, the staff there are likely to be extremely influential. Their tenure may be longer than that of the members, and consequently their expertise may be greater as well.

The CBO is headed by a director who is appointed by the speaker of the House and the president pro tempore of the Senate for a four-year term. Among the CBO's functions are (1) to monitor the economy and estimate its impact on the budget, (2) to improve the flow and quality of budgetary information, and (3) to analyze the costs and effects of alternative budgetary choices. In this sense the CBO is a legislative equivalent to the executive's Office of Management and Budget, which does most of the work in formulating the budget. Indeed, the creation of the CBO illustrates one of the classic observations about bureaucracy: bureaucratization increases within a society, because it takes bureaucracy to control bureaucracy. (Remember the Law of Control Duplication from Chapter 2.) Congress has created its own bureaucracy in an effort to check effectively the OMB and gain more control over federal spending.[46] The question of who will control the CBO and the budget committee staffs, however, is not so easily answered. Undoubtedly the director of the CBO, like that of the OMB, will become powerful, as will the office itself. But the "power of the purse" will hardly return to the elected. In the future, Congress is likely to have more and better information available when it evaluates the executive's budgetary proposals, but at the same time it will also be reacting to the assumptions, analyses, advice, data, and alternatives presented to it by the new legislative budget bureaucrats. The current system may improve upon the past, but bureaucratization continues apace. Today it seems little more than quaintly charming that the founders thought they were protecting the people by requiring that all revenue bills originate in the House of Representatives and that an account of government spending be published on occasion![47]

It is too early to develop a more profound assessment of the CBO. The important point, however, is that bureaucratization appears to be the direction of the legislative future. Indeed in 1972, even as President Nixon was phasing out its White House Office counterpart, Congress created the Office of Technology Assessment to provide technical evaluations of pending legislation. Although small, the office represented still another administrative answer to a legislative problem. Almost wherever one turns within the legislative branch, whether to observe the creation of new administrative units or the expansion of old, the number and importance of the unelected is constantly growing. Where does this leave the voters?

THE ELECTED AND THE PUBLIC

The organization of Congress contributes to several of its inherent limitations as a political institution in a democratic polity. Bureaucratization has placed the typical member of Congress in the position of a director who oversees a staff. He or she relies on others to supply information, ideas, proposals, and policy alternatives; to write letters, speeches, bills, and articles; to handle the media; to do casework. As Congress lost its initiative in legislation, its chief power became that of saying "no" to the president—hence the rise of the legislative veto.[48] As individual members have lost much of the initiative for ideas and action to their unelected staffs, their chief power likewise has become saying "no." A congressman may still work almost alone to develop an idea, transform it into a legislative proposal, and push for its acceptance—but this is the exception rather than the rule.

Perhaps the most fundamental question in this regard is whether our bureaucratized legislature is nevertheless a representative institution. The concept of representation is one of the most perplexing in the social sciences. Part of the problem is that "representation, taken generally, means the making present *in some* sense of something which is nevertheless *not* present literally or in fact."[49] Although the idea of representation is somewhat paradoxical, there are two general approaches to understanding and using this term.

DELEGATE REPRESENTATION

The representative as "delegate" of the represented is probably the more common concept of representation in the United States. According to this approach, a good representative is one who faithfully represents the wishes and desires of his or her constituents. The closer the agreement between the legislator's voting and the constituency's attitudes, the greater the representation. An inherent problem here, however, is whether a delegate representative should reflect the opinions of a majority of constituents, or the collective thinking of them all. The latter approach would assign some weight to minority opinions, especially where they are intensely held.

The findings of research that takes minority opinions into account are by no means conclusive.[50] However, they do suggest that representation by members of Congress fits the delegate concept only to the extent that the issue involved is highly salient to the constituency. Even then the agreement between constituencies and their congressmen is far from perfect. Figure 5–3 provides a summary diagram of one set of findings. It shows the relationship between the votes of members of the House on civil rights questions and the attitudes of their constituencies on the same matters. The correlation coefficient (statistical relationship) between representatives' votes and constituencies' attitudes is .57, which on the whole means that the attitudes of constituencies account for only a small part of the reasons why representatives vote the way they do.* The figure also suggests some reasons why this is the case. It is evident that the electoral process does not select representatives whose personal attitudes reflect

* This conclusion is based on the statistical concept of *variance*, a measure of the relationship between variables. In this case the relationship is between representatives' votes and constituencies' attitudes. Variance is computed by taking the correlation coefficient, squaring it, and multiplying by 100 to arrive at a percentage. With a correlation coefficient of .57, the variance is 32.49 percent.

those of their constituency. Rather, the route to representation in the House is for congressmen to try to understand the position of their constituencies on an issue and then vote in accordance with this perception. Of course, the congressmen's understanding of their districts' positions would have to be accurate in order to produce forceful delegate representation. But in fact, as Figure 5–3 shows, congressmen do not fully know what their constituents think.

There are important reasons why they do not. First, congressmen tend to hear most often from the more articulate segments of their constituencies. Yet there is little reason to expect that voters who write letters, send telegrams, and make phone calls are representative of a majority. After all, only about 15 percent of the population has *ever* written a letter to a congressman, and approximately 3 percent of the population writes two-thirds of all congressional mail.[51] Second, congressmen generally hear most often from those who agree with them.[52] Third, congressmen generally assign greater weight to the opinions of newspapers and economic and social leaders than to those of ordinary citizens. Finally, because it is

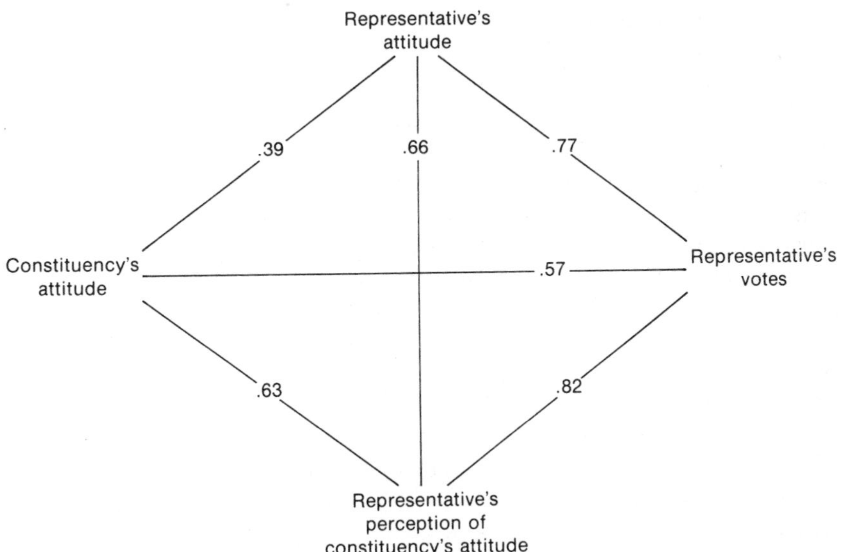

Figure 5–3 **Constituency's Attitudes and Congressmen's Votes on Civil Rights Issues**

SOURCE: Warren E. Miller and Donald E. Stokes, "Constituency Influence in Congress," *American Political Science Review*, 57:1 (March 1963), 45–56; as presented in Thomas R. Dye and L. Harmon Zeigler, *The Irony of Democracy*, 3rd ed. (North Scituate, Mass: Duxbury Press, 1975), p. 175.

the congressman's staff who read, interpret, and categorize communication and information for their boss, there is even more room for distortion. Many, often most, of a congressman's Washington staff are neither from the district nor familiar with it. Not only is their feeling for the constituency likely to be less sensitive than that of the elected representative, but they may filter information in such a way as to make it more pleasing to the boss. All in all, there is great room for misinterpretation and misunderstanding.[53]

Delegate representation is even further limited by the fact that even when members of Congress think they understand their constituencies' attitudes, they may not vote in accordance with them. Among the factors that commonly influence congressional votes are committee recommendations, presidential positions, the congressman's own attitude, the position of the party leadership, the position of the party in the district, how other members of the state delegation intend to vote, the pressure exerted by an interest group or a campaign contributor, and of course, the recommendations of the personal, committee, and administrative staffs of the legislature.

The fact is that Congress shows a moderate degree of delegate representation on issues like civil rights, which are highly salient and often arouse intense emotions in the population as a whole. However, in areas concerning social welfare and foreign policy, which contained no emotional issues when the research was conducted, much weaker relationships were found between the attitudes of a constituency and its congressman's votes. Here the constituency's view becomes less important and the other factors influencing a congressman weigh more heavily. The vast bulk of laws concern such nonemotional issues. Therefore, for the most part the House of Representatives cannot be said to provide strong delegate representation. It is reasonable to assume that the Senate, with larger districts and longer terms, behaves similarly.

TRUSTEE REPRESENTATION

Given the prevailing thinking about representation, this leaves two additional possibilities: either Congress provides "trustee representation," or Congress does not really represent the public's attitudes in accordance with any accepted concept of representation. In trustee representation a member of the legislature represents the "best" interests of his or her constituency or of the nation as a whole. The basic notion is that a representative ought to rise above the sometimes selfish or shortsighted concerns of a constituency and act as a leader in behalf of the public good.[54] In doing so the trustee might ultimately fashion comprehensive policies for resolving political, social, and economic problems. It is crucial to this concept that at some point the voters have a chance to express their approval or disapproval of the trustee, for otherwise there would be no element of democracy in it. However, while it might be assumed that popular disapproval would lead to the rejection of "trustees'" reelection bids, this has not been the case in recent years.

Table 5–4 compares the percentage of the public giving Congress a positive rating with the percentage of incumbents in each house who have been reelected in the years covered. The question is, if so little of the population thinks well of Congress, why are incumbents so successful in getting reelected? How has it happened that "since World War II nearly

TABLE 5–4

Popular Support for Congress and Reelection of Incumbents

YEAR	PERCENT OF PUBLIC EXPRESSING POSITIVE RATING OF CONGRESS	PERCENT OF SENATE INCUMBENTS REELECTED	PERCENT OF HOUSE INCUMBENTS REELECTED
1954		85	95
1956		86	96
1958		65	91
1960		96	94
1962		90	96
1964		93	88
1965	64		
1966	49	96	90
1967	38		
1968	46	83	96
1969	34		
1970	34	88	95
1971	26		
1972	24	84	93
1974	29	92	90
1976	*	64	97
1978	*	68	95

SOURCES: Data through 1974 from *The Irony of Democracy, An Uncommon Introduction to American Politics* by Thomas R. Dye and L. Harmon Zeigler. © 1975 by Wadsworth Publishing Company, Inc., Belmont, Ca. 90042. Reprinted by permission of the publisher, Duxbury Press. 1976 and 1978 data from *Newsweek*, Nov. 20, 1978, p. 50; *New York Times*, Jan. 12, 1979.

* Although not strictly comparable, Louis Harris surveys report that 10 to 18 percent of the population expressed "high confidence" in Congress during these years.

90 percent of all incumbents have sought reelection in any given election, and approximately 90 percent of all those who ran were successful"?[55]*

There are many possible explanations, but none of which supports the idea that members of Congress fill the role of trustee representatives. First, it may be that nonvoters and voters differ sharply in their opinions of the performance of Congress. Nonvoters are a majority of the public in congressional elections, but since they do not vote, they have little influence upon the success of incumbents or any other candidates. Voters, on the other hand, may have considerably more faith in Congress, and they may perceive more direct benefits resulting from the work of their senators and representatives. But even if this is the case, congressmen cannot be considered trustee representatives because they cannot induce most eligible voters to legitimize their position—or even to express confidence in them.

Second, it may be that a majority of Americans have little faith in Congress as an institution, yet like the way *their own* congressmen operate. This interpretation has a certain appeal, because in fact much of what Congress does is parochial in nature. Congressmen seek to gain electoral majorities by bringing various benefits (in congressional lingo, "pork"), such as highways, dams, bridges, contracts, grants, and subsidies, back to their districts. For instance, in 1975 "Fewer than 75 of the 435 members of the House of Representatives [did] *not* have a major defense plant or a military installation in their district."[56] It may be that many Americans appreciate the efforts of their own congressmen in this connection, but oppose those of legislators from other districts and states. Indeed, it is even possible that many people distrust Congress as an institution because of its various pork-barrel projects, while rewarding their own congressman for getting them some. As one Senate staffer expressed it, "Their constituents don't judge them on how well they supervise the Department of Interior [for example], but only on the number of land reclamation projects they get for their state."[57] If this is the case, it would be impossible to argue that Congress as a whole provides trustee representation. And it would be difficult to maintain that individual congressmen are serving the public interest as judged by the public as a whole. It would also reinforce the contention that the structure of Congress militates against the successful performance of its major roles.

* It should be noted, however, that a trend toward shorter service may be beginning. From 1974 to 1978 the total turnover in the House was 49 percent and in the Senate, 48 percent. It should also be noted that nonincumbents are not necessarily new to Congress. The 96th Congress includes at least thirty-eight members who once worked in some staff capacity in the institution. Seven of these were elected in 1978. Some former staffers now hold leadership positions. See *Newsweek*, Nov. 20, 1978, p. 56, and *New York Times*, Nov. 19, 1978, p. 80.

Third, and more critical for a democratic government, the gap between the public's confidence in Congress and the reelection of incumbents may be explained in terms of the character of elections. Generally, incumbents have substantial advantages in running for reelection against their opponents (if any). Tables 5–5 and 5–6 present the proportion of incumbents in the House and Senate who won at least 60 percent of the majority party vote in elections in selected years during the post–World War II period. When an individual receives this proportion of the vote, the political competition is generally considered minimal and the seat is regarded as "safe." It is evident that incumbents in the House tend to be safer in this sense than those in the Senate. However, a substantial proportion of both are unlikely to face a serious challenge at the polls. Throughout the periods under consideration, between three-fifths and three-fourths of the House incumbents have held safe seats. So have about one-third to one-half of the incumbents in the Senate.

What explains the advantages of incumbents? One line of reasoning is that they have continuing benefits in their quest for reelection:

- The Use of the "Postal Frank" The volume of franked mail sent out by congressmen doubled from about 100 million pieces in the early 1960s to about 200 million a decade later.[58] Free mail, which is unavailable to a nonincumbent challenger, brings the incumbent's name and face into many households in the congressman's district.
- Facilities in Congress to Make Radio and Television Clips at Cost Except during election periods, these are likely to be broadcast free as a public service.
- Staff Activity As we have seen, much of the activity of personal staffs is aimed at public relations and constituent services. Although the sole purpose of "casework" may be to foster reelection, the expense is borne by the taxpayer.
- Electoral Dynamics For much of the time that incumbents have spent in the legislature, no one from the opposition party has been nominated to run against them. A challenger often has a great deal of trouble becoming established as a credible alternative to the incumbent. This is especially true in the Senate. Hence there is little to counteract the incumbents' own public relations efforts.

Together these advantages are regarded as providing incumbents with about a 4 to 6 percent vote advantage.[59] While the monetary value of incumbency is difficult to assess, one observer places it at $480,000.[60]

These explanations for the gap between low public confidence in Congress and the reelection of incumbents are not mutually incompatible.

TABLE 5–5

Decline in Marginality in House Elections, 1956–1974

YEAR	PROPORTION OF INCUMBENTS WINNING AT LEAST 60 PERCENT OF THE MAJOR PARTY VOTE	NO.
1956	59.1%	403
1958	63.1	390
1960	58.9	400
1962	63.6	376
1964	58.5	388
1966	67.7	401
1968	72.2	397
1970	77.3	389
1972	77.8	373
1974	66.4	383

SOURCE: From *Congress Reconsidered,* edited by Lawrence C. Dodd and Bruce Oppenheimer, copyright © 1977 by Praeger Publishers, a division of Holt, Rinehart and Winston Publishers. Reprinted by permission of Holt, Rinehart and Winston.

TABLE 5–6

Changes in Marginality in Senate Elections, by Region, 1946–1974

	PROPORTION OF INCUMBENTS WINNING AT LEAST 60 PERCENT OF THE MAJOR PARTY VOTE			
Election Triplets	South	North	Total	No.
1946–1950	100.0%	23.9%	42.6%	61
1952–1956	100.0	18.5	35.4	82
1958–1962	86.4	24.2	40.5	84
1964–1968	72.2	41.9	48.8	80
1970–1974	76.9	37.1	44.0	75

SOURCE: From *Congress Reconsidered,* edited by Lawrence C. Dodd and Bruce Oppenheimer, copyright © 1977 by Praeger Publishers, a division of Holt, Rinehart and Winston Publishers. Reprinted by permission of Holt, Rinehart and Winston.

In a provocative treatise, Morris Fiorina draws upon them all in constructing a more general theory concerning Congress. In his view,

> The growth of an activist federal government has stimulated a change in the mix of congressional activities. Specifically, a lesser proportion of congressional effort is now going into programmatic activities and a greater proportion into pork-barrel and casework activities. As a result, today's congressmen make relatively fewer enemies and relatively more friends among the people of their districts. . . .
>
> Congress does not just react to big government—it creates it. All of Washington prospers. More and more bureaucrats promulgate more and more regulations and dispense more and more money. Fewer and fewer congressmen suffer electoral defeat.[61]

Moreover, in Fiorina's view, casework is so important to the congressmen's new role that it is a major reason for the growth of personal staff: "We have seen a doubling of personal staff resources during the past fifteen years, most of which occurred at the same time the marginal districts [unsafe seats] were disappearing."[62] While recognizing the value in the congressman's new ombudsman role, Fiorina points out that it is equally important for us to be aware that "the general, long-term welfare of the United States is no more than an incidental by-product of the system."[63]

In sum, congressmen provide only limited delegate representation, and most cannot be considered trustees of the public good. Voters do not have an equal chance of electing a new face or reelecting the old. Incumbents have substantial advantages; they tend to run for reelection in overwhelming numbers; they are overwhelmingly successful in their bids; many hold safe seats. If the public felt overwhelming confidence in Congress, perhaps these conditions would not be so important. But given the low confidence in Congress that Americans express in opinion polls, at least one conclusion is inescapable: Many elected members of Congress have been able to turn the bureaucratization of that institution to their own electoral advantage.

Conclusion The Congressional Dilemma

In the early 1970s several reforms were proposed and adopted by Congress. For example, the practice of making committee assignments by seniority was formally reduced in stature from almost a law to little more than a norm. The speaker was given more power, as were the rank-and-file Democrats. Subcommittees were given a "bill of rights" ensuring, among other things, their existence and adequate staffing.[64] By 1979, however, the shortcomings of these reforms were evident. Seniority has in fact remained dominant. The speaker's new powers have hardly helped coordinate activity among the presidency, the Senate, and the House, even though Democrats controlled these institutions. Staffs keep growing, as do their functions.[65]

The reforms are largely inconsequential because they take the congressional structure as given, and attempt to modify some aspects of the process by which Congress operates. Thus as long as there are standing committees, formulas for assigning members to them will be needed. Seniority, while not apolitical in its effect, is convenient in that it reduces intense conflict over each and every desired position. As long as there is specialization, there will be veto points. As long as there is a leadership hierarchy, there will be inequality among members. As long as Congress seeks to check the executive branch by duplicating its bureaucratic structures, power will continue to accumulate in the hands of the committee, personal, and administrative staffs. As long as incumbents can use their staffs and other institutional benefits to their own advantage in elections, challengers will face a difficult task in attempting to unseat them. In short, Congress has become bureaucratic, and its structure has come to dominate its activity.

Congress does not legislate, represent, or oversee the executive branch well. It does provide useful services for constituents. It can act as an important check on presidential proposals for legislation. And through its amendment of these proposals, Congress has a major impact on our lives. But the legislature will not change fundamentally without a fundamental change in its bureaucratized structure. If its bureaucratization were to be reversed, however, Congress would undoubtedly be even less forceful, especially with regard to its power as a check on the presidency. And if it were less effective in this respect, the executive branch bureaucracy would be all the more powerful. Here again we see the dilemma of our bureaucratic age: it takes bureaucracy to control bureaucracy.

NOTES

1. See Joseph Clark, *The Sapless Branch* (New York: Harper and Row, 1965); and Drew Pearson and Jack Anderson, *The Case against Congress* (New York: Pocket Books, 1969).

2. See *Powell v. McCormack*, 395 U.S. 486 (1969) for the Supreme Court's interpretation.

3. Norman Ornstein, Robert Peabody, and David W. Rohde, "The Changing Senate: From the 1950s to the 1970s," in Lawrence C. Dodd and Bruce I. Oppenheimer, eds., *Congress Reconsidered* (New York: Praeger, 1977), p.15.

4. Lawrence C. Dodd and Bruce I. Oppenheimer, "The House in Transition," ibid., p. 37. The number of committees and subcommittees is subject to change by the legislature. Historically, a reduction in the number of committees has been associated with an increase in the number of subcommittees.

5. Garrison Nelson, "Assessing the Congressional Committee System," *Annals of the American Academy of Political and Social Science*, 411 (January 1974), 120–132.

6. See *Wesberry v. Sanders*, 376 U.S. 1 (1964).

7. U.S., Congress, Senate, Commission on the Operation of the Senate, *Legislative Activity Sourcebook: The United States Senate*, 94th Cong., 2d Sess., 1978, p. 38.

8. Michael Mabin, "Congressional Committee Staffs: Who's in Charge Here?" *The Public Interest*, 47 (Spring 1977), 36.

9. For an excellent discussion of "constituency," see Grant McConnell, *Private Power and American Democracy* (New York: Knopf, 1966), esp. chap. 4.

10. Ornstein, Peabody, and Rohde, "The Changing Senate," in Dodd and Oppenheimer, *Congress Reconsidered*, p. 15.

11. Nevertheless, because the rank-and-file party members now play a greater role in the selection process, chairmen may be more responsive to their wishes. See *New York Times*, Nov. 19, 1978, p. 31.

12. Morris P. Fiorina, *Congress: Keystone of the Washington Establishment* (New Haven, Conn.: Yale University Press, 1977), p. 63, observes that in 1973, on the average, one out of every two Democrats in the House chaired a subcommittee, and every Senate Democrat chaired an average of two subcommittees. Of course, some subcommittees are more important than others. See also Randall B. Ripley, *Congress: Process and Policy*, 2nd ed. (New York, Norton, 1978), p. 168. Ripley observes that even though the full Democratic membership of House committees has been able to vote on the assignment of subcommittee chairmen since 1973, seniority on the full committee remains the most important criterion for selection.

13. William J. Keefe and Morris S. Ogul, *The American Legislative Process*, 4th ed. (Englewood Cliffs, N.J.: Prentice-Hall, 1977), pp. 277–278.

14. See ibid., p. 232; and Bruce I. Oppenheimer, "The Rules Committee: New Arm of Leadership in a Decentralized House," in Dodd and Oppenheimer, *Congress Reconsidered*, p. 97.

15. Ibid.

16. See David J. Vogler, *The Third House* (Evanston, Ill.: Northwestern University Press, 1971).

17. Quoted in Michael Scully, "Reflections of a Senate Aide," *The Public Interest*, 47 (Spring 1977), 42.

18. James Reston, "Backstairs in the Congress," *New York Times*, Jan. 12, 1979, p. A23.

19. See *New York Times*, July 17, 1977, p. 6E, for a discussion of the "Koreagate" episode. It should be noted that both committees were special, rather than standing.

20. *Newsweek*, Jan. 17, 1977, p. 20.

21. Scully, "Reflections of a Senate Aide," pp. 46–47.

22. *Newsweek*, Jan. 17, 1977, p. 20. Quoting Harrison Fox, Jr.

23. In 1977 the Senate adopted a ban on employment discrimination for the first time. See Daniel P. Moynihan, "Imperial Government," *Commentary*, 65 (June 1978), 27.

24. Harrison Fox, Jr., and Susan Hammond, "The Growth of Congressional Staff," in Harvey Mansfield, ed., *Congress against the President* (New York: Academy of Political Science, 1975), p. 118.

25. Fiorina, *Congress*, p. 57.

26. Harrison W. Fox, Jr., and Susan Webb Hammond, "Congressional Staffs and Congressional Change," paper to *American Political Science Association*, New Orleans, September 4–8, 1973.

27. *New York Times*, Nov. 20, 1978, p. 7.

28. Scully, "Reflections of a Senate Aide," p. 46.

29. Malbin, "Congressional Committee Staffs: Who's in Charge Here?" p. 17.

30. Fox, Jr., and Hammond, "The Growth of Congressional Staff," in Mansfield, *Congress against the President*, p. 123.

31. Keefe and Ogul, *The American Legislative Process*, p. 195.

32. *New York Times*, May 17, 1978, p. A9.

33. *Newsweek*, Jan. 17, 1977, p. 20.

34. Ibid., p. 21.

35. Ibid.

36. Ibid.

37. See *New York Times*, May 17, 1978, p. A9, and Dec. 4, 1977, p. 19.

38. Malbin, "Congressional Committee Staffs," p. 19.

39. Ibid., p. 31.

40. *New York Times*, Dec. 3, 1978, p. 90; about 3,000 were enacted.

41. See Richard E. Brown, *The GAO* (Knoxville, Tenn.: University of Tennessee Press, 1970), for a detailed discussion.

42. See "The GAO Has Much More Than Ledger Domain," *New York Times*, June 25, 1978, p. E3. The report was made public at the request of the Democratic majority in the House. It was released the day of the Carter-Ford foreign policy debate in 1976.

43. Quoted in Keefe and Ogul, *The American Legislative Process*, p. 407.

44. Timothy H. Ingram, "The Billions in the White House Basement," in Stanley Bach and George Sulzner, eds., *Perspectives on the Presidency* (Lexington, Mass.: D. C. Heath, 1974), pp. 333–347.

45. John Ellwood and James Thurber, "The New Congressional Budget Process," in Dodd and Oppenheimer, *Congress Reconsidered*, p. 170.

46. Daniel P. Moynihan, "Imperial Government," p. 26, points out that the creation of the CBO coincides with a period in which Congress seeks to spend more money than does the president.

47. But even this protection has been eroded. See *United States v. Richardson*, 418 U.S. 166 (1974).

48. Moynihan, "Imperial Government," p. 30, points out that in 1975 alone, congressional veto provisions were incorporated into fifty-eight laws. See Chapter 4 for a more detailed discussion.

49. Hannah Pitkin, *The Concept of Representation* (Berkeley, Calif.: University of California Press, 1967), pp. 8–9.

50. See, among others, J. W. Kingdon, *Congressmen's Voting Decisions* (New York: Harper and Row, 1973); Aage R. Clausen, *How Congressmen Decide* (New York: St. Martin's, 1973); D. Mayhew, *Congress: The Electoral Connection* (New Haven, Conn.: Yale University Press, 1974); R. Erikson, "The Electoral Impact of Congressional Roll Call Voting," *American Political Science Review*, 65 (December 1971), 1018–1032; and R. Weissberg, "Collective versus Dyadic Representation in Congress," ibid., 72 (June 1978), 535–574. The research upon which we are reporting is W. Miller and D. Stokes, "Constituency Influence in Congress," ibid., 57 (March 1963), 45–56.

51. Thomas Dye and L. Harmon Zeigler, *The Irony of Democracy*, 3rd ed. (North Scituate, Mass: Duxbury Press, 1975), p. 328.

52. Ibid., p. 330; originally from V. O. Key, Jr., *Public Opinion and American Democracy* (New York: Knopf, 1961), p. 418.

53. Richard F. Fenno, *Home Style: House Members and Their Districts* (Boston: Little, Brown, 1978), finds that while congressmen are oriented toward their constituents, the latter's views and advice often provide ambiguous guidance.

54. Roger Davidson, *The Role of the Congressman* (New York: Pegasus, 1969), p. 117, suggests that 28 percent of members of the House see themselves as "trustees," compared with 23 percent who view themselves as "delegates." Forty-six percent thought of themselves as combining the two approaches.

55. Fiorina, *Congress*, p. 5.

56. Dye and Zeigler, *Irony of Democracy*, p. 331.

57. *New York Times*, Jan. 30, 1977, p. E3.

58. Fiorina, *Congress*, fig. 2, p. 20.

59. See ibid. for a discussion and alternative interpretation which is summarized in the text below.

60. Leroy Rieselbach, *Congressional Reform in the Seventies* (Morristown, N.J.: General Learning Press, 1977), p. 99.

61. Fiorina, *Congress*, pp. 46, 49.

62. Ibid., p. 57.

63. Ibid., p. 49.

64. Ibid., pp. 63–67.

65. See *New York Times*, Jan. 30, 1977, p. E3; and June 12, 1978, p. A18, "The Watergate Window," for a discussion of the inefficiency of reform.

6

The Judicial Branch

The Bureaucratization of Justice

It is a central thesis of this book that the power of the administrative staffs of the various branches of government has been expanding substantially. Equally central is the proposition that for the most part, the overall structure of these institutions has become bureaucratic. When we turn our attention to the judiciary and the administration of justice, we can observe a somewhat different but nevertheless related process. While the administrative component of the judiciary has in fact grown perceptibly in terms of size and power, the more pronounced changes involve process rather than structure. The most democratic feature of the administration of justice, the jury, has been severely reduced in importance by the process of "plea bargaining." This process enables public prosecutors to make decisions regarding whether an individual receives criminal punishment and how much. Judges often do no more than ratify agreements struck by public prosecutors and court-appointed public defenders. In addition, the federal judiciary has begun to issue large numbers of unpublished decisions in recent years. This procedure is at marked variance with traditional legal values, which stress explication and development of the law through judicial reasoning. Unpublished opinions are somewhat more akin to those traditionally made by administrative officials rather than judges. Finally, there has been a revolution in the nature of court-ordered remedies in some kinds of cases. It is now far more common for a court or a judge to engage in ongoing supervision of an administrative operation, such as a school or a prison system. This places the judiciary in a position similar to that of any other public-sector managerial executive. Thus while the judicial system has always been bureaucratic in terms of structure, it is now operating in an increasingly bureaucratic fashion as well.

JUDICIAL POWERS

The United States judiciary is an independent and constitutionally co-equal branch of the federal government. Federal judges are appointed by the president, with the advice and consent of the Senate, for continual service during "good behavior." In practice, the only constitutional method of dismissing judges—that is, impeachment—has been awkward.* Indeed, no Supreme Court justice has ever been successfully impeached. Moreover, the Constitution stipulates that the salaries of judges cannot be reduced during their terms of office. The security afforded by the Constitution has clearly served to foster judicial independence from the other two branches, although substantial checks on the federal courts' jurisdiction remain. Such formal independence is unusual; in several democratic countries the judiciary is part of the ministry of justice, and judges are a special category of civil servant.

A second basis of judicial power is also constitutional in nature. The Constitution contains a broad grant of power to the "third branch":

> The judicial Power shall extend to all Cases, in Law and Equity, arising under this Constitution, the Laws of the United States, and Treaties made, or which shall be made under their Authority;—to all Cases affecting Ambassadors, other public Ministers and Consuls;—to all Cases of admiralty and maritime Jurisdiction;—to Controversies to which the United States shall be a Party;—to Controversies between two or more States; . . . [and] between Citizens of different States.

While much litigation and legal thought has been devoted to several aspects of this grant, such as what constitutes a "case" or a "controversy," and although judicial procedure and authority is subject to modification by statute, the Constitution's provision gives the judiciary wide power broadly protected against encroachment by the other two branches.† In order to modify its basic power, a constitutional amendment would have to be adopted.

Third, and within the context of judicial independence and authority, the extra or implied constitutional power of judicial review has been created. Judicial review is the power of the federal courts to declare acts and actions of the federal and state governments unconstitutional. Although

* A startling example occurred in the 1970s when Federal Judge Otto Kerner, a former governor of Illinois, was convicted of crimes involving political corruption and sentenced to jail. Rather than go through the formalities of an impeachment proceeding, the government induced him to resign his judgeship, perhaps in return for some sort of beneficial treatment.

† It is important to note that the Constitution establishes only the Supreme Court. Other federal courts are created by statute.

it is relatively infrequently exercised, it is the greatest single power held by courts in the United States, and in fact has been used to remake our political life. For example, the "Warren Supreme Court" (1953–1969), which was activist in using judicial power, accomplished the following: outlawed racial segregation and discrimination in public schools and in other situations where government action was involved; enunciated the "one man, one vote" doctrine which required widespread reapportionment of state and federal legislative districts and brought greater influence to the urban population; continued the trend toward making most of the Bill of Rights, which had previously been regarded as constraining only the federal government, binding on the states as well; ruled out voluntary religious exercises in public schools; sustained the right to disseminate and receive birth-control information; and more generally, expanded the protections afforded citizens by the First, Fourth, Fifth, and Sixth Amendments.[1] Had the court done nothing more than require racial integration and reapportionment, it would have had a major impact on American society. At other times in our history the exercise of judicial review has had a similarly great influence on national politics.

Judicial review is a power of tremendous importance. In a very real sense it places the judiciary above the other branches of government, because it enables judges to declare the actions of Congress and the president to be unconstitutional and consequently unenforceable through the courts. Indeed, situations have arisen in which a single federal district judge has ruled against Congress or the president. Thus the power of judicial review has a strange quality. Allowing unelected officials, holding office for life, to thwart the will of the elected branches of government is contrary to democratic values. The Constitution binds the nation to decisions made in 1787; the judiciary maintains the importance of those decisions and adapts them to contemporary circumstances. Conceivably a slim majority of five to four on the Supreme Court could force the nation to go through the arduous process of amending the Constitution to obtain some widely desired end. In addition, and at least equally perplexing, is the fact that the Constitution itself does not mention the power of judicial review.

JUDICIAL REVIEW

Although the founders discussed the possibility of establishing a function similar or equivalent to judicial review, they never placed it in the final draft of the Constitution. Indeed, to the extent that they considered it at all, they thought of having some sort of Council of Revision, which would include nonjudicial members as well as judges.[2] The founders' omission created a great opportunity for John Marshall, who is generally considered to have been the strongest chief justice of the Supreme Court in the nation's history.

The vehicle for Marshall's assertion of the power of judicial review came in the complex case of *Marbury v. Madison* (1803).[3] Just before leaving office in 1801 after his defeat by Thomas Jefferson, President John Adams appointed a number of supporters of his own Federalist Party to various administrative positions. He named William Marbury to be justice of the peace of the District Court of Washington. Unfortunately for Marbury, in the rush of final business Adams's secretary of state—none other than John Marshall, who for a brief time was both secretary of state and chief justice—failed to deliver Marbury's commission to him. Upon taking office, Jefferson instructed Marshall's successor, James Madison, not to give Marbury his commission. Marbury in turn took his case directly to the Supreme Court and asked for a writ of mandamus (a writ, or order, requiring a public official to perform a specific duty). He thought he had the right to do this under section 13 of the Judiciary Act of 1789.

The suit placed the court in a difficult position. If it granted Marbury his writ, Jefferson and Madison might very well ignore its decision, and the court would lose face and probably power as well. If the specter of a president ignoring the Supreme Court seems odd, remember that at the time, the place of the court in American political life was highly ambiguous. It did not yet enjoy the prestige it would have later, and because it was dominated by the opposition party, Jefferson might well have dismissed its ruling as an act of partisanship. Indeed, a later president, Andrew Jackson, made a show of ignoring the court.[4] Even in our day President Nixon could declare that he would obey a "definitive" decision of the Supreme Court, leaving in doubt what he would do if the court were divided or equivocal.[5] On the other hand, to simply rule that the secretary of state's earlier failure to deliver the commission had the effect of denying Marbury's appointment would require strained legal reasoning and set a peculiar precedent for the future.

Faced with this dilemma, Marshall argued that while Marbury might have some right to his commission and office, the remedy he sought was inappropriate. It was inappropriate because by giving the court "original" jurisdiction (that is, authority to be the first court to hear the case) in such cases, Congress had expanded by statute the extent of original jurisdiction granted the court by the Constitution. According to the Constitution the court has original jurisdiction in cases involving ambassadors, other public "ministers," and states. Although it might have been possible to read the Constitution as allowing Congress to expand but not contract this original jurisdiction, Marshall chose to construe the situation as a conflict between the statute and the Constitution. In such a conflict, he asked, which should prevail? In order to have meaning as anything other than a guide, Marshall argued, a written constitution must prevail over any laws which are contrary to its provisions. Hence his conclusion was that the Constitution is the "supreme law of the land" and therefore that the section of the statute involved must be null and void.

Impeccable though such logic may be, it nevertheless fails to answer the question of why it is the judiciary rather than Congress or the president that determines the meaning of the Constitution and statutes in this context. Marshall's answer, and that of our history as well, was that it is the courts' duty to decide what the law is. In other words, in the normal course of their functioning, the courts must interpret the laws and the Constitution. Thus the power to review laws for their constitutionality becomes *judicial review*, and is a direct outgrowth of the constitutional separation of powers. In this fashion the Supreme Court, while denying that it had the power to issue the writ in question on the basis of original jurisdiction, asserted the far greater and more important power of judicial review. At the same time, Marshall and the Federalists momentarily solved their political problem with Jefferson.

Yet *Marbury v. Madison* only explains the origins of judicial review; it hardly accounts for its continuance. Understanding why Americans have both tolerated and relied heavily upon the use of judicial review requires a fuller explanation of the role of the Supreme Court in the political system and of the checks which can be placed upon it. There is no doubt that allowing "nine old men," appointed for life, to decide what the polity can and cannot constitutionally achieve does not harmonize with democratic values. There is not a shred of majoritarianism in the scheme. Aware of this, the Supreme Court has generally used its power of judicial review with considerable restraint. For the most part, the court has exercised the power of judicial review to overturn *state* laws and *local* ordinances found in violation of the *federal* Constitution. Yet this function is hardly controversial at all. Several other federal political systems have an equivalent mechanism, simply because there can be no national supremacy without it. If state laws could override the Constitution, the states would not be constrained by that document and the United States as we know it would certainly not exist. Politically, when the judiciary, often called the "least dangerous" branch of the government,[6] overturns a state statute, it does not directly challenge a national majority in the process. Rather, it challenges a majority in that particular state. When national laws and national majorities are involved, however, it is a different matter.

There have been long periods in our history when very few federal laws were declared unconstitutional. Between 1789 and 1857, for example, only two such laws were found invalid. One was in *Marbury v. Madison* (1803); the other was in *Dred Scott v. Sandford* (1857), in which the Missouri Compromise of 1820 was struck down and the likelihood of civil war was increased.[7] In another period, 1940–1964, only nine federal laws were declared unconstitutional.[8] Indeed, only in the period from 1890 to 1936 did the Supreme Court engage in a protracted battle against a national majority. The fundamental issue at stake was "economic liberalism," and the court stood firmly on the side of entrenched economic power in declaring regulations such as those concerning workmen's compensation and prohibiting child labor unconstitutional. In all, forty-six federal laws were declared unconstitutional during this period. The confrontation came to a head during the 1930s, when the court rejected much New Deal legislation.

The court's weakness, however, was brought out in the very process of asserting its strength. Frustrated by its opposition to his recovery programs, President Franklin D. Roosevelt developed a plan to "pack" the court with new justices. Since the number of justices is fixed by law rather than by the Constitution, such an expansion is always a possibility. Shortly after F.D.R. began advocating his plan (which in fact was not adopted), in what has been dubbed "the switch in time that saved nine," one of the justices—Owen J. Roberts—who had typically sided with a five-to-four majority on economic issues began to join with the dissenting bloc, thereby giving it a majority.[9]

The prolonged conflict of the 1930s is just one example of how the court can lose in a major confrontation with a national majority as reflected in Congress and the presidency. By one set of calculations, Congress has reversed the court in about two-thirds of these confrontations by rewriting legislation or initiating constitutional amendments.[10] The court's greatest single weakness may be that its "original" jurisdiction is established by the Constitution and is quite limited in scope. The remainder of its jurisdiction is called appellate jurisdiction. This is the power to hear cases appealed to it from lower federal and state courts. In both numbers and importance, the vast majority of cases the court hears fall within appellate jurisdiction. However, this jurisdiction is *fixed by law* and therefore can be modified by law. The Constitution says so explicitly in Article III, Section 2: "The Supreme Court shall have appellate jurisdiction, both as to Law and Fact, with such Exceptions, and under such Regulations as the Congress shall make."

There is some dispute among constitutional scholars about whether this section would allow Congress to deprive the court of appellate jurisdiction in specific categories of cases, such as those involving equal protection or free speech. Certainly historical precedent holds out the possibility. In *Ex Parte McCardle* (1869) this is precisely what Congress did with the court's appellate jurisdiction in cases of habeas corpus.[11] Moreover, even though Congress altered the appellate jurisdiction after the court had heard the case but before it issued a decision, the court upheld the constitutionality of Congress's action.

The court's position, then, is precarious. Its power to use judicial review is no longer disputed, but its lack of restraint in employing this power can make it vulnerable to far-reaching sanctions by the elective branches. Two of its crucial elements—its size and appellate jurisdiction—are fixed by law and therefore relatively easily changed. At the same time that the court is weak compared with the other branches, elected officials who are more vulnerable to the electorate have paradoxically tended to thrust the court into highly controversial policy areas. While this tendency gives the court greater influence, dealing with controversial issues also makes it more subject to political attack.

POLITICAL ISSUES AND THE COURTS

The problem of the court's involvement in political disputes stems from two major factors. First, as a political community, Americans tend to "constitutionalize" issues. That is, they tend to address political issues from the perspective of whether the Constitution requires or allows a particular approach. Thus, with the exception of foreign affairs, virtually every major policy area has been heavily litigated. Among them have been economic regulation, civil liberties, civil rights, capital punishment, reapportionment, the rights of those accused of crimes, pornography, and abortion. Obviously these issues are intensely emotional, which brings us to the second factor. Elected officials are most closely watched and criticized by the public on issues of high visibility or emotional content (see Chapter 5). Consequently they tend to channel these issues to (nonelected) bureaucrats or to judges. When frustrated by Congress, interested groups and parties take their cases to the courts. The result is that such matters as desegregation, reapportionment, affirmative action, and the right to have an abortion are decided in an unelected and socially unrepresentative branch of government. No matter how the Supreme Court rules on such issues, it is bound to provoke serious opposition. Hence the court tends to be selective in choosing the cases it will hear and cautious in its decision making.

Part of the Supreme Court's use of restraint lies in its ability to avoid deciding cases brought to it. Unless four or more justices want to hear a case, the court can generally avoid taking it. And even when it does accept a case, there are several ways of avoiding the central issue. To successfully bring suits before the Supreme Court, individuals or groups must be able to demonstrate that they have "standing" to sue. Although the rules of standing have been changed over the years, and have sometimes been haphazardly applied, essentially one must show that a particular injury was done by the government (national, state, or local) to oneself or to a class one represents.[12] This injury must be different from injuries shared by virtually everyone else, such as by all taxpayers. But even if one can show standing, the court may avoid deciding the merits of the case by declaring that it is a "political question" suitable for resolution in another branch of government;[13] that the issue is not "ripe" for resolution;[14] or perhaps that the issue has become moot—that is, deprived of practical significance by a change in the status of a litigant, such as by death or receipt of the action sought.[15] Moreover, if the court does deal with the merits of the case, it may produce a narrow opinion that resolves the specific dispute at hand but not the wider issues involved. By using these techniques, the court can avoid an issue or even pass it back to elected officials.

The Supreme Court's position differs from that of the lower federal courts. While they too can avoid the merits of cases, they have greater difficulty in refusing to hear the cases themselves. Having less control over their dockets and dealing with more cases, district and appeals court judges may also be less given to restraint. They have the luxury of knowing, however, that on most major issues their decisions will not be the final word.

In sum, the chief power of the federal judiciary is its ability to exercise judicial review. Given the nonmajoritarian nature of this branch of government and the important checks Congress and the president can place upon it, judicial review is mostly exercised with restraint. Although there have been major exceptions, the courts have historically been reluctant to confront a clear national majority on a particular issue. They have usually waited until the emotional intensity surrounding a question abates.

ORGANIZATION: THE HIERARCHY OF JUSTICE

It has been said that "the federal judicial system displays most of the attributes of Max Weber's ideal type of *bureaucracy*."[16] This is true in terms of both structure and process, although it is in the area of process that bureaucratization has been most striking in recent years. Structurally there are several similarities between bureaucracy in general and the organization of the federal judiciary:

> The organization's basic subunits are its courts. Each has a unique geographical and/or functional jurisdiction [specialization]. Lower courts are linked to higher courts through appellate review [hierarchy]. Judges, in particular, but other court officials as well (including lawyers), must meet certain technical qualifications. Selection of permanent court officials is by appointment. Remuneration for the most important of these officials—the judges—is by set income that cannot be diminished. It is of such a scale that it is their primary

> or sole source of income. Judicial authority extends only to official acts. All official acts are set down as written transcripts, orders, rules, and opinions. The whole system is permeated by rigid rules relating to such matters as jurisdiction, procedure, admissibility of evidence, remedies, and appellate review.[17]

The bureaucratic model does not explain the amount of discretion allowed judges and especially Supreme Court justices, perhaps because of their political roles. Nor, as noted in Chapter 2, can the Weberian model deal effectively with informal relationships. Nevertheless, the bureaucratic nature of the structure of the federal judiciary is evident from Figure 6–1 on the next page.

THE SUPREME COURT

The major structural units of the federal judiciary can be grouped into the following categories: Supreme Court, courts of appeals, district courts, special and other courts, and administrative units. The Supreme Court sits at the pinnacle of the judicial hierarchy. In 1789 it consisted of a chief justice and five associate justices, but its size has been fixed at nine members since 1869. The court begins its regular annual term in October and continues, with periodic recesses, into the following June. On occasion the chief justice may convene a special summer session. The court's importance lies in the nature of the decisions it renders and its hierarchical position in the federal judiciary rather than in the quantity of its work. Typically it disposes of about 3 percent of all cases handled by the federal courts. Although this amounts to about 5,000 dispositions per year, most of them are very brief. For example, the court may dismiss a case for "want of a federal question" with no further explanation. In about 200 or 250 of its cases, however, it deals with issues of considerable national importance and concern.[18]

When it is in session, the Supreme Court meets for four hours a day, three days a week, two weeks a month for oral argument. Once a case is docketed, or scheduled for hearing, a full record is supplied to each of the justices so that they can study it before the oral argument. During oral argument each side is commonly given an hour or less to state its case. The justices are free to interrupt, lead, or harass counsel as they see fit. Although oral argument is sometimes called archaic in our litigious age, it can also be described as the court's only meaningful official contact with private citizens (lawyers).[19]

Friday has traditionally been the court's day of decision. The justices talk over the cases heard during the week in strict secrecy; no one else is present. The chief justice opens the discussion of each case; the others

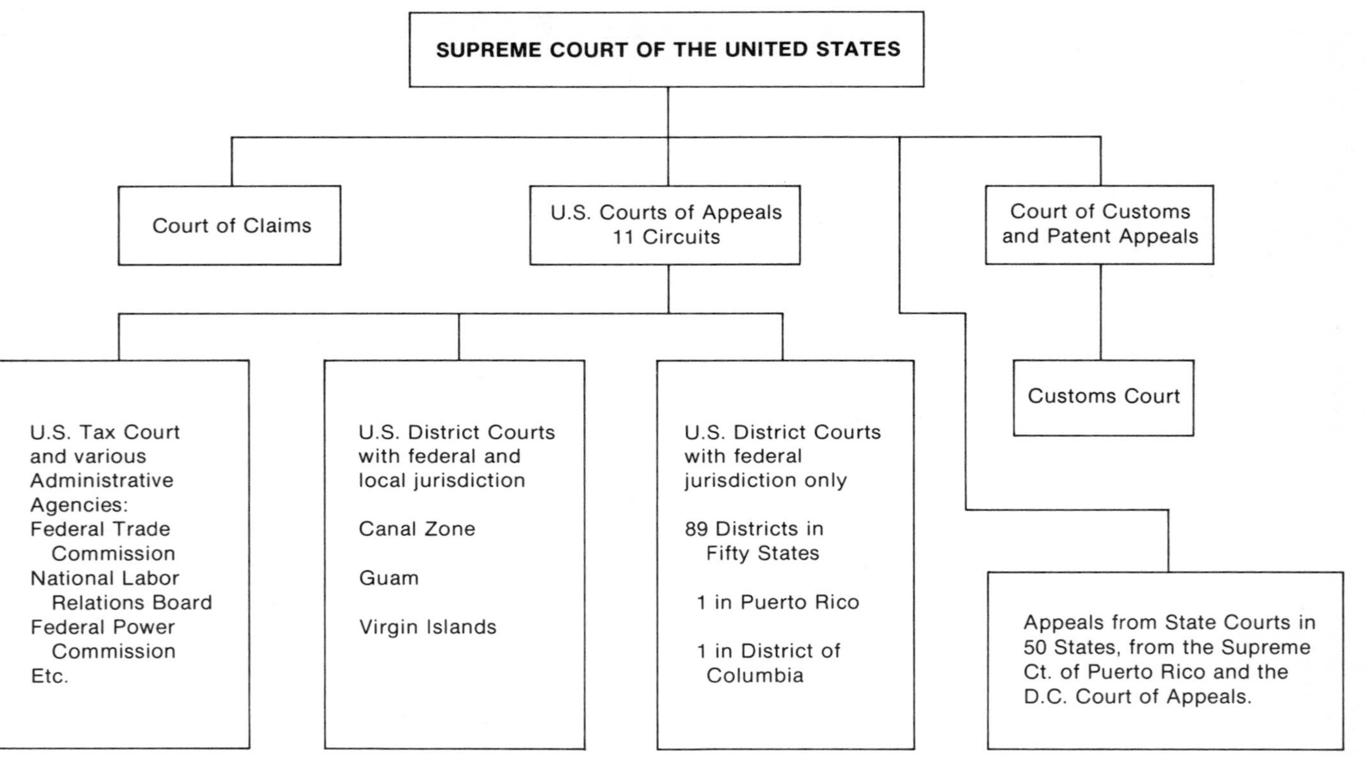

Figure 6–1 **The United States Court System**

SOURCE: Reprinted with permission from Fanny Klein, *Federal and State Courts Systems: A Guide*, copyright 1977, Ballinger Publishing Company.

give their opinions in order of seniority on the court. Voting follows the opposite order: the least senior votes first, the chief justice last. This traditional procedure gives the chief justice some added leverage, for by opening the discussion he can attempt to frame the issues, and by voting last he can make his decision with near certainty of how the case will go. When he votes with the majority, the chief justice assigns the writing of the court's opinion. It is possible therefore that if his colleagues were divided 5–3, for example, prior to his vote, the chief justice might join the majority solely for the purpose of using his power of opinion assignment to obtain one which is closer to his views. When the chief justice is in the minority, the most senior justice in the majority assigns the writing of the opinion. Once opinions are in draft form, they are circulated among the justices for comment and may subsequently be revised. A justice may change his vote at any time before the announcement of the opinion. In the earliest years it was customary for each justice of the Supreme Court to give a separate opinion. Chief Justice Marshall began the practice of issuing a single opinion for the court, but this has been successful only in periods of strong leadership and basic policy consensus. Nowadays justices are free to write concurring and dissenting opinions as they see fit. Sometimes the court is so divided that it has to decide a case without majority opinion, amid a flurry of concurrences and dissents.[20] If the court is divided equally on a decision, the opinion of the lower court stands. A justice may disqualify himself from hearing a case if he feels that there is some conflict of interest, but short of impeachment, this depends solely on his discretion.

As mentioned earlier, the court has different types of jurisdiction.[21] Original jurisdiction comes from the Constitution and is of two types. *Exclusive original jurisdiction* includes disputes between two or more states and cases in which a foreign ambassador, public minister, or one of their domestic servants is being sued. Such cases can be originated only in the Supreme Court. Cases arising under *concurrent original jurisdiction*, on the other hand, can be brought in the Supreme Court originally, but by statute Congress can also permit them to be tried in the lower federal courts. Concurrent original jurisdiction includes (1) a suit *by* a foreign ambassador or minister, (2) disputes between the federal government and a state, and (3) disputes between a state and citizens of another state or against aliens.

The court's appellate jurisdiction has been far more important politically. Within the area of appellate jurisdiction, the court may take a case under two procedures. The first is by *appeal*. This is a matter of right where a lower federal court has held a state statute to be invalid under the United States Constitution, treaties, or laws. In addition, when the highest court having jurisdiction over a matter in a state has questioned the validity of a federal statute, an appeal may be taken to the Supreme Court. The court will also hear appeals from the decisions of some federal administrative agencies.

A second means of bringing cases within the court's appellate jurisdiction involves the writ of *certiorari*. Review under this procedure is not a matter of right, but a privilege based on the court's discretion. Under rule 19 of the Supreme Court, certiorari is most likely to be granted when (1) there is a conflict among circuit court decisions, (2) a lower federal or state court has passed on a matter of federal law which had not previously been considered by the Supreme Court, (3) a lower federal court has dealt with a matter in such a fashion as to conflict with previous Supreme Court decisions, or (4) a lower federal court has radically departed from acceptable canons of judicial procedure. Since 1925 certiorari has been granted when four justices favor it. Certiorari now accounts for most cases heard by the court during a typical term. Finally, the court may review a case by *certification* when a court of appeals requests instructions on dealing with the legal issues in it.

The Supreme Court's position in the federal judicial hierarchy does not rest upon the quality of its opinions, performance, and prestige alone. As can be seen from the nature of its appellate jurisdiction, it has widespread supervisory power over the lower courts. It can overrule them even where the matter is obviously one of interpretation and political preference rather than legal technicality. In deciding cases, it also instructs other courts on how to behave in the future with regard to the whole range of questions involving procedures and substantive interpretation. In addition, the court has rule-making authority. Although rule making is basically legislative in nature, the constitutionality of this power, which is derived from statutes passed in the late eighteenth century, has been upheld by the Supreme Court. Rules that are proposed by the court go into effect within ninety days if Congress does not act upon them. Such rules can affect virtually all phases of judicial activity, from questions of evidence, to pleadings and motions, to trials, to judgments, to the behavior of district court clerks. So far, Congress has rarely shown interest in amending or rejecting proposed rules.

UNITED STATES MAGISTRATES

Whereas the Supreme Court ranks highest in the federal judicial hierarchy, United States magistrates occupy the lowest level of the system. The position was created in 1968 when U.S. commissioners, who played a related role in the judicial system, were phased out of existence. Today there are about 600 magistrates, whose duties include the trial of all but a few federal misdemeanors, the administration of oaths and affirmations, and the setting of conditions, other than bail, for the release of accused persons. Magistrates can be directed to perform other duties by the district courts as well. They handle over 250,000 matters a year. While many magistrates have worked only part time, the current trend is to convert these positions into full-time jobs. Full-time magistrates must be lawyers.[22]

DISTRICT COURTS

Moving up the hierarchy, district courts are the workhorses of the federal judicial system. Including those in Puerto Rico, the District of Columbia, the Canal Zone, Guam, and the Virgin Islands, there were in 1978 ninety-three district courts. Each state has at least one, and there are over 400 district judges, though this number will rise: the appointment of an additional 117 was authorized in 1978.[23] District courts have jurisdiction in the following matters:

1. Admiralty and maritime cases
2. Bankruptcy proceedings
3. Cases arising under the patent or copyright laws
4. Cases involving a fine, penalty, or forfeiture under federal law
5. Proceedings against consuls or vice consuls of foreign states
6. Seizures (on land or upon the waters) not within admiralty and maritime jurisdiction[24]

In addition, the district courts have concurrent jurisdiction with state courts where a controversy arises under federal laws, treaties, or the United States Constitution, and where more than $10,000 is involved. Such cases are often referred to as "federal question jurisdiction." Concurrent jurisdiction is also available in "diversity" cases; that is, cases in which the dispute is between citizens of different states, or citizens of one or more states and a foreign state or foreign subjects. Again, however, more than $10,000 must be at stake. About one-fourth of all cases before the district courts involve diversity of citizenship. The original theory behind diversity jurisdiction was that state courts might be biased in favor of their own citizens, but the economic, social, political, and cultural integration of American life makes it unlikely that such bias would present a serious problem today. Nevertheless, the district courts remain burdened by the need to resolve disputes of a minor and local nature according to the prevailing state law. Several proposals for changing this condition have been under consideration, and it is likely that diversity jurisdiction will be modified in the future.[25] Another third of the cases before district courts involve the United States as a party.

Since 1903 there have been certain circumstances in which three-judge district courts have been impaneled. This development was an outgrowth of a case in which a single federal district court judge had enjoined a state officer to perform duties under a state law which the judge had declared unconstitutional. The ability of a single judge to determine what a state may not do was widely protested. Congress responded by requiring that cases involving applications for injunctions restraining the enforcement activities of state or federal officers on constitutional grounds be heard by a district court composed of three judges. Such courts also came to fulfill other functions. Today they are used when (1) required by a specific law, such as the Voting Rights Act of 1965 and the Civil Rights Act of 1964, and (2) the apportionment of congressional districts or seats in a state legislature is being challenged. Some cases can be appealed from three-judge district courts directly to the Supreme Court.

APPEALS COURTS

In 1891 Congress established the United States Courts of Appeals as an intermediate step in the judicial process between the district courts and the Supreme Court. The basic purpose of these courts has been to relieve the Supreme Court of the necessity of hearing all appeals in the federal system. Today, in fact, they are the courts of last resort for the vast majority of litigation before the federal judiciary. In recent years, however, as appeals from district court decisions became more common—indeed, became standard procedure—the number of appeals court decisions became large enough to create new problems. Foremost was the growing pressure on the Supreme Court to deal with the inevitable increase in conflicts among appeals courts of the eleven judicial circuits (see Figure 6–2). Some students of the problem have urged that a national court of appeals be created to screen all petitions for review now filed directly with the Supreme Court and to decide cases involving intercircuit conflicts.[26] Such a step would add another level to the judicial hierarchy and increase its bureaucratic tendencies. It might, as many have argued, also produce undesirable changes in the role of the Supreme Court.

There are about 100 court of appeals judges divided among the various circuits.[27] An additional 35 were authorized in 1978. Although there are three to fifteen appellate judges per circuit, a panel of three generally hears and decides cases. Supreme Court justices are each assigned one or more circuits to supervise, although for the most part this function is only a formality.

SPECIAL COURTS

In addition to the district courts, courts of appeals, and the Supreme Court, there are several more specialized courts. The United States Court of Claims, created in 1855, provides a forum in which an individual can

Figure 6–2 **The Eleven Federal Judicial Circuits in 1978**

sue the federal government for money damages, providing that Congress has waived the government's sovereign immunity. It is composed of a chief judge and six associate judges appointed by the president with the approval of the Senate. They serve during good behavior. The court has a heavy docket of cases, many of which deal with such matters as taxes paid under protest and the government's roles as employer and allocator of contracts. The United States Customs Court hears complaints regarding the rate of duty or exclusion of merchandise imported into the country. The Court of Customs and Patent Appeals hears appeals from decisions of this court and also reviews some decisions of the Patent Office and of the Tariff Commission. In addition, there are two courts attached to executive departments. The Tax Court of the United States gives individuals an opportunity to litigate Internal Revenue Service findings that they have been deficient in paying federal taxes. The Court of Military Appeals, which is part of the Department of Defense, hears questions of law concerning military justice.

ADMINISTRATIVE UNITS

Bureaucratization of the federal judiciary is also shown by the increasing number of administrative units incorporated into that branch. The prestigious Judicial Conference of the United States grew out of the Conference of Senior Circuit Judges, which was established in 1922. It is chaired by the chief justice of the Supreme Court and includes the chief judge of each of the circuits, the chief judges of the Court of Customs and Patent Appeals and the Court of Claims, and other judges elected for three-year terms by their circuits. Chief circuit judges are selected on the basis of seniority. Therefore here, as in Congress, seniority is a fundamental criterion for the distribution of political influence. The conference meets twice a year to deal with administrative matters, to propose, for pro forma approval by the Supreme Court, changes in federal court procedural rules, and to recommend legislation to Congress. The conference has stressed specialization in fulfilling its mission. By 1974 it was assisted by nineteen standing committees, four subcommittees, and several ad hoc committees comprising over 220 judges, lawyers, and law teachers appointed by the chief justice.[28] The conference has been vitalized by Chief Justice Warren E. Burger's interest in administrative matters. The Judicial Conference of the Circuit plays a similar role at that level.

A major step in the bureaucratization of the federal judicial system occurred in 1939 when the Administrative Office of the United States Courts was created. The office has several crucial organizational functions, including the preparation of the judicial budget and the hiring, compensation, and supervision of the judiciary's clerical personnel, probation officers, referees in bankruptcy, and court reporters. It also compiles and publishes statistical information on the operation of the federal courts, and supplies this to the Judicial Conference and the legislature. The director of the office acts as liaison between the Judicial Conference and Congress. Both the director and the deputy director are appointed by the Supreme Court.

Another organizational unit is the Federal Judicial Center, established in 1967. The center functions as the research arm of the Administrative Office and the Judicial Conference. It is supervised by a board of directors which includes the chief justice, other members of the judiciary, and the director of the Administrative Office. It is charged with the following responsibilities: educating and training federal judges and other court personnel, conducting and stimulating research on judicial administration, developing and recommending proposals for court reform, staffing and aiding the Judicial Conference, and improving the administration of justice by the application of computers. The center's budget increased rapidly in the past decade.[29]

In addition to these structural units, two positions which are indicative of the overall trend toward further bureaucratization of the judiciary were created in the early 1970s. Circuit court executives were authorized for each of the eleven circuits in 1971. By 1977, ten circuits had appointed executives, who are officials trained in court management. They may play a role in assigning judges, arranging dockets, and supervising court personnel, depending on the extent to which these functions are delegated to the executive by the Judicial Council of each circuit. The council consists of the appeals judges of the circuit, who meet as a committee at least twice a year and who previously were responsible for the administrative aspects of the various circuit and district courts. While the executive is unlikely to emerge as a kind of circuit "boss" of judicial personnel, in the future judges will undoubtedly be sharing more and more of their traditional administrative functions with the new court managers.[30] Just as has occurred in the Administrative Office, the centralization of information and increased specialization afforded by such managerial units give them authority and a continually increasing scope of influence.

A second position that shows the trend toward bureaucratization of the judiciary is the post of administrative assistant to the chief justice. Created in 1972, the job is intended to give the chief justice assistance in fulfilling many of his responsibilities as the head of the entire federal court system. While the addition of one person to the judiciary's payroll is hardly a bureaucratic act in itself, the new position represents another government office and another case in which the authority and influence of the politically appointed may begin to devolve into the hands of managerial staff.

CLERKS

Clerks are another group that often has a good deal of influence upon federal judges and justices. Their number and influence have been growing with the increasing case load of the federal judiciary. At the Supreme Court level each justice is authorized to hire three clerks. The chief justice has four. Clerks are also assigned to judges of the district and appeals courts. In the latter, the court executives may have permanent clerks. Clerks appointed to the Supreme Court are typically outstanding products of the best legal training available in the United States. They bring energy and intellect to the court and play an important part in several of its functions, including opinion writing. Most clerks serve for one year, thereby assuring a constant influx of new talent. (The chief justice has a permanent clerk.) Their duties are not fixed; they are assigned whatever work the justice pleases.

The amount of a clerk's influence may be very little or may extend to almost total control of a justice's opinion. Justice Powell's use of clerks provides one illustration:

> He . . . picks out fifteen to eighteen cases he thinks will be particularly important and has his clerks do extra research on them. Each case is assigned to a clerk. Then, during the court term, on the day before the case is to be argued, Powell sits down with the clerk in charge of the case and reviews the issues.
>
> Once Powell is assigned an opinion, either he or his clerk roughs out a draft opinion. Who does the first draft depends on what the workload is in the office at the time. The opinion then goes back and forth between the justice and his clerk like a shuttlecock, being worked and reworked, drafted and redrafted, until both are satisfied. Then the opinion is given to a second clerk, who goes over it like an editor, looking for mistakes, poor reasoning, unclear writing. Then the opinion is sent to the print shop. Then a third clerk reads the opinion, acting as an editor-proofreader. Finally, when everyone in the Powell chambers is satisfied with the quality of the opinion, it is circulated to the other justices.[31]

Most clerks also play a role in screening the petitions for cases being appealed to the court. Thus they can be instrumental in determining which cases and issues are even brought to the justices' attention. At the appeals level, they may do the screening that determines which cases receive oral argument. As useful and necessary as the clerks are, it is undeniable that they present another instance of political authorities sharing their functions with staff personnel.

Even though clerks are rotated on a yearly basis, it is feared by some that the Supreme Court will become substantially more bureaucratized with the continual addition of a few more clerks. Moreover, some justices have become alarmed by the chief justice's use of a permanent clerk and by his requests for more legal officers to aid in processing the court's business. In the words of one observer, some justices are concerned that "all the new people being added to the court's staff are creating a government bureaucracy that will eventually stagnate the court."[32] The use of permanent clerks may lower the intellectual quality of the interaction among justices and clerks and increase the likelihood of processes slipping into inviolable routines. Yet unless the work load is somehow cut, permanent clerks will undoubtedly be more common in the future.

THE DEPARTMENT OF JUSTICE

Although it is part of the executive branch, no discussion of the organization of the federal judiciary would be complete without mention of the Department of Justice (DOJ). Structurally, as Figure 6–3 indicates, the DOJ can be thought of as three relatively distinct bureaucracies headed by the attorney general, his deputy, and his associate.* Functionally, the department's activities include dealing with broad policy matters, policing activities, and litigation. We are most concerned with litigation here because it can be considered an integral aspect of the federal judicial system. Organizationally, this function involves: (1) the Solicitor General's Office, (2) several divisions of the department that are involved in the management of litigation on behalf of the federal government, and (3) United States attorneys and marshals, both of whom, along with their staffs, are attached to the various district courts.

The solicitor general, officially ranked as the third-highest official in the Department of Justice, is the highest-ranking federal official who performs exclusively as a lawyer. The Solicitor General's Office argues all cases before the Supreme Court in which the United States is a party. In order to emphasize the importance of a case, the solicitor general may personally present the government's case in that forum. In addition, where the United States is not a party, the Solicitor General's Office may intervene by submitting a "friend of the court" brief. Furthermore, the solicitor general is instrumental in determining which other public or private organizations will be permitted to present their own views through such briefs. Since the United States is an official party to about half of all the cases argued before the Supreme Court, the Solicitor General's Office

* Former Attorney General Griffin Bell found it frustrating to attempt to control the DOJ. When asked whether Vice President Mondale was actually running the department, Bell replied, "Maybe he is. I'd hate to take an oath swearing that I am." *New York Times,* Jan. 8, 1978, p. E3.

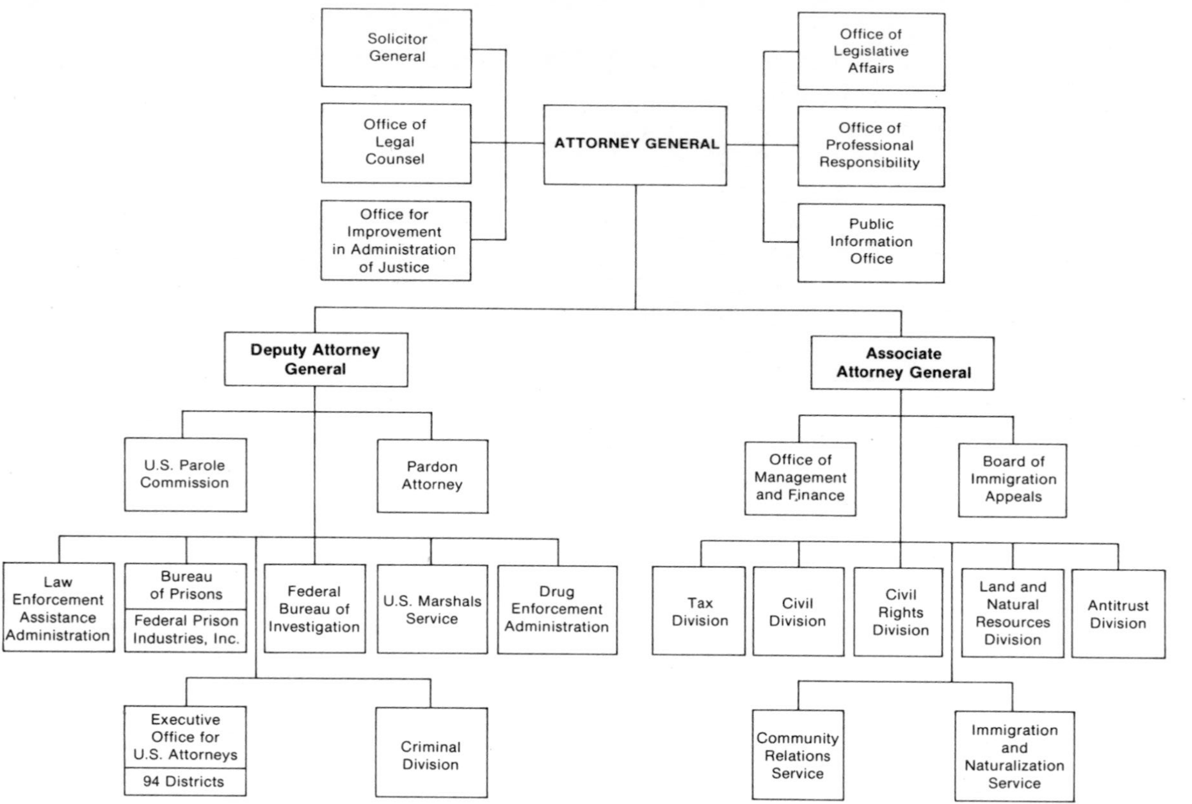

Figure 6–3 Department of Justice

SOURCE: *U.S. Government Manual,* 1978–1979, p. 332.

is of obvious importance. Its power is augmented by the fact that the government cannot appeal cases involving the United States to a higher court without the solicitor general's approval. This restriction permits the Solicitor General's Office to play a major role in shaping the judicial issues of the day. The office's activity has been summarized by Glendon Schubert: "During the 1970s as had been true also in the 1960s, the solicitor general's staff (1) participated in over a third of *all* cases docketed by the Supreme Court; (2) participated in well over half the cases that went to oral argument; and (3) was successful in about two thirds of the cases decided on the merits."[33] Schubert concludes: "The solicitor general is by far the most frequent, as well as one of the most successful, of the lobbyists with the Supreme Court."[34] Indeed, the office has so many advantages over other litigants that a fundamental question of fairness is raised when the United States is a party to a case. The solicitor general is a presidential appointment, but the bulk of the legal personnel in the office are not politically appointed. They currently number nineteen, and since they are a mixture of outstanding recent law school graduates and senior government lawyers, the office commands general respect.

The divisions of the Department of Justice involved in the federal judicial system can be summarized as follows:

- ANTITRUST DIVISION Enforces federal antimonopoly laws through the prosecution of criminal and civil suits against companies that it decides are in violation. Sometimes the division negotiates settlements with these firms, thereby making it unnecessary to go to court. The Antitrust Division also reviews the proceedings and orders of several regulatory agencies.
- CIVIL DIVISION Deals with miscellaneous issues, including admiralty and shipping, tort and contract claims against the United States, frauds, patents, copyrights, customs, and more general matters. The Civil Division handles literally thousands of cases per year and has a high success rate.
- CIVIL RIGHTS DIVISION Works toward "the day when the quality of American life will no longer be marred by discrimination against any of our people on account of their race, color, national origin, sex, or religion."[35] Its primary activities are to enforce voting rights legislation and regulations requiring nondiscrimination in public schools, in places of public accommodation, such as hotels and restaurants, and in facilities partially funded by the federal government, such as airports and hospitals. The division's staff grew rapidly during the late 1960s as a result of a nationwide effort to enforce nondiscrimination. In the early 1970s it had over 300 employees, most of whom were lawyers.

- CRIMINAL DIVISION Supervises and directs United States attorneys in the field of criminal matters arising under close to a thousand federal statutes—for example, those against bank robbery and kidnapping.
- INTERNAL SECURITY DIVISION Was abolished in the wake of the Watergate scandal. This unit used to have enforcement responsibility for matters involving subversion of the government, including the laws against treason, sedition, and espionage. It also had authority in some civil matters, such as the dismissal of subversive federal employees.
- LAND AND NATURAL RESOURCES DIVISION Supervises all suits and civil matters in courts at all levels relating to the real property (land) of the United States. The division is also responsible for criminal prosecutions in the areas of air and water pollution.
- TAX DIVISION Handles criminal and civil litigation involving federal taxation.

United States attorneys work under the general supervision of these divisions. They are the government's front-line lawyers in criminal and civil litigation in the district courts. They are political appointees with four-year terms, but they can be removed at will by the president. While the activities of some U.S. attorneys have attracted national attention, most have not. Similarly, in some cases their staffs are far more important than in others. There has been pressure to depoliticize the appointment of U.S. attorneys, but so far nothing has come of it.[36] Marshals are the enforcement officers of the federal courts.

In summarizing the organization of the federal judicial system, we can return to our opening theme. Structurally the judicial system is bureaucratic: heirarchy, specialization, formalism, and seniority are important in its organization. In addition, the number, size, and influence of its administrative units have proliferated in recent years. Furthermore, much of the system's operation is intermeshed with the activity of the Department of Justice's bureaucratic units. Finally, as the number of nonjudges in the system has grown, so too has the influence of the judges' aides, including clerks, administrative assistants, legal officers, and court executives. There is no doubt that federal bureaucrats in the Department of Justice decide which laws will be vigorously enforced and how. United States attorneys and the Solicitor General's Office decide how the government's case should be argued. Administrative units such as the Federal Judicial Conference, the Judicial Center, and the Administrative Office propose many of the court reforms that are ultimately adopted. And clerks play a substantial role in determining which cases will be taken and what the specific content of judicial opinions will be. Many, if not most, of these conditions are dictated by the increasing work load of the federal judiciary.

THE BURGER COURT

Because of its immense importance in the federal judicial system, as well as in American political life generally, a great deal of interest has traditionally focused on the Supreme Court. Moreover, partly as a result of personnel and partly due to the agenda of political concerns before the nation at any given time, the court often develops a distinctive character. Thus, it is commonplace to associate the Marshall Court with building the foundations of judicial power and national supremacy and the Earl Warren Court with vast expansions of civil rights and civil liberties. While it is still too early to characterize the Burger Court, at least one tendency is apparent: the leadership of Chief Justice Warren E. Burger is likely to be remembered in connection with court reforms and decisions and procedures designed to limit or reduce the work load of the federal judiciary. To some extent, these involve the creation of administrative units and positions to facilitate the judiciary's work. But they also modify some fundamental aspects of the courts' decision-making processes.

The major problem facing the federal courts, according to Chief Justice Burger, is either too many cases or too few judges. In other words, the case load is too heavy to attract and keep the best-qualified judges or enable them to make the best possible decisions. As Burger sees it, the federal judicial system is being inundated by an "appalling mass of litigation."[37] With a backlog of 125,000 cases, the average number of cases handled by district court judges per year increased from 285 in 1968 to 349 in 1973. For appeals judges the increase was from 85 to 156. In the chief justice's view, the nation still needs more federal judges to keep abreast of the continually increasing amount of litigation. The problem is exacerbated by the fact that many federal judges and potential appointees find the job unsatisfactory. Although high in prestige, judgeships are relatively low in pay. Moreover, one study indicated that the judges most likely to resign are those who are confronted by the heaviest case loads.[38] The Supreme Court in particular is besieged; it now handles over 5,000 cases a year. Burger predicted that by 1984, "unless we find some solution we may well see the nine Justices facing a case load exceeding 7,000 cases a year, nearly one new case every hour of the day and night, weekdays and weekends included."[39] Consequently in Burger's view, "We must face up to the flinty reality that there is a necessity for choice: If we wish to maintain the Court's historic function with a quality that will command public confidence, the demands we make on it must be reduced to what they were a generation ago [about 1,000 cases a year]."[40]

The increasing concern with the case loads of the federal judiciary was compatible with President Nixon's approach to staffing the Supreme

Court. The selection of most federal judges is a political act, tempered by evaluation by the American Bar Association acting as a spokesman for the legal community. Democratic presidents appoint an overwhelming proportion of Democrats to openings on the bench; Republicans appoint Republicans. Liberal presidents may seek liberal judges, while conservatives may appoint those who will maintain the status quo or even turn back the clock. Historically most federal judges, and especially Supreme Court justices, have been of high-status social backgrounds.[41]

President Nixon had the opportunity to appoint a chief justice and three associate justices. He also had definite ideas about how he wanted to use this authority. Disenchanted with the "liberal" decisions rendered by the Warren Court and the growth of the Supreme Court's role in national politics, Nixon stressed the need for "strict constructionists." As he put it, "The duty of a judge [is] to interpret the Constitution, and not place himself above the Constitution or outside the Constitution. He should not twist or bend the Constitution in order to perpetuate his personal, political and social views."[42] Such an approach contrasts with former Chief Justice Earl Warren's contention that justices should be guided not only by the Constitution, but also by their "consciences" and their view of the "public interest."[43] Despite Nixon's failure to gain Senate confirmation of two of his nominees, Judges Clement Haynsworth and G. Harrold Carswell, the evidence to date suggests that his appointees do in fact reflect his general judicial philosophy.*

Once all four Nixon appointees were on the bench, the court became clearly divided into three groups: the Nixon appointees, comprising Chief Justice Burger and Justices William Rehnquist, Lewis Powell, and Harry Blackmun; the "liberal bloc," composed of Justices William Douglas, William Brennan, and Thurgood Marshall; and Justices Potter Stewart and Byron White, who provided the "swing votes." As early as the 1973–1974 term, the court's division was fully evident. The Nixon bloc was in the majority on all but one of the 103 occasions in which they voted together. This constituted about 75 percent of all cases decided. Justice White agreed with the Nixon appointees 85 percent of the time, Justice Stewart 82 percent. On the other side, the liberal bloc voted together 74 percent of the time. However, 37 percent of their bloc votes were cast in minority opinions. Each member of the liberal bloc dissented about fifty times, as compared with a high of twenty-five dissents by Rehnquist among the remainder of the court. These differences appeared in virtually everything

* There is no doubt that the notion of "strict construction" is difficult to implement in practice and that in some ways it is a euphemism for conservatism.

that the Supreme Court did. By 1975 Justice John P. Stevens had replaced Justice Douglas and had more or less aligned himself with the Nixon appointees. During the 1977–1978 term, however, the cohesiveness of this bloc diminished, perhaps as a result of the justices' shifting positions on issues involving criminal justice.[44]

Nevertheless, the "strict constructionism" of the Burger Court has been borne out in two general ways. First, the court has been seeking a *narrower* role for the judiciary in the life of the nation. This is manifested in the court's deference to the policy judgments of Congress, executives, and the states. The Burger Court has preferred not to substitute its judgment on the wisdom of policies for that of other political officials or institutions. In some areas it has simply announced that, whatever the precedents, it will no longer entertain cases. For example, despite some twenty years of legal precedents to the contrary, the court pronounced in a 1976 case:

> The federal court is not the appropriate forum in which to review the multitude of personnel decisions that are made daily by public agencies. We must accept the harsh fact that numerous individual mistakes are inevitable in the day-to-day administration of our affairs. The United States Constitution cannot feasibly be construed to require federal judicial review for every such error.[45]

While not quite so blatant, a similar approach has been adopted concerning the rights of prisoners.[46] Along with this general trend, the court has also tightened standards for "standing," thereby selectively reducing access to the federal courts.[47]

Second, the court has issued a number of decisions in the areas of civil rights and civil liberties which have upheld or even rolled back the status quo.[48] At the same time, these decisions have served notice on judicial pressure groups, and others seeking to achieve political and social change through the courts, that they are unlikely to obtain a sympathetic hearing. Indeed, many civil rights groups were reluctant to see a case involving "affirmative action," *Board of Regents v. Bakke* (1978), reach the court.[49] Such groups have increasingly turned their efforts to the executive and legislative branches. This is precisely what Burger believes they should do.

The Burger Court's judicial philosophy is congruent with the chief justice's desire to limit the work load of the federal judiciary. "Strict construction," however, is not the sole means by which the federal courts are attempting to accomplish this end. Indeed, like other bureaucracies, they have adopted bureaucratic methods for controlling their work load.

THE BUREAUCRATIZATION OF LITIGATION

The bureaucratization of justice in the United States is relatively recent. Despite earlier flirtations with "slot-machine justice,"[50] it is only since the work loads of the federal courts increased dramatically that the judiciary has redefined the nature of its "services" along bureaucratic lines. This has been most pronounced in three contexts: (1) the courts' reliance on unpublished opinions, (2) "plea bargaining," and (3) the provision of ongoing judicial remedies.

UNPUBLISHED OPINIONS

The hallmark of legal development in the Anglo-American tradition has been the written, published judicial opinion explaining the court's reasoning in a case. It is largely through this means that the United States Constitution has been adapted to the vast changes that have taken place since the founders met in 1787. Similarly, doctrines such as "separate but equal," "clear and present danger," and "due process," which have shaped the political life of the nation for generations, were first expressed or defined by the judiciary. The meaning of the law at any given moment consists of judicial concepts and precedents that have evolved over the whole history of Anglo-American legal development. Today, however, in a direct effort to cope with their work loads, the federal courts are adopting a different way of announcing their actions on a large number of cases.

At the Supreme Court level this new approach is seen in the tendency to decide cases "summarily," without hearing arguments on them and without issuing written opinions. It is a trend opposed by Justices Brennan and Marshall, who maintain that important issues are being ignored or ill-treated and that the court is providing inadequate legal guidance in its cryptic disposal of such cases.[51] The approach, however, is well suited to Burger's desire to reduce the court's work load.

That a similar trend is apparent in the courts of appeals is evident from Table 6–1. Increasingly the federal appeals courts are disposing of cases without published opinions. Indeed, in some circuits the published judicial opinion is becoming exceptional. In the third, fourth, ninth, and tenth circuits, less than one-third of all dispositions entail published opinions in some years. What is perhaps more remarkable is the extent to which the use of the unpublished opinion has grown since 1972, when the chief justice decided to curtail the publication of judicial decisions.[52] As Table 6–1 shows, in 1973, 54 percent of all circuit court opinions were

TABLE 6–1

Appeals Disposed of by Published Opinions in United States Circuit Courts

Circuit	1973			1974			1975			1976		
	Total Appeals[1]	Published Opinions[2]	% Published	Total Appeals[1]	Published Opinions[2]	% Published	Total Appeals[1]	Published Opinions[2]	% Published	Total Appeals[1]	Published Opinions[2]	% Published
District of Columbia	723	276	38.2	551	253	45.9	404	218	54.0	443	219	49.4
First	222	123	55.4	268	179	66.8	349	146	41.8	269	166	61.7
Second	696	390	56.0	774	432	55.8	702	380	54.1	918	407	44.3
Third	790	296	37.5	707	273	38.6	591	174	29.4	870	273	31.4
Fourth	520	249	47.9	1,151	285	24.8	1,129	290	25.7	951	365	38.4
Fifth	1,780	1,192	67.0	1,774	1,016	57.3	2,262	1,386	61.3	1,865	963	51.6
Sixth	749	355	47.4	872	340	39.0	951	388	40.8	906	270	29.8
Seventh	590	223	37.8	857	437	51.0	712	347	48.7	697	312	44.8
Eighth	490	361	73.7	713	485	68.0	525	334	63.6	567	415	73.2
Ninth	1,262	820	65.0	2,320	791	34.1	1,885	496	26.3	1,902	501	26.3
Tenth	627	278	44.3	670	254	37.9	615	182	29.6	678	224	33.0
Total[4]	8,449[3]	4,563	54.0	10,657	4,745	44.5	10,125	4,341	42.9	10,066	4,115	40.9

SOURCE: Administrative Office of U.S. Courts, *Annual Report on Operations of the Circuit Courts Opinion Publication Plans,* table B (Washington, D.C., 1976).

[1] Cases disposed of after hearing or submission.

[2] Includes signed opinions, per curiam opinions, and published memoranda.

[3] This figure does not include 978 cases reported as "all other" disposition in 1973.

[4] Percent "totals" are averages of circuits' percentages.

published, whereas by 1976, the proportion of published opinions had dropped to slightly less than 41 percent. Here is an example of the bureaucratic approach: the system's work load is controlled by providing less service for consumers but without giving up any authority over them.

The rules concerning unpublished opinions vary among the circuits. So far, studies have not revealed any marked distinctions between the substance of unpublished and published opinions. Nevertheless, the widespread use of unpublished opinions is a major deviation from past judicial practice. Indeed, unpublished opinions are more akin to the traditional bureaucratic way of disposing of cases. This is especially true where, as in some circuits, unpublished opinions *cannot be cited* in other cases. Such opinions have no meaningful value as precedents—the decision of a court at one time cannot be brought to bear on its disposition of a related issue at some other time. This is precisely how some federal bureaucratic agencies operate. Most notably, the United States Civil Service Commission's Appeals Review Board never considered itself bound by precedent in its judgments on equal employment opportunity appeals.[53]

Unpublished opinions may be a viable means of reducing work loads. And they may be acceptable in bureaucratic agencies, where the development of the law is not a primary function and where there is generally a subsequent appeal to the federal courts. However, it is difficult to see how they serve the cause of justice in the judicial setting. Not only must unpublished opinions stand outside the realm of legal development, since they are not widely circulated, but where they cannot be cited they operate against the citizen's right to due process of law. It is entirely possible that an individual's case could be helped by an unpublished opinion previously handed down, but that the person either does not have access to it or is prohibited from citing it. So apparent are the pitfalls of issuing unpublished opinions that lawyers have been highly critical of this practice, especially where a no-citation rule is in effect.[54] In passing, it should be noted that the courts are also increasingly relying on summary dispositions without written explanations, and that they are curtailing oral argument in an effort to cope with their work loads.

"PLEA BARGAINING"

The unpublished opinion is only one sign of the judicial system's growing tendency to behave like a bureaucracy. Far more important has been the bureaucratization of the decision-making process itself. This development, which is also rooted in the increasing case load of a crime-ridden and litigious society, is manifested in the ubiquitous reliance on "plea bargaining." Plea bargaining is exactly what the phrase suggests: the defendant and the public prosecutor bargain over whether the defendant will plead guilty or not guilty. Each may have something that the other wants. The defendant, by pleading guilty, can save the prosecutor and the courts the time, effort, and expense of the full-fledged jury trial to which every citizen is entitled under the Fifth, Sixth, and Seventh Amendments to the Constitution. The prosecutor in turn has the authority to reduce the charge against the defendant or to decrease the penalty sought. When the defendant believes that the prosecutor has made the best offer obtainable, and that the certainty of the reduced penalty outweighs the risk of greater punishment upon conviction after a jury trial, the defendant will plead guilty. About 80 percent of all federal criminal cases are handled in this fashion.[55] However, while plea bargaining serves to reduce the work load of the federal judicial system, it does not always serve the needs of justice.[56] A major consequence of plea bargaining is that the most representative element in the federal judicial system—the jury—is excluded from the decision-making process. Determining who gets punished and how severe the punishment will be is mostly up to the public prosecutor (U.S. attorney). This official, who is employed by the Department of Justice, largely has bureaucratic functions. In practice, plea bargaining creates a situation in which the defendant is not likely to seek a hearing before a jury of his peers. Hence a relatively closed bureaucratic system asserts almost total control over defendants. Plea bargaining occurs for several reasons. First, most defendants have limited resources, in both money and knowledge, for challenging the system. Second, prosecutors may first "trump up" the charges only to reduce them later in an effort to make a bargain more acceptable to the defendant. Third, many defendants cannot afford legal counsel and are assigned a lawyer by the court. While many public defenders conscientiously try to give their client the best defense possible, others are more interested in good relationships with prosecutors and judges.[57] They may work only in the courtroom and spend very little time with their client. A Justice Department study found that "many defense attorneys consider the plea bargain a vital part of their service to the defendant"[58] and generally encourage the defendant to take the best deal offered by the prosecutor. Finally, the deck is heavily stacked against the defendant who insists on going to trial. As Goldman and Jahnige write:

> An obviously guilty defendant is discouraged from going to trial not only by the advice of his lawyer, but also by considerations of time and outcome. If he is not able to provide bail, the time spent in jail prior to a trial judgment is normally not deducted from any subsequent prison term. . . . Even more important in a defendant's calculation in deciding whether to plead guilty are the differences in sentences of those pleading guilty compared to those convicted by trial. . . . In every offense category those sentenced after trial received more severe treatment than those sentenced after pleading guilty. . . . Sentences after trial convictions were often two to three times more severe than sen-

> tences after guilty pleas for comparable crimes and defendants. There seems little doubt, therefore, that a trial—where the prosecution may "throw the book" at the defendant and the judge "discipline" him with a harsh sentence for "wasting" the court's time—can be a risky business for the obviously guilty.[59]

But for exactly the same reasons, a trial appears to be risky even for the innocent, poor, minority, or previously convicted defendant who has little faith in the fairness of the judicial process in the first place.

It is important to note that prosecutors and judges involved in plea bargaining are likely to be aware of its faults as a means of dispensing justice.[60] It inspires little confidence in the system and hardly guarantees that the punishment will fit the crime (if any). But these public officials are even more likely to point out that plea bargaining is a necessity if the judicial system is to keep working under its present case load. The Constitution guarantees accused people a "speedy" trial—something hardly attainable even when the vast majority of all criminal cases are plea-bargained. Hence unfairness to the individual is tolerated in order to protect "the system." This, of course, is the very essence of bureaucratic impersonality and goal displacement. Rather than arranging the system to serve the individual, the individual's needs are sacrificed to maintain the system. While some apologists for plea bargaining may take comfort in the belief that those coerced or induced into pleading guilty are probably guilty of some crime anyway, the plain fact is that their "guilt" is established as part of a bargain rather than before a jury of their peers. The opportunity to determine guilt or innocence has largely passed out of the hands of the citizenry as represented in juries and into those of public prosecutors and judges.

ADMINISTRATION BY THE JUDICIARY

In a third aspect of the bureaucratization of justice, judges have begun to take on administrative functions traditionally reserved for public bureaucrats and political executives. This occurs when the courts are asked to order large-scale changes in institutions such as prisons, mental hospitals, and public schools. Rather than ending such cases by commanding the parties to perform certain acts, the federal courts "have assumed a more active role in the implementation of their orders to assure that their decrees become more than paper pronouncements."[61] A federal judge may appoint a committee to oversee changes in an institution, or may almost single-handedly attempt to create the changes himself. In either event, it is the judge who will be responsible for the key administrative decisions concerning reforms. In this fashion judges begin to act like high-level public bureaucrats such as commissioners of schools, health, and prisons, and establish themselves as "super" administrators. Judicial remedies of this type enable the courts to take on executive functions. This process may violate our notions about the traditional separation of powers. But it is a striking example of the judiciary's attempt to function in a bureaucratized nation. In order to assert power in the bureaucratic polity, one must take on the role of bureaucrat.

Conclusion Bureaucracy versus Justice

In his classic essay on bureaucracy, Max Weber argued that the "quantitative extension" of administrative tasks provides "the proper soil for . . . bureaucratization."[62] This proposition is well illustrated by the bureaucratization of the federal judiciary. As the work load of the federal courts increased dramatically in recent years, more administrative units were created and more aides appointed. The logic of the development is clear, as Chief Justice Burger explains: "In any complex activity specialization is essential. . . . Clearly, no one person can today master the techniques of administration in addition to the rapidly expanding world of law."[63] But although the purpose of increased bureaucratization is to help judges dispense justice, inevitably specialization and formalization breed influence and power. Consequently the influence of administrative officials and other personnel, such as clerks, expands. Reacting to the emergence of court management as a fledgling profession, several judges claim that court executives have been "conjured up as an assault on judicial independence and an attempt to demean the status of the judge to that of a glorified civil servant."[64] Specialists are always added to provide the chief political functionaries with the organizational assistance to perform their jobs better. But whether in Congress, in the presidency, or in the courts, the staffs emerge as an important power element in their own right.

The impact of the quantitative extension of tasks upon the process of justice is even more pronounced. As the number of docketed cases has risen dramatically at all levels of the federal court system, the system has responded by adopting short-cuts in the bureaucratic mold. Thus, it has taken to the widespread use of unpublished opinions, which reduces not only costs and labor but also the body of effective precedents. Even more telling, the trial process has been avoided through the use of plea bargaining in over 80 percent of all criminal cases. Consequently there is far less expense and reliance on juries. But does this bureaucratization serve the needs of justice?

It is difficult to argue that it does. Unpublished opinions deny the parties to a case ready access to precedents or even the ability to use them in support of their claims. Plea bargaining often amounts to little more than coercing the accused into pleading guilty to a crime he or she did not commit or to a charge that is inappropriate. On its face, it would seem, then, that perhaps these practices should be abolished or used far more sparingly. Yet such practices do speed the process of handling cases, and as Chief Justice Burger maintains, "Delay itself, with the loss of witnesses and the clouding of memories, diminishes the ability of the courts to do justice."[65] Thus the judicial system is in a serious bind. Bureaucratization provides one approach for keeping the system going when it is being swamped with work. Two other possibilities have been suggested as well.

First and simplest, creating more judgeships and courts might go a long way toward solving the problems created by the judiciary's work load. If there were more courts and judges at the district and circuit levels, cases could be processed more rapidly. Of course, the cost would be higher, but since the judiciary receives less than 1 percent of the total federal budget, some shifting of priorities might be in order. This approach was endorsed in 1978 when 152 more federal judgeships were authorized.[66] However, even multiplying judges and courts will not resolve the problem entirely. More district courts, coupled with less plea bargaining and more rapid processing of civil cases, will result in more appeals. These in turn will create more intercircuit conflicts and more appeals to the Supreme Court.[67] In bureaucratic structures the various units and levels generate work for each other. A national court of appeals has been proposed to help reduce the work load of the Supreme Court, but it would also reduce that court's role in American politics. Obviously such an approach deals with the symptoms of the problem rather than its cause.

A second suggestion comes closer to the heart of the overall difficulty. It is to decriminalize whole categories of activities. As Edward Gallas expresses it:

> Criminal dockets become buried under a morass of litigation more appropriately assigned to a social work agency, a hospital, or a treatment facility, including cases involving victimless offenders such as narcotic addicts, alcoholics, traffic offenders, gamblers, prostitutes, and consenting adult homosexuals. . . . The required processing of such cases by the courts deflects attention from other litigation.[68]

While much of the decriminalization argument applies best at the state and local levels, it has potential utility for the federal courts as well. Of course, treating such cases—and perhaps some civil matters, such as divorce and family affairs—outside the courts creates pressures for further bureaucratization elsewhere in the society. And in the view of some observers, there are no "victimless" crimes, because prostitution, gambling, and various forms of deviant behavior have social costs.[69]

We have seen how the presidency, the executive branch, Congress, and the federal courts have become bureaucratized. Is it naïve to assume that the administration of justice can follow prebureaucratic patterns? As Chief Justice Burger put it, "In the supermarket age, we [the judicial system] are like a merchant trying to operate a cracker barrel corner grocery store with the methods and equipment of 1900."[70] In supermarkets one looks for speed, standardization, and low prices, not for individualized treatment. Yet it is treatment suited to each particular case that the jury and adversary system are intended to provide. As the courts become bureaucratic and the judges function as bureaucrats in black robes, perhaps our expectations will change. Bureaucratic justice, as noted in Chapter 2, is different from democratic justice. But the irony is that the bureaucratization of justice is unlikely to reduce crime, which is a major contributor to the increased work load of the courts. This is because the bureaucratic system has discarded the goal of rehabilitation, and to a considerable extent that of incapacitation as well,* in an effort to maintain current dockets.[71] Hence the circle becomes complete; the bureaucratized judiciary provides adequate service neither to the accused nor to society but mainly serves its own needs and contributes to its own growth.

NOTES

1. There are too many cases involved to cite more than a few. Among these are *Brown v. Board of Education,* 347 U.S. 483 (1954); *Baker v. Carr,* 369 U.S. 186 (1962); *Engel v. Vitale,* 370 U.S. 421 (1962); *Poe v. Ullman,* 367 U.S. 497 (1961); *Mapp v. Ohio,* 367 U.S. 643 (1961); *Miranda v. Arizona,* 384 U.S. 436 (1966).
2. See Winton U. Solberg, ed., *The Federal Convention and the Formation of the Union of the American States* (Indianapolis: Bobbs-Merrill, 1958), pp. 78, 97–101.
3. 1 Cranch 137 (1803).
4. Jackson is reputed to have said, "John Marshall has made his decision, now let him enforce it." See C. Herman Pritchett, *The American Constitution*, 3rd ed. (New York: McGraw-Hill, 1977), p. 83.
5. See Frank Mankiewicz, *U.S. v. Richard M. Nixon* (New York: Ballantine, 1975).
6. Alexander Hamilton in *The Federalist*, No. 78, and Alexander Bickel, *The Least Dangerous Branch* (Indianapolis: Bobbs-Merrill, 1962).
7. 19 Howard 393.
8. See Robert S. Ross, *American National Government* (Chicago: Markham, 1972), pp. 42–43. The information in the remainder of the paragraph is from this source.
9. See Pritchett, *American Constitution,* p. 40.
10. Robert Dahl, *Democracy in the United States,* 2nd ed. (Chicago: Rand McNally, 1972), p. 202. See pp. 200–210 for a discussion.
11. 7 Wall 506.

* Incapacitation in the sense of long incarceration. Plea bargaining leads to shorter sentences by having defendants charged with lesser offenses.

12. For some examples, see *Massachusetts v. Mellon*, 262 U.S. 447 (1923); *Flast v. Cohen*, 392 U.S. 83 (1968); *Sierra Club v. Morton*, 405 U.S. 727 (1972).

13. See, among others, *Luther v. Borden*, 7 Howard 1 (1849); *Colegrove v. Green*, 328 U.S. 549 (1946); *Baker v. Carr*, 369 U.S. 186 (1962); *Powell v. McCormack*, 395 U.S. 486 (1969).

14. *Poe v. Ullman*, 367 U.S. 497 (1961); *Griswold v. Connecticut*, 381 U.S. 479 (1965).

15. *DeFunis v. Odegaard*, 416 U.S. 312 (1974).

16. Sheldon Goldman and Thomas Jahnige, *The Federal Courts as a Political System* (New York; Harper & Row, 1971), p. 43.

17. Ibid., pp. 46–47.

18. Fannie J. Klein, *Federal and State Court Systems—A Guide* (Cambridge, Mass.: Ballinger, 1977), pp. 168–170.

19. Kenneth Turan, "Court's Oral Arguments a Scary Thing," *Roanoke Times*, Feb. 2, 1975; in Annual Editions, *Readings in American Government* (Guilford, Conn.: Dushkin, 1975), pp. 165–167. In the past century Supreme Court justices were obligated to "ride the circuit," during which they acted as other federal judges in the various federal courts distributed throughout the nation.

20. See *Elrod v. Burns*, 427 U.S. 347 (1976); *Board of Regents v. Bakke*, 46 *Law Week* 4896 (1978).

21. The following comes from Klein, *Federal and State Court Systems*, pp. 171–172.

22. U.S. Federal Judicial Center, *Developments in Judicial Administration* (August 1974), p. 6. It has been proposed that magistrates be allowed to act as judges in any civil proceeding or criminal misdemeanor if the parties to the case so agree. See *New York Times*, Jan. 1, 1978, p. 15.

23. *New York Times*, Dec. 31, 1978, p. 8. Some opposition arose on the grounds that it would allow one (Democratic) president to appoint a large number of new judges. The chief justice believes 900 judges should be authorized. See *New York Times*, Jan. 7, 1974, p. 16, and Jan. 1, 1978, p. 15.

24. Klein, *Federal and State Court Systems*, p. 180.

25. *New York Times*, Jan. 1, 1978, p. 15.

26. Charles Black, "The National Court of Appeals: An Unwise Proposal," 83 *Yale Law Journal* 883 (1974). See also *New York Times*, Dec. 5, 1978, p. A18, for the views of some Supreme Court justices.

27. *New York Times*, Dec. 31, 1978, p. 8.

28. Federal Judicial Center, *Developments in Judicial Administration*, p. 1.

29. Ibid., p. 3. It went from $700,000 in fiscal year 1971 to over $2,000,000 in 1974.

30. For a general discussion of developments in this area, see ibid., p. 6, and "Court Administration: The Newest Profession," 10 *Duquesne Law Review* 220 (1971).

31. Nina Totenberg, "Conflict at the Court," in Annual Editions, *Readings in American Government 77/78* (Guilford, Conn.: Dushkin, 1977), p. 145.

32. Ibid.

33. Glendon Schubert, *Judicial Policy Making* (Chicago: Scott, Foresman, 1965), p. 58.

34. Ibid.

35. Ibid., p. 60.

36. See Goldman and Jahnige, *The Federal Courts*, pp. 78–86, for a more extensive discussion. See also James Eisenstein, *Counsel for the United States* (Baltimore: Johns Hopkins, 1978).

37. *New York Times*, Jan. 7, 1974, p. 16.

38. Cited by Chief Justice Burger in *U.S. News and World Report*, March 31, 1975. See Annual Editions, *Readings in American Government 77/78*, p. 139.

39. *New York Times*, Jan. 7, 1974, p. 16.

40. Ibid., Aug. 14, 1975, p. 31.

41. See Goldman and Jahnige, *The Federal Courts*, chap. 3. See also Harold W. Chase, *Federal Judges* (Minneapolis: University of Minnesota Press, 1972).

42. K. Miller and N. Samuels, eds., *Power and the People* (Pacific Palisades, Calif.: Goodyear, 1973), p. 252.

43. Quoted in James F. Simon, *In His Own Image* (New York: David McKay, 1973), p. 2.

44. *New York Times*, July 1, 1974, p. 10, and July 5, 1978, pp. 1, 13. The Nixon appointees

voted together in 36 percent of the cases. The previous year they had voted together 67 percent of the time.

45. *Bishop v. Wood*, 426 U.S. 341, 349–350. See David H. Rosenbloom, *Federal Service and the Constitution* (Ithaca, N.Y.: Cornell University Press, 1971), for earlier precedents.

46. *Stone v. Powell*, 428 U.S. 465 (1976); *Wolff v. Rice*, 428 U.S. 465 (1976).

47. But this has not been accomplished in uniform fashion. See *U.S. v. Richardson*, 418 U.S. 166 (1974); *Sierra Club v. Morton*, 405 U.S. 727 (1972); *U.S. v. S.C.R.A.P.*, 412 U.S. 669 (1973); *Singleton v. Wulff*, 428 U.S. 106 (1976).

48. See Arthur S. Miller, "The Court Turns Back the Clock," *The Progressive*, October 1976; and Paul Bender, "The Techniques of Subtle Erosion," *Harper's*, December 1972. But see *Kaiser v. Weber*, 47 *Law Week* 4851 (1979) in which the legality of voluntary "affirmative action" in the private sector was upheld by a five-to-two margin (Justices Powell and Stevens not participating).

49. "Minority Goals in Education," *New York Times*, June 9, 1977.

50. "Slot-machine justice" assumes that upon learning the facts of a case a judge need only consult past precedent to reach a decision in the public interest. See Walter F. Murphy and C. Herman Pritchett, *Courts, Judges, and Politics* (New York: Random House, 1961), pp. 3–10, for a brief discussion of perceptions of judicial role.

51. *New York Times*, Nov. 9, 1976, p. 24.

52. *Hearings before the Commission on Revision of the Federal Court Appellate System, 2d Phase (1974–5)*, vol. I, p. 520.

53. Robert G. Vaughn, *The Spoiled System* (New York: Charterhouse, 1975), p. 84.

54. Administrative Office of the U.S. Courts, Memorandum to the Subcommittee on Federal Jurisdiction, Dec. 23, 1976.

55. See Goldman and Jahnige, "Input," *The Federal Courts*, for a discussion.

56. Plea bargaining has come under serious attack. See *New York Times*, Dec. 18, 1977, p. E8.

57. The same may be true of attorneys associated with "legal clinics" of the high-volume, low-cost genre.

58. Goldman and Jahnige, *Federal Courts*, p. 125.

59. Ibid., p. 126.

60. For a good account, see Judge Lois G. Forer, "View from the Bench: A Judge's Day," *Washington Monthly*, February 1975.

61. "The Wyatt Case: Implementation of a Judicial Decree Ordering Institutional Change," 84 *Yale Law Journal*, 1338 (1975). See also A. Chayes, "The Role of the Judge in Public Law Litigation," 89 *Harvard Law Review*, 1281 (1976); D. Bazelon, "The Impact of the Courts on Public Administration," 52 *Indiana Law Journal*, 101–110 (1976); and Donald L. Horowitz, *The Courts and Social Policy* (Washington, D.C.: Brookings Institution, 1977).

62. H. H. Gerth and C. W. Mills, eds., *From Max Weber* (New York: Oxford University Press, 1958), p. 209.

63. "Foreword: Symposium on Judicial Administration," *Public Administration Review*, 31 (March/April, 1971), 112.

64. 10 *Duquesne Law Review*, 220, 233, (1971).

65. *Public Administration Review*, 31 (1971), 112.

66. *New York Times*, Dec. 31, 1978, p. 8. According to Chief Justice Burger, these judges will not all be "in place" and in peak performance for 3 to 5 years.

67. Chief Justice Burger is aware of this and believes that "these problems should be faced without waiting for a crisis." *New York Times*, Dec. 5, 1978, p. A8.

68. Edward Gallas, "The Court as a Social Force," *Public Administration Reviews*, 31 (March/April 1971), 130.

69. See Alan Wertheimer, "Victimless Crimes," *Ethics*, 84 (July 1977), 302–318.

70. Quoted in Nesta Gallas, "Court Administration: A Discipline or a Focus," *Public Administration Review*, 31 (March/April 1971), 144.

71. See James Q. Wilson, "If Every Criminal *Knew* He Would Be Punished If Caught," *New York Times Magazine*, Jan. 28, 1973.

Part III

BUREAUCRATIC POLITICS

7

Campaign Management

The Decline of Political Parties

Like the formal institutions of government set up under the Constitution, American political parties are undergoing a period of change. Some observers believe that this change reflects a transformation of the American electorate, a consequence of which is "an astonishingly rapid dissolution of the political party as an effective 'guide,' or intervenor between voter and the objects of his vote at the polls."[1] At the same time, political parties are playing a diminishing role in what used to be regarded as their major function—campaigning. Forming an exception to the general tendency of the political system to become more bureaucratized, political parties do not provide candidates for public office with a viable bureaucratic apparatus. Consequently the candidates rely increasingly on their personal campaign organizations. These are run by electioneering technocrats, such as campaign managers, advertising and public relations specialists, media experts, pollsters, and administrative staffs. The technocrats utilize methods and strategies common to large-scale organizations, including long-term planning, market research, budgeting, monitoring, and public relations.

These developments, coupled with the changing roles of elected officials, have been interpreted as a sign that the United States is entering an era of "a new politics." The new politics has been described as

> the contemporary contest for power, characterized by primary reliance on personal organizations in preference to party machinery, emphasis on consolidating voters rather than dividing them along traditional lines of class and region, projection of political style above issues and exploitation of the full range of modern techniques of mass communication.[2]

We can recognize here the early steps toward the penetration of elections by bureaucracy. At the same time, the new politics provides vehicles for shifting power out of the hands of the traditional party leaders.

THE PARTY TRADITION IN AMERICAN POLITICS

About four decades ago, an influential student of American politics, E. E. Schattschneider, argued that "the political parties created democracy and that modern democracy is unthinkable save in terms of the parties. . . . The parties are not therefore merely appendages of modern government; they are the center of it and play a determinative and creative role in it."[3] This argument was based on the proposition that, generally speaking, political parties enable citizens to participate in the process of governing. Parties organize the "public will," imbue individuals with civic awareness and civic responsibility, link government with public opinion, and select political leaders. Even though the parties themselves were not fully democratic in structure and process, it was widely accepted that they served democracy insofar as there was free competition among them. As Avery Leiserson put it, "Just as the corporation has been labelled the representative institution of capitalist enterprise, so the political party may be designated as the representative institution of political enterprise."[4]

Empirically speaking, the most important activity of political parties in the United States has been the recruitment, nomination, and election of office holders. American parties are interested first in winning elections and only second in policy issues and representing the public. Accordingly, the political parties could be simply defined as "organized attempts to win electoral office."[5] By providing structured opportunities for competition for public office, political parties organize and channel conflicts in specific directions. The possibility of winning office at the national level depends upon nomination by either of the major parties. Indeed, one justification for the two-party monopoly is that with more parties, the level of political conflict would increase and threaten the nation's stability.

A procedure that perpetuates the two-party system has been the single-member legislative district. Typically each district is entitled to only one seat in the House of Representatives. The candidate receiving a plurality of votes in the district wins the office. Such a procedure, commonly referred to as "winner takes all," discourages lasting third-party movements because minority parties gain neither political power nor legislative seats through electoral contests. Only a party that has a realistic chance of obtaining the most votes has lasting reason for bearing the expense of electoral competition. The electoral college system has a similar effect on the number of parties. Since only one party can win the presidency in any given election, there is little incentive to vote for a candidate of a party that has no chance of winning.

The two-party system, it is commonly argued, structures and limits conflict in another way as well. Allegiance to a party diminishes extreme ideological differences within the electorate and among the party's leadership. For example, Senator Jacob Javits and Ronald Reagan, who are at opposite ends of the Republican Party's ideological spectrum, cooperate on both procedural matters and substantive issues. Hence partisan affiliation can unify people and aid in the process of governance. Congress and state legislative bodies use partisan affiliation in organizing themselves, and some states have systems in which parties retain strong controls on legislators' voting behavior.

Many observers, however, have criticized party performance and the influence that the parties have had on American political life. Scholarly criticism has focused mainly on the lack of party responsibility in government. A comprehensive statement of the doctrine of party responsibility is found in a report of the committee on political parties of the American Political Science Association, *Toward a More Responsible Two-Party System*, published in 1950. The report called for a party system that is "democratic, responsible, and effective."

> Party responsibility means the responsibility of the two parties to the general public, as enforced in elections. Party responsibility to the public, enforced in elections, implies that there be more than one party, for the public can hold a party responsible only if it has a choice. . . . When the parties lack the capacity to define their actions in terms of policies, they turn irresponsible because the electoral choice between the parties becomes devoid of meaning. . . . An effective party system requires, first, that the parties are able to bring forth programs to which they commit themselves and, second, that the parties possess sufficient internal cohesion to carry out these programs.[6]

Two central assumptions underlie this concept of responsible political parties. The first is that democracy is maintained by popular control over government rather than by popular participation in the immediate activities of government. Government by responsible parties is an expression of majority rule. The second assumption is that popular control of government requires that the citizenry be given a choice between competing, effective, and cohesive parties capable of assuming collective responsibility to the public for the actions of government. In other words, a responsible party system would "enable the people to choose effectively a general program, a general direction for government to take, as embodied in a set of leaders committed to the program." This system would help to "energize and activate" public opinion, and "it would increase the prospects for popular control by substituting the responsibility of the party as a whole for the individual responsibility assumed by individual office holders."[7]

To achieve such a responsible party system, the report recommended a transformation of national party organizations, party platforms, congressional party organization, intraparty democracy, nominations, and elections. The two American political parties have changed little in structure since the days before the Civil War, but if the recommendations advanced by the committee were implemented, the party system would have almost no resemblance to its present form. The major attributes of the new parties would be

> . . . the national quality of their organization, a much greater degree of centralization of party power, a tendency for party claims to assume primacy over individual constituency claims in public policy formation, a heightened visibility for the congressional parties and their leadership, and for the President's role as party leader, and a greater concern over party unity and discipline.[8]

Central to this report as well as to other proposals for party reform is the organization of the parties. Certainly national party organizations as they now stand are not models of effectiveness. In fact, some observers take the position that there is a semantic trap in joining the words "organization" and "party": "Organization in the sense of a bureaucratic institution which possesses recognizable personnel and ethos, permanence, continuity and some uniformity in its operations is basically absent from the American party system."[9] And because it is absent, political parties have become less effective even in their principal function—campaigns. Candidates for office now rely less on them, and the proportion of voters identifying with either party has declined.

PARTY ORGANIZATION

The national party organizations are confederations of county, village, township, city, ward, and precinct units. Typically, each of them has a high degree of autonomy vis-à-vis other units. Moreover, they are personalized, relatively open, and informal—a style suitable to attract party activists and workers. Some years ago the term "stratarchy" was coined to describe the parties. A stratarchy is "a diffusion of power within each level of the party organization such that power resides in and is exercised at each level."[10] Furthermore, the formal structure of the party parallels the organization of electoral districts. Some states have ward or city council district organizations as well.

PRECINCT ORGANIZATION

The basic unit of party organization is the election district, or precinct (usually containing 600 to 900 voters), within which the polling place is located. Party precinct officials (who are elected in some states, appointed in others) are the basic link between the party and the electorate. They are responsible for getting to know the voters and identifying those who regularly support the party's candidates. In addition, the precinct leader forms a precinct election board and represents the party at the polling place on election day. With the declining role of parties in local elections, the scope and intensity of precinct party activity have also diminished.

COUNTY PARTY ORGANIZATION

In many places the most powerful local party official is the county chairman. Different states specify different selection methods for this official. The chairman may be elected by a county convention, by precinct officials, by all party voters, by the members of a popularly elected county committee, or by the party candidates for elective office. The county organization is important because many public officials are elected and many government functions are implemented at this level. The county committee is an intermediary between the state party organization and the lower levels of local organization.

STATE PARTY ORGANIZATION

Party organization at the state level includes state party conventions, state committees, and state chairmen. State committees are created by various procedures, including election in the party's primaries, election by a lower committee, or election by a party convention.

State party committees usually call and organize party conventions, draft party platforms, and select the party's presidential electors, national convention delegates, and alternates. Together they elect the national party chairman. At the head of the state committee is the state chairman. This official is the chief executive officer in charge of state party headquarters. The chairman is formally responsible for the day-by-day activities of the state organization and plays an important role in fund-raising campaigns at the state level. Indeed, state chairmen view campaigning as their most significant task. They see the parties almost exclusively as electoral organizations. The dominant concern in establishing a state party organization "seems to be its usefulness in helping the state administer the electoral processes rather than its viability as a healthy and on-going political organization."[11]

At the state level a number of systematic attempts to establish broader party organizations through professional staffing were made in the 1960s. For instance, Michigan Republicans were urged to develop a bureaucratic party organization by a special report prepared for the state's Republican Central Committee. The report said: "The dilemma of the Michigan GOP can largely be attributed to its failure and inability to develop political techniques necessary to cope with the vastly changing conditions."[12] It described professional staffers as "skilled political tacticians" who can provide organizational permanence: "Not transitory, crash-program campaign organization, but continuing, permanent year-round organization that makes its influence felt in every county, city, township, and village—organization that not only wins the new votes needed to win elections, but wins the new Republicans needed to sustain a working majority."[13] The report advised the state central staff to engage in research, education, press relations, advertising, promotion, and field organization.

NATIONAL PARTY ORGANIZATION

The national party organization is a loose confederation of local and state parties. Formally, each party's presidential nominating convention is its highest governing body. At the national conventions, delegates establish committees, commissions, and task forces that will meet during the interelection period. Authority to initiate, formulate, and implement party rules and regulations are delegated to these groups. In the 1970s the Democratic Party placed great emphasis on making the convention delegates more representative of the party's supporters. By employing a quota system, the Democrats brought more minorities, women, and young party members to the convention.

Ongoing national party leadership rests in each party's national committee. These consist of national committee members from each of the fifty states, plus the District of Columbia, Puerto Rico, the Virgin Islands, and until very recently in the case of the Democrats, the Canal Zone. Usually the national committee meets two or three times a year. As might be expected, the members

> . . . have very little collective identity, little patterned interaction, and only rudimentary common values and goals . . . the national committees may be thought of not so much as groups, but as lists of people who have obtained their national committee memberships through organizational processes wholly separate in each state.[14]

The national committee selects the national party chairman. In practice the chairman is designated by the party's presidential nominee, and this choice is confirmed by the national committee and the national convention. The term is for four years, and the chairman has a permanent staff of about one hundred, organized in a rather loose manner, to direct the work of the national party organization. However, the nature of the position is such that the tenure of many chairmen has been shorter than four years, and few have served longer. To a large extent the effectiveness of the national party organization depends on this officer. Under strong chairmen the normally weak national party organizations tend to assume greater significance.

The performance of national chairmen is usually evaluated in terms of their public relations skills. If chairmen

> . . . are to do the job well, they must be, first and foremost, good public-relations men . . . the national chairmen, whether in-party or out-party, whether personally colorful or not, have a job which is fundamentally and increasingly that of directing and coordinating the public relations efforts of the many different people and groups who bear the labels "Democrat" and "Republican."[15]

National chairmen play a smaller role in managing presidential campaigns. They are supposed to be neutral and should not take part in the preconvention campaign, except in the case of an incumbent president who enjoys overwhelming party support.

CONGRESSIONAL CAMPAIGN COMMITTEES

National party organization is further fragmented by a campaign committee in each house of Congress. The Democratic congressional committee was created in 1842 as a joint House-Senate group to publish "a declaration of principles for General Harrison's administration."[16] Republicans established a joint committee of congressional Republicans to aid their candidates during Lincoln's first administration. The two parties adopted permanent congressional organizations in 1866. When popular election of senators began (after the ratification of the Seventeenth Amendment in 1913), both parties formed separate senatorial campaign committees.

The campaign committees are similar in composition. The Republican Congressional Campaign Committee includes one member from each state that has even a single Republican member of Congress. The entire state delegation from the party chooses its representative. The Democrats in the House have a similar procedure, except that the chairman may appoint representatives from states not having any Democratic members of Congress. The senatorial campaign committees both have up to ten members, usually drawn from the group of senators whose term is not up in the coming election.

The objective of these campaign committees is to help reelect incumbents and, when possible, to assist nonincumbents whose chances of winning seem reasonable. The committees allocate funds, send party speakers to the states to endorse colleagues who are up for reelection, and provide legislative histories, roll-call data, and campaign literature.

The national committees have to compete with the congressional campaign committees of their parties for funds and appropriate issues. At the same time, the campaign committees must establish working relations with state and regional party organizations. But there is no organic relationship among all these committees, and the relationships are by and large informal and personal. As a result there is considerable duplication and overlapping of effort. The congressional campaign committees have resisted encroachment by the national committees and have succeeded in retaining their autonomy. Congressional leaders want the national committee to confine itself to fund raising and public relations work, leaving them to operate as they see fit. Furthermore, members of Congress often disagree with the policies and positions advocated by the national committee. The overall effect of these tensions has been lack of party unity, dispersion of power within the party organization, failure of the party to hold its public officials accountable, and conflict between the public officials and the party leaders.

Figure 7–1 presents an official Republican Party organization chart—but charts like this do not convey the actual structure of the parties. Frank Sorauf has observed:

> We have every right to call the party "organization" by that name, but it is an inescapable and central fact that the parties, chief among our social institutions, have resisted the development of "big," efficient, centralized organizations. . . . They lack the hierarchical control and efficiency, the unified setting of priorities and strategy, and the central responsibility we associate with contemporary large organizations. . . . In large part . . . the "under-organization" of American parties results from their fundamental character as parties. They have been pragmatic electoral parties, involved chiefly in supporting candidates for public office and active mainly during campaigns.[17]

The desirability of professionalism and bureaucratization in party organization is by no means universally accepted. The characteristics of bureaucracy are opposed to those of democracy. Moreover, bureaucratization does not guarantee efficiency and effectiveness. But the lack of bureaucratic organization in the political parties, now that other social and political institutions are bureaucratized, has weakened them as an apparatus for winning elections. It is inevitable that candidates for public office have turned to other methods of campaigning.

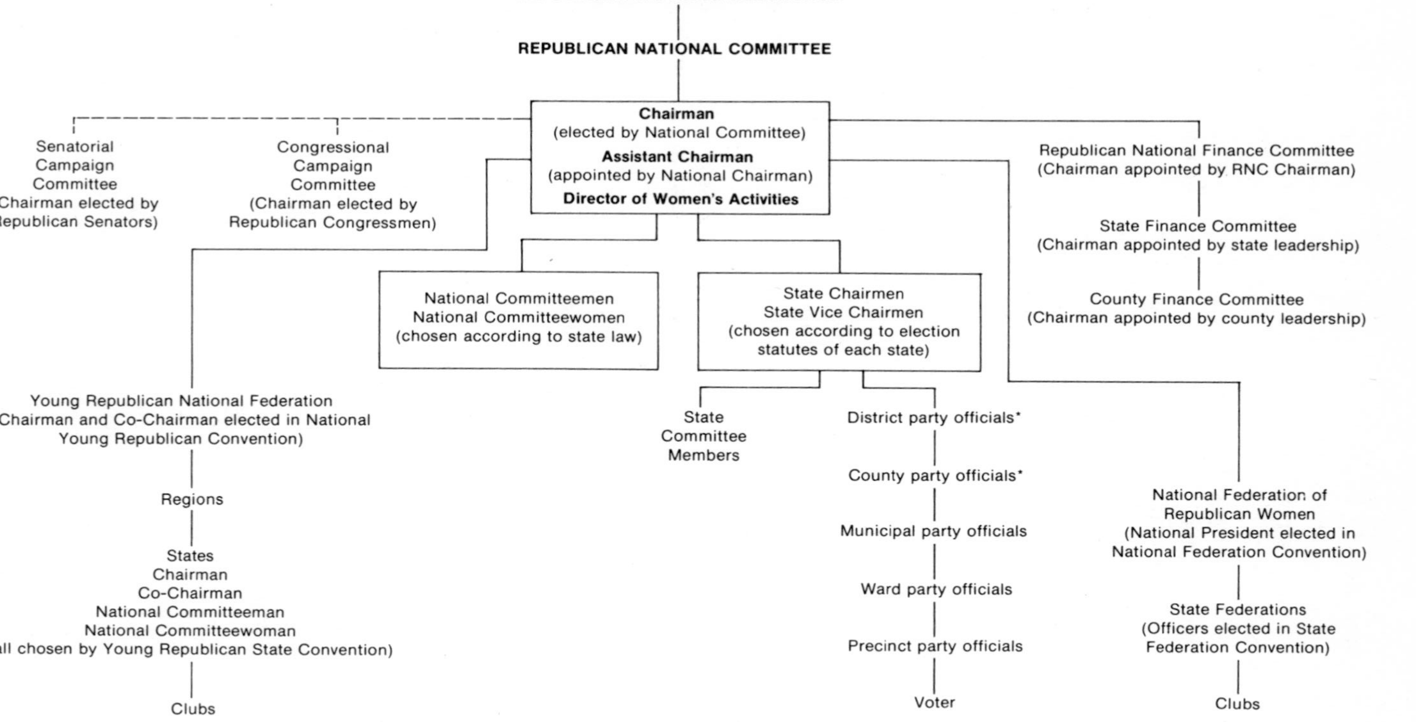

Figure 7–1 **Official Republican Party Organizational Chart**

SOURCE: Republican National Committee, Washington, D.C.

THE DECLINE OF PARTY IDENTIFICATION

At the same time that political parties have become less viable linkages between citizens and government, voting in national, state, and local elections has been declining. Turnout in presidential elections is the only formal political activity for even a slim majority of eligible voters.

Among the people who do vote, what factors cause them to choose one candidate over another? There is no simple answer, but an accumulating body of research demonstrates that party identification has had more influence on a person's voting decision than any other consideration. *Party identification* is the subjective attachment of an individual to a political party. In the United States, unlike other Western democracies, party identification does not require formal membership in a political party. On occasion the partisans of one party may even vote for candidates of another without changing their self-perceived party identification. Party identification, it is generally believed, serves an important psychological function for the voter:

> To the average person the affairs of the government are remote and complex, and yet the average citizen is asked periodically to formulate opinions about these affairs. At the very least, he has to decide how he will vote, what choice he will make between candidates offering different programs and very different versions of contemporary political events. . . . Having the party symbol stamped on certain candidates, certain issue positions, certain interpretations of political reality is of great psychological convenience.[18]

Americans have tended to inherit the party identification of their parents, particularly when mother and father identify with the same party. In cases where the parents agree on their party identification, two-thirds to three-fourths of all adult Americans consider themselves members of their parents' party. Americans whose parents have different party identifications or have changed their party identifications are more likely to be political independents. Moreover, party identification is more likely to develop in children when their parents are interested in politics and participate in elections. Indeed, party identification is acquired early in life. Some 30 to 50 percent of elementary school children express a party identification, and a larger proportion of children who do so are from relatively affluent families.[19]

The distribution of party identification in the United States from 1952 to 1974 is shown in Table 7–1. It is evident that a sizable portion of the electorate participates in the two-party system. Yet the total number of people identifying with either party is declining, while the number classifying themselves as independents is on the rise. The proportion of the

TABLE 7–1

Party Identification in the United States, 1952–1974 (Percents)

PARTY IDENTIFICATION	1952	1960	1968	1972	1974
Democrats	47	46	45	41	41
Republicans	27	27	24	23	18
Independents	22	23	29	34	40
Other	4	4	2	2	1
	100%	100%	100%	100%	100%

SOURCE: Institute for Political Research (Ann Arbor, Mich.: University of Michigan).

electorate identifying with the Democratic Party reached its highest level in 1952, when 47 percent said that they were Democrats. A gradual decline in Republican support started in 1968. At the same time, the number of people who view themselves as independent has increased substantially, reaching 40 percent in 1974. Consequently independents have emerged as a group occupying the decisive center of elections and holding the balance of power between the two major parties. Not only do more voters than ever now call themselves independents, but more of them are youn-

TABLE 7–2

Split-Party Victories in States Electing Governor and U.S. Senator at the Same Time

YEAR	NUMBER OF STATES ELECTING GOVERNOR AND SENATOR AT SAME TIME	NUMBER OF STATES ELECTING GOVERNOR AND SENATOR OF DIFFERENT PARTIES	PERCENT OF SPLIT VICTORIES
1950	19	3	16
1952	20	6	30
1954	25	5	20
1970	23	11	48
1972	12	6	50
1974	26	11	42

SOURCE: *Parties, Politics and Public Policy in America*, 2nd ed., by William J. Keefe. Copyright © 1976 the Dryden Press, Hinsdale, Ill., a division of Holt, Rinehart and Winston. Copyright © 1972 Holt, Rinehart and Winston. Reprinted with permission.

TABLE 7–3

Support for the Parties among Voters

	1968	1970	1972
Q.: How much do you feel that political parties help make the government pay attention to what the people think?			
A.: A good deal	37%	33%	26%
Total	(1,342)	(911)	(2,191)

SOURCE: Institute for Political Research (Ann Arbor, Mich.: University of Michigan).

ger voters—a fact that partly explains the overall growth in independents.[20]

The declining role of parties as stable, salient symbols to a large proportion of Americans is also seen in *split-ticket voting*. As shown in Table 7–2, ticket splitting has become increasingly common. This makes it more difficult for one party to win a range of offices in the same election.

The immediate result of the rise in split-ticket voting and the expanding number of independents is that party control over elective officials is further declining, because the value of party endorsement and support is diminishing. Candidates for office at all levels increasingly proclaim their independence from political parties, even though they wear party labels in the hope of attracting more voters. Consequently Americans are still electing Republicans and Democrats to office, even though fewer view the parties as effective mediators between the people and their government (see Table 7–3).

CAMPAIGN MANAGEMENT: THE PROFESSIONALIZATION OF ELECTIONS

The decreasing effectiveness of political party organization on the one hand, and the decline of party identification on the other, has led candidates for public office to mobilize their own electorates by using professional specialists in organization, management, information, and media. As Robert Agranoff has observed, "The acquisition of campaign resources, the campaign organization, strategy formulation and media selection have become the province of the candidate instead of the party organization."[21] Candidates employ professional campaign management firms, which have become a nationwide industry selling a wide range of services "from a candidate's announcement of availability to his post-election victory party."[22]

ORIGINS OF THE CAMPAIGN INDUSTRY

The first professional campaign management firm, Campaigns, Inc., was established in California in 1933 by Clem Whitaker (a journalist, lobbyist, and public relations expert) and Leone Baxter. One of the first major beneficiaries of Campaigns, Inc., was the Republican Earl Warren, who served for ten years (1943–1953) as California's governor before his appointment as chief justice of the United States Supreme Court. Between 1933 and 1955 Campaigns, Inc., won seventy of the seventy-five political campaigns it managed.[23] The company's success at turning political campaigning into a profitable business stimulated the rise of other campaign management firms. These became a permanent part of California's political system about twenty years ago, and the state became a model of modern campaign management.

It was not incidental that professional campaign management firms were born in California. The conditions there provided incentives and opportunity for them to develop. Political reforms made by the Progressive movement in 1910–1920 restricted the activities of political parties, so that party organizations became difficult to maintain. Candidates could not rely upon precinct and ward party organizations to deliver votes. Furthermore, the Progressive reforms encouraged numerous referenda. Extensive advertising was needed in order to familiarize voters with the issues. In addition, massive migration during the Great Depression brought to California large numbers of eligible voters who had no party identification and were substantially indifferent to party and issue appeals. This group "comprised a rootless electorate that was particularly susceptible to mass advertising appeals."[24]

The large-scale growth of campaign management firms in other areas of the country is a more recent development. However, by the 1960s it had turned into a nationwide industry. The rise of this industry is associated with the weakening of traditional party organizations and the increase in the numbers of independent voters. Party organizations have less and less control over the critical aspects of the electoral process—candidate selection, policy positions, the development of strategies, and the allocation of campaign resources. This has become obvious at all electoral levels. In the presidential nominating process, for example, contenders use their own personal organizations to mobilize committed supporters to become convention delegates. Long before the convention they place pressure on state party leaders and delegates to support them by initiating news coverage of their activities, by seeking nationwide television coverage of states with primaries, and by using public opinion polls to demonstrate their support in the electorate. It is often pointed out that as the party's control over the selection of delegates to the national convention is further reduced, party leaders will have even less influence over presidential selection. Thus the process of choosing a president has been shifting away from the party organizations to the electorate and to individual delegates known to be committed to certain candidates. Furthermore, the national party organizations have been losing their influence in determining policy positions. Instead, the strong candidates dictate their own positions and campaign strategies to the parties.

ACTIVITIES AND ORGANIZATION

Professional campaign management firms perform several important functions for their clients. They attempt to structure and control campaigns by publicizing a client's assets and disguising his or her liabilities. In marketing the candidate, these firms enter all phases of the political contest. Here is a partial list of the types of professionals they typically employ.[25]

MANAGEMENT

- Public relations counselor
- Advertising agent
- Advance person
- Fund raiser
- Management scientist
- Industrial engineer
- Telephone campaigner
- Organizer

INFORMATION

- Market researcher
- Public opinion pollster
- Political scientist
- Social psychologist
- Psychologist
- Computer programmer
- Demographer
- Statistician

MEDIA

- Journalist
- Media advance agent
- Radio and television writer
- Radio and television producer
- Film documentary producer
- Radio and television time buyer
- Newspaper space buyer
- Television coach
- Radio and television actors
- Direct-mail advertiser
- Computer printing specialist

MANAGEMENT

Campaign management requires both management and consultant personnel. Management personnel are "directly involved in planning and guiding all features of a campaign . . . [they] try to attain an overall view of the campaign, assess elements of strength and weakness, and adjust accordingly."[26] Some candidates hire campaign managers who plan and coordinate the overall effort and who contract out such specialties as advertising, public opinion surveying, and fund raising. Other candidates purchase a full-service campaign managing firm that "performs the planning, organization, financing, research, advertising, and publicity."[27] Organizations that have no expertise for handling a particular service may subcontract it. Typically subcontracting involves activities such as television production or door-to-door canvassing. Larger campaign management companies, such as Publicom, Inc., have specialists on legislation, lobbying, and public opinion surveying, so that a candidate can shop within the firm for any number of services.

Consultant personnel provide more limited and specialized services. Campaign consultants are employed for tasks such as speech writing, research, and developing position papers. Technical specialists perform specific services, including canvassing precincts and designing and distributing direct-mail advertising. One California firm circulated petitions to get a particular proposal on the ballot at a cost of 50 cents per signature.[28]

Since campaign management companies, like other profit-making corporations, search for salable products, they become involved in the process of political recruitment itself. So far their activities have been limited to screening candidates who seek expert advice; they have not yet aggressively searched for sure winners. From their point of view, "The ideal candidate is an attractive young Republican or Democrat who has accumulated no political 'record' of possible liabilities."[29] The various firms have different policies concerning the political affiliations of prospective clients. Some companies work for candidates of both parties. For example, Baus and Ross Company managed the campaigns of Republicans Richard Nixon and Barry Goldwater and the Democrat Edmund G. Brown, former governor of California. Other companies work exclusively for Democrats or for Republicans. Spencer-Roberts and Associates, for instance, manages campaigns only for Republicans. Matt Reese, a professional campaign manager, says that he works "only for Democrats whom I approve."[30] There is also a tendency among management firms to refuse to handle a campaign for a candidate whose views are so unpopular as to ensure defeat. Like other successful business enterprises, management firms try to protect their reputations by screening prospective clients.

There are no accepted standards or ground rules covering the campaign management industry. Indeed, conflict of interest does occur in cases where a firm or a campaign manager works for candidates of both parties simultaneously in a single state, or in cases where consultants perform overlapping services for two or more employers.

INFORMATION

Some observers believe that there has been a shift of political skill from "party leaders, political brokers, and special interest group leaders to those who are information and communication experts."[31] According to William Roberts, cofounder of Spencer-Roberts, "Too many campaigns try to fly by the seat of their pants. Good old Charley Brown who knows that district like the back of his hand just isn't good enough for this day and age."[32]

Reliable information is a necessary requirement for an effective campaign strategy. Spencer-Roberts begins a campaign by collecting and sorting as much data about the constituency as possible, including facts on incomes, education, race, ethnicity, religion, opinions, and past voting patterns. The information is often collected in a "unit data book," which is a potentially significant campaign document. Agranoff compiled a table of contents for a typical county data book:[33]

1. Name of county: congressional and legislative districts, population of county, county seat.
2. Chairman and members of county board and their political affiliations.
3. Name of city, population of city, mayor of city, and key members of the cities' councils in the county.
4. Names, addresses, and phone numbers of the statewide candidates' chairmen in the county.
5. Names, addresses, and phone numbers of party officials, including precinct leaders.
6. Names, addresses, phone numbers, and the responsibilities of other persons involved in the campaign.
7. Composition of state legislative delegation, addresses and phone numbers, and candidates for these offices.
8. Radio stations in the county and those outside with 50 percent or more coverage in the county.
9. Television stations in the county.
10. Daily and weekly magazines, including papers outside the county which have substantial circulation in the county.
11. General descriptive statistics: population trends, voting trends, election indexes, vote ranking, swing rate, vote proportions.
12. Major plants: size of work force, shift times, number in each shift.

13. Names of officers of important organizations.
14. Location and date of county fairs or other civic celebrations.
15. Airports: length of runways, when lighted, radio facilities, mechanical services, nearest all-weather field.

Campaign managment firms and professional campaign managers acquire the necessary information for handling a campaign in much the way any other business does. Increasingly information systems are being stored and processed by computer, which is "today's functional equivalent of the ward and precinct leaders' personal knowledge of their neighborhoods."[34]

Information specialists have emerged as key persons in political campaigns. In many cases they become confidants and close advisors to the candidates and the elected officials. Key campaign decisions, such as which issues to stress or ignore, which media markets to concentrate upon, and which groups of voters to appeal to, are made with the active participation of information experts. It is "the function of these advisors, the candidate's brain trust, to coach him in the use of his 'campaign bible'!"[35] The "campaign bible" presents facts, arguments, interpretations, and conclusions in two major areas: First, it summarizes all issues which the candidate might wish to address or might be questioned about by constituents, reporters, or opponents. Second, it describes the attributes and opinions of groups who support or oppose the candidate. In this way the well-briefed candidate can impress the voters by showing awareness of and sympathy with their concerns.

MEDIA

One of the nation's largest campaign management firms, Baus and Ross, views the political campaign as a "war" for voters' minds: "It starts with the battle plan. That is the strategy. Then there are the tactics." Many tactics center on public exposure of candidates through the mass media, particularly television.* Today practically all candidates for major office use television, radio, and newspapers in campaigning. The media are now the largest single cost in campaigns.

The growing significance of mass media in elections stems from a number of interrelated factors. First is the sheer size of the media audience. No other means of mass persuasion offers the same potential for reaching large numbers of voters in a short period of time. Second, most

* There are two kinds of campaign media: controlled and uncontrolled. *Controlled* media refers to communications which candidates and their media specialists can create, produce, purchase, and place. *Uncontrolled* media are communication activities over which the campaigner has limited influence—news coverage, newspaper stories, and editorials.

of what Americans know about politics and political campaigns comes to them through the mass media. Table 7–4 shows that television and newspapers are the major source of information, while magazines and radio are less important.

Third, the mass media, and especially television, bring the candidate into direct communication with a large proportion of the electorate. As political party organization becomes less effective for winning elections, the media become the vehicle for campaign communications. Samuel Eldersveld, for example, found that in the Detroit area, only 17 percent of the Democratic precinct leaders and 25 percent of the Republican leaders performed all three campaign tasks of voter registration, canvassing, and getting out the vote.[36] This low degree of party contact fosters a greater reliance on campaign media. Fourth, the mass media can influence and convert some voters in a campaign. At the same time, media campaigning reinforces the opinions and the convictions of committed voters, minimizing the risk that they will cast their ballots for another candidate on election day.

Finally, the media, but most notably television, have a considerable influence on the voters' perceptions of the personal qualities of the candidates. Candidate-oriented messages create the candidate's image. The image in turn has assumed greater importance in the voters' decisions:

> Prior to 1972, partisan attitudes had been one of the most important factors explaining the vote decision. Yet, although the 1972 election marked the first occurrence of a substantial decline in the correlation between party identification and the two-party presidential vote, a long-term trend toward both de-

TABLE 7–4

Percent of People Exposed to Campaign Media in Three Presidential Election Years

MEDIA	1952	1964	1972
Newspapers	79.1 (N=1,707)	78.1 (N=1,437)	57.1 (N=1,115)
Radio	70.1 (N=1,703)	48.1 (N=1,441)	43.1 (N=1,116)
Magazines	40.1 (N=1,703)	39.1 (N=1,438)	33.1 (N=1,117)
Television	51.1 (N=1,634)	89.1 (N=1,446)	89.1 (N=1,116)

SOURCE: Institute for Political Research (Ann Arbor, Mich.: University of Michigan.)

creased importance of partisan attitudes and increased importance of candidate images as predictors of the vote has been taking place.[37]

From the voters' perspective, the candidate's image includes factors such as personal appearance (age, health, and other background characteristics), competence (experience and ability), trustworthiness (honesty, integrity), reliability (decisiveness, stability), and leadership appeal (communicativeness, likableness, ability to inspire). Obviously such factors are subject to manipulation by the controlled campaign media, as exemplified by television campaigns.

Television Campaigns. Television is now the preeminent medium of what is commonly labeled "image politics." Indeed, the professionals do not view television as a means of informing the electorate, but as an audience-delivery business. Television sponsors purchase time, and broadcasters guarantee a large audience in exchange for the price of the commercial message.

Television specialists operate on the assumption that *projected* personalities win votes. To this end they attempt to create an image-candidate. Voters who say that they vote for the person, not the party, are likely to be the targets of the image-persuasion approach. The overt strategy of the image makers is "contrived spontaneity, the effort to appear uninhibited, candid, open and credible without running the risk of an unrehearsed performance."[38] The public is not exposed to the entire public record and character of the candidate, but to those aspects that, according to careful research, attract more voters. Moreover, as Robert MacNeil, a veteran television correspondent, has commented, "Nonachievements can be projected almost as effectively as real ones and an impression of experience and qualification can be constructed that has little basis in fact."[39] By research, rehearsal, and the control and staging of events, the candidate is transformed into a composite image. This image is a blend of his or her television performance, political role, and personal qualities. Image messages are usually short (10 to 60 seconds in length); they involve simple themes; and they are placed in slots adjacent to popular programs. Indeed, campaign television advertising is adjusted to the habits of the audience, and these are systematically researched before producing the messages and planning the advertising campaign.

CAMPAIGN ORGANIZATION

Campaign organizations vary in size, structure, form, and patterns of decision making. The typical congressional campaign organization has about five paid employees and as many as 350 volunteer workers. Tasks are divided among several generalists, there are few hierarchical levels, and decision making is centralized. A study of 102 congressional campaign organizations found that in four of the five campaign policy areas investigated, at least 75 percent of all the decisions were made by either the candidate or the campaign manager.[40]

On the other hand, President Nixon's reelection campaign in 1972, featuring the Committee to Re-elect the President, was perhaps the most extensively organized campaign in history. Commanding a budget of over $60 million, it marshaled 337 paid staff members and thousands of volunteers in a highly differentiated organizational structure with a sophisticated division of labor. It included a finance division, an advertising department, a polling agency, 11 direct-mail and 250 telephone centers throughout the country, an advance division, a number of citizens' divisions and subdivisions, and a security division. Members of the security force, it will be recalled, burglarized the national Democratic headquarters in the Watergate Building. Figure 7–2 is a chart of Nixon's reelection campaign organization.

Generally speaking, the type, size, and style of campaign organizations vary with the environment, the setting, and the campaign strategy. Campaigns for higher-level offices, covering large and heterogeneous constituencies and using various persuasion tactics, are more elaborately organized and have larger staffs than those for low-visibility offices in relatively small and/or homogeneous constituencies. Thus a candidate for the U.S. Senate running against an incumbent is likely to develop a large-scale, highly specialized, multimedia organization. But an incumbent legislator at the state level seeking reelection in a safe district does not need a vast organizational apparatus; a small staff with members who are influential in the district might suffice. And of course, the amount of money available dictates the kind and number of activities that a campaign organization can undertake; this in turn influences its size, structure, and style.

Although the ultimate purpose of the campaign organization is to elect the candidate, the candidate himself or herself is not an integral member of the organization. Though most candidates are involved in the selection of the campaign manager and the key campaign staff, often "a candidate is not so much a member as an object of the organization."[41] The candidate is busy campaigning in the field and does not take part in the daily routine of the organization. As with other organizations, but perhaps more so, there is much uncertainty in the environment in which campaign organizations operate. Furthermore, there is a tendency among staffs to depersonalize their commitment to the candidate as an individual:

> Staff members will speak of "the candidate," "the boss," "the senator," "the governor" and so on. They will come to think of their candidate as a body that gets moved around from place to place and says the lines he or she is told to

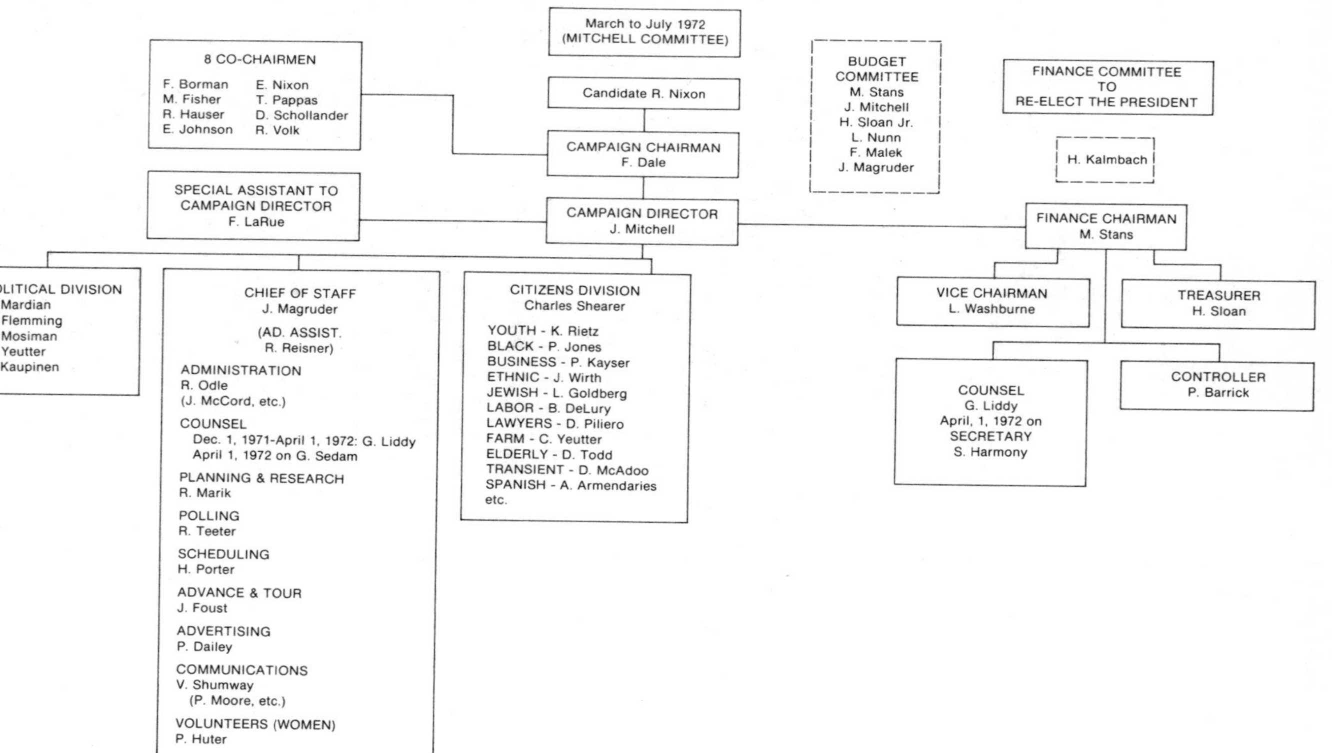

Figure 7–2 **Committee to Re-Elect the President (President Nixon's 1972 Campaign Organization)**

> say. If a line is missed or an impromptu one inserted, it increases the sense of frustration felt by some in the organization.[42]

Thus the bureaucratic norm of impersonality seeps into the waging of campaigns.

ORGANIZATION FORMS

There have been several attempts to classify the various kinds of campaign organizations along one or more central dimensions. Robert Agranoff draws a distinction among four forms:[43]

1. *Functional-specialist organizations* in which the various activities are divided throughout the campaign, allowing for their expansion and contraction as deemed desirable.
2. *Generalist organizations* in which the staff performs whatever tasks are necessary, in any part of the constituency, to implement the overall strategy. With few exceptions, all workers in such an organization are generalists. This form of organization maximizes the efforts of campaign workers. But it does not effectively utilize the special training or abilities that campaign workers bring to the campaign. Furthermore, the lack of specialization may leave some important activities unperformed or only partially completed.
3. *Areal organizations* characterized by a loose division of labor at the top and in which area units perform a number of tasks for the campaign management.
4. *Large-scale organizations* that combine specialist divisions with subunit generalists who perform only a limited number of campaign activities. Usually the various specialty divisions are coordinated with each other at the higher organizational levels. Presidential campaigns and many gubernatorial and U.S. Senate campaigns are organized in this fashion.

Another classification has been advanced by Xandra Kayden. In this scheme the critical factor is the degree to which organizations are responsive to the candidate:

> Organizations whose members reflected the personal style of the candidates more than they did the tasks of the organization . . . can be called *personalized* campaigns; organizations whose members reflected the tasks they performed more than the style of the candidate and maintained some distance between themselves and their roles in the organization can be called *professionalized* campaigns.[44]

Typically in a personalized campaign the professional staff is carefully selected by the candidate from a relatively homogeneous group of people. They are coached by the campaign manager and expected to accept the candidate's ideas. The advantage of such an arrangement is that it eases communication problems, because the staff has a common base of experience and a common language. In the professionalized campaign, on the other hand, there is a division of labor, a number of hierarchical levels, and a sense of distance among the staff members and between them and the candidate. Conflicts between the various specialists are settled at higher levels of the organization's hierarchy. At the same time, the more specialized the organization, the greater the problems of communication and coordination among the subdivisions.

Not enough information is available to attempt to conclude which forms of campaign organizations are more effective in what situations. Research in this area is scant, and the development of candidate-centered campaign organizations is relatively recent. The general trend seems to be toward more professionalism, specialization, and bureaucratization, and the use of methods and technologies characteristic of nonpolitical, large-scale, complex organizations. But the impact of these newer campaign organizations and of the electioneering industry in general has been easier to detect. Reflecting specifically upon the presidency, James Barber makes the following observation:

> The process of electing a president has become a high-powered business enterprise, a technical, organized, systematic production. The strong focus on getting elected has somehow increasingly divorced that problem from the problem of governing. For all the manipulation of sentiment, the election process has acquired a technocratic tone which seems to work against emotional expression. The resonance between candidate and people is shallow, temporary, calculated—and known to be calculated. The steam has gone out of the drama. What is left is the image of the clean machine, the blinking computer.[45]

THE COST OF ELECTIONS

Electioneering firms sell their services at soaring prices. To mention only a few items, campaign organization, management firms, research, polls, broadcast media time, film producers and editors, and computers and their technicians are expensive. The cost of presidential elections since 1932 is reported by party in Table 7–5. Total campaign spending in all primary and general elections for all offices at the three levels of government increased from $140 million in 1952 to $500 million in 1976. Significantly,

TABLE 7–5
Costs of Presidential General Elections

YEAR	REPUBLICAN	DEMOCRAT
1932	$ 2,900,052 (Hoover)	$ 2,245,052 (F. Roosevelt)*
1936	8,892,972 (Landon)	5,194,741 (F. Roosevelt)*
1940	3,451,310 (Willkie)	2,783,654 (F. Roosevelt)*
1944	2,828,652 (Dewey)	2,169,077 (F. Roosevelt)*
1948	2,127,296 (Dewey)	2,736,334 (Truman)*
1952	6,608,623 (Eisenhower)*	5,032,926 (Stevenson)
1956	7,778,702 (Eisenhower)*	5,106,651 (Stevenson)
1960	10,128,000 (Nixon)	9,797,000 (Kennedy)*
1964	16,026,000 (Goldwater)	8,757,000 (Johnson)*
1968	25,402,000 (Nixon)*	11,594,000 (Humphrey)
1972	59,500,000 (Nixon)*	35,000,000 (McGovern)
1976	22,000,000 (Ford)	22,000,000 (Carter)*

SOURCE: Herbert E. Alexander, *Political Finances* (Minneapolis: Burgess, 1972), p. 6; for 1972, Alexander, *Financing the 1972 Elections* (Lexington, Mass.: Heath-Lexington, 1975).

*Denotes Winner.

the rise during the last thirty years is not associated with the expansion in the size of the electorate or with inflationary cycles in the economy.[46]

As the table shows, election outcomes are not exclusively determined by the amount of money spent. Nonetheless, campaign funds are an important political resource that has been used to gain influence over public policy and government activities. It is these aspects of "political money" that are of major concern in democratic elections.

DISPARITIES IN SPENDING

Campaign spending is unequally distributed. More money is spent for executive offices than for legislative ones. For example, in the 1972 presidential race, primary and general election campaign expenditures were estimated at $115 million. In the same year primary and general election outlays to elect one-third of the Senate were about $30 million, and about $46 million was spent to elect the entire House.[47] This disparity in spending further enhances the prestige and the public's expectations of the president at the expense of the legislature.

Campaign money also flows to competitive rather than noncompetitive races. From the perspective of the candidates and the donors, this disparity is understandable: more money is spent in those elections where it can make a difference between defeat and victory. But

> A vicious circle develops in which a candidate wins an election, becomes stronger because of incumbency and the political composition of his district, and finally becomes almost invulnerable because few of the usual sources of campaign funds are willing to gamble on his long shot opponent. These secure officeholders do not feel accountable to voters in elections.[48]

Another significant disparity in campaign spending is between incumbents and challengers. In 1972, for instance, incumbent United States senators outspent their opponents by an average of $495,000 to $244,100. Democratic incumbents had an average $381,100 to $312,400 edge over Republican challengers, while Republican senators outspent Democratic opponents $559,700 to $205,700. A similar trend prevailed in House races.[49] And the financial edge that officeholders have over challengers is accompanied by other advantages, as discussed in Chapter 5.

SOURCES OF CAMPAIGN FUNDS

Political reformers have long argued that candidates should be supported by many donors giving no more than $10, $25, or $100 each. They maintain that candidates would then be free from the pressures brought by large contributors—wealthy individuals, interest groups, big corporations, and organized labor. Efforts to increase small campaign contributions, most notably through direct-mail techniques, have met with some success. But as shown in Table 7–6, the number of donors is rather small even in presidential campaigns, and campaign treasuries have usually been filled by a relatively small number of large contributions. From 1952 to 1960, donors of $10,000 or more numbered about 100 in each presidential year, and their gifts totaled $1.6 million to $2.3 million per election. In the 1968 campaign, the number of donors contributing $10,000 or more increased to 424, and their total contributions exceeded $12.2 million. The Nixon reelection campaign in 1972 was the most heavily dependent on very large donations. Of a total of $19.9 million raised before April 1972, 87 contributors donated a total of $12.4 million; of the $43.3 million raised later, a total of $4.4 million was given by 37 contributors. These large donors contributed almost 28 percent of all Nixon's campaign funds.[50]

Table 7–7 compares the contributions of large and small donors to the 1972 congressional elections in relation to the expense of the contests. The less expensive the race, the greater the reliance on small donors. As the cost of the campaign grows, dependency on the larger contributors increases.

TABLE 7–6

Contributions to Presidential Campaigns

YEAR	TOTAL NUMBER CONTRIBUTING	PERCENT OF ADULT POPULATION
1952	3,000,000	4.0
1956	8,000,000	9.0
1960	10,000,000	10.5
1964	12,000,000	12.0
1968	8,700,000	8.0
1972	6,400,000	5.3

SOURCE: U.S. Senate Committee on Rules and Administration, 93rd Congress, *Public Financing of Federal Elections* (Washington, D.C.: U.S. Government Printing Office, 1973), p. 237.

Large contributions come from wealthy individuals with strong ideological or personal commitments to the candidate, individuals expecting payoffs or favors if the candidate wins, and special interest groups. An example of ideological commitment is provided by Stewart Mott's 1968 letter to Hubert Humphrey. Mott is the son of one of the founders of General Motors and a multimillionaire. He was one of the

TABLE 7–7

Funding Sources by Expense of Contest, U.S. House Races, 1972

EXPENDITURE LEVEL	SHARES OF FUNDS DERIVED FROM	
	Small Donors and Party Committees* (Percent)	Large Contributors and Interest Groups† (Percent)
Up to $30,000	57.9	27.1
$30,000–$70,000	50.6	34.6
$70,000–$120,000	46.7	36.5
$120,000 and above	39.1	40.4

SOURCE: U.S. Senate Committee on Rules and Administration, 93rd Congress, *Public Financing of Federal Elections* (Washington, D.C.: U.S. Government Printing Office, 1973), p. 337.

* Small donors were defined as those giving under $1,000; the funds provided by party committees are included in this statistic.

† Large contributors were defined as those giving more than $1,000. This included funds provided by special interest committees.

most important contributors to Eugene McCarthy's campaign. After McCarthy failed to win the Democratic party nomination, Mott was unwilling to contribute to the campaign of Hubert Humphrey unless he was satisfied with Humphrey on ideological grounds. Following are excerpts from Mott's letter:

> I've spent over $325,000 this year in politics. . . . Yet I am still not convinced that I should give money and time to your campaign. . . . The least we on the McCarthy Finance Committee could do for you would be to give you a hearing—a personal private interview of an hour's length—in order to question you about your own view of the nation's future and what it ought to be. We will be meeting you next Wednesday evening with an open mind and a sense of fair play. . . . We have the capacity to give $1,000,000 or more to your campaign—and raise twice or three times that amount. But we will each make our own individual judgment on the basis of how you answer our several questions and how you conduct your campaign in the following weeks.[51]

It is a violation of federal law to offer public employment as a reward for any help given a party in an election campaign. Yet the relationship between high federal posts, particularly ambassadorships, and substantial campaign contributions is strong. The Nixon administration was explicit about trading ambassadorships for contributions. After his reelection, Nixon appointed nine noncareer envoys who had given large sums to his campaign (see Table 7–8).

TABLE 7–8

Ambassadors and Campaign Contributions to Nixon's 1972 Reelection Campaign

COUNTRY	AMBASSADOR	CONTRIBUTION
England	Walter H. Annenberg	$250,000
Switzerland	Shelby Davis	$100,000
Luxembourg	Ruth L. Farkas	$300,000
Belgium	Leonard K. Firestone	$112,600
Holland	Kingdon Gould	$100,000
Austria	John P. Humes	$100,000
France	John N. Irwin II	$ 50,000
France	Arthur K. Watson	$300,000
Ireland	John D. Moore	$ 10,442
Total		$1,323,042

SOURCE: Congressional Quarterly Service, *Dollar Politics* (Washington, D.C.: Congressional Quarterly, 1974), vol. II, p. 15. Reprinted with permission.

The extent, dimensions, and implications of interest-group and corporate contributions to campaigns are obviously difficult to document systematically. Some well-publicized cases, however, have resulted in the conviction of several participants.* These incidents involved some of the best-known names in American industry and business:

- American Airlines The airline made an illegal contribution from corporate funds to the Nixon reelection campaign after personal solicitation by Herbert Kalmbach (Nixon's fund raiser and personal legal representative), who asked for $100,000.
- American Ship Building Company This corporation made an illegal donation of $100,000 to Nixon's reelection campaign under pressure from Kalmbach.
- 3M (Minnesota Mining and Manufacturing Corporation) The 3M company maintained a secret political fund starting in the 1950s. In 1972 it made an illegal corporate contribution of $36,000 to the Nixon campaign.
- Northrop Corporation Two of this major defense contractor's officers illegally contributed $150,000 in corporate funds to the Nixon campaign.
- Ashland Oil The corporation made a $100,000 cash donation (via a Swiss bank) from corporate funds to Nixon's reelection campaign.

Criminal charges were brought against these and some other companies caught in the most obvious attempts to buy political influence.[52]

Money may not only buy campaign victories; it may also purchase influence and access to elected officials, especially when the contributions are large. Yet some elected officials may be consistently disappointing to their contributors. Henry C. Frick, president of the United States Steel Corporation, was unhappy with his investment in Theodore Roosevelt's presidential campaign: "He got down on his knees to us," Frick complained. "We bought the son of a bitch and then he did not stay bought."[53] In other cases the payoffs are promptly delivered. For example, in 1970 representatives of the American Milk Producers, Inc., wrote President Nixon that they had contributed $135,000 to Republican congressional candidates and that they were interested in channeling $2 million to his campaign. In the same letter they protested about Nixon's slowness in approving import quotas on ice cream and other dairy products. Within two weeks the quotas were approved.[54]

* The regulations governing campaign funds are discussed in the next section.

REGULATING CAMPAIGN FINANCING

Until the 1970s the core of federal control over financing federal elections consisted of the Federal Corrupt Practices Act (1925) and the Hatch Act (1939, as amended in 1940). The Federal Corrupt Practices Act codified relevant statutes and required candidates for the Senate and House to disclose their receipts and expenditures. The act did not apply to presidential campaigns. Political and campaign committees functioning in more than one state came under the act's provisions, and spending ceilings for Senate ($10,000 to $25,000) and House ($2,500 to $5,000) contests were established. Minor modifications in the act were made in 1944, 1947, and 1948. The Hatch Act placed a limit of $5,000 on individual contributions, and a $3 million ceiling on the expenditures of political committees for federal candidates.

These regulations were ineffective both in limiting the cost of elections and in controlling the sources and kinds of financial donations. Congress was not eager to improve and enforce the acts and, with the exception of occasional incidents, law enforcement agencies have never been interested in political money. Mechanisms to circumvent the law have also been developed. For example, the limits on contributions to individual campaign committees are commonly evaded by establishing scores of committees for a single candidate. Thus each committee can accept the legal maximum contribution. The prohibition on contributions by corporations is evaded in two major ways: First, many firms solicit contributions from their executives, collect these individual checks, and give the substantial total to a candidate. Second, executives have been issued inflated bonuses or expense-account payments with the understanding that they will contribute to a designated candidate. Payments made to executives become part of their own private resources rather than corporate funds.

PUBLIC FINANCING

The 1970s were an era of campaign financing regulation. The 1976 presidential campaign was mounted on the foundation of public money. Nomination aspirants began their campaigns under the Federal Election Campaign Act of 1974. Although the Supreme Court struck down provisions of the law that limited campaign expenditures and curbed candidates' contributions to their own campaigns, it upheld the limits on contributions by individuals and groups and the sweeping requirements for disclosure of campaign finances.[55] The major provisions of the new legislation are listed below:

- Contribution Limits Individuals may give up to $1,000 to each candidate in each federal or primary election; up to $5,000 per year to a political action committee, such as those sponsored by corporations or labor unions; and $20,000 per year to a national political party committee. Total contributions by one person are limited to $25,000 a year. Political action committees may contribute $5,000 to a candidate in each election.
- Public Financing Presidential—but not Senate or House—candidates have the option of accepting federal money to pay for general elections or primaries, as did both major party candidates in 1976. To qualify, a candidate must raise $5,000 in each of twenty states in contributions of $250 or less, for an overall total of $100,000. In addition, public funds may be used to pay $2 million to each major political party to finance their national conventions.
- Spending Limits Presidential candidates who accept federal funds are limited to a ceiling, set at $21.8 million each in the 1976 general election, and they can accept no private contributions. For each candidate in the presidential primaries, the spending limit in 1976 was $10.9 million, in both private contributions and federal matching funds.
- Disclosure Candidates must file periodic reports with the government disclosing the names and addresses of all donors of more than $100 and listing all expenditures of more than $100.
- Federal Election Commission The law created a new bipartisan six-member Federal Election Commission to enforce the campaign finance laws and administer the public financing machinery.

These provisions are the most comprehensive in American history. Only time will tell how they will change the conduct of election campaigns. But one inevitable consequence will be in the domain of bureaucratic regulations. The Federal Election Commission (FEC) was established as a regulatory commission to implement the law, and as such it can make rules concerning the financing of elections. In 1975–1976, for example, it was called upon to rule on the issue of whether President Ford's political travels had to be financed from his campaign funds, or whether they could be charged to his presidential expense account. In addition, all candidates for federal elective office must file reports on their finances with the FEC. There is every reason to expect that over time the FEC will develop into a bureaucratic organization, processing cases, issuing regulations, and adjudicating questions with a heavy reliance on formalization.

Conclusion The Paradox of the Parties

Regardless of variations in emphasis, the consensus among observers of American politics is that the political parties have weakened in recent years. Party organizations are less effective in elections; their control over the nominating process has weakened; there are more voters who regard themselves as independents today than ever before; and there are more successful independent candidates now than in the past. At the same time, campaign management firms and candidates' personal organizations are now an integral part of the election process. In sum, the parties have been losing influence over the recruitment, campaign, and election stages of the political process. As a result, an increasing number of important political and public issues lie beyond the influence of the parties; many public policies are defined, articulated, advocated, and acted upon outside the party system.

The under-bureaucratization of the national parties has placed them in a less competitive position vis-à-vis the more bureaucratically organized social and political institutions. The parties have not developed large, centralized, cohesive, and effective organizations. The decentralization of the party organization has persisted despite the centralization of government power and the bureaucratization of other political institutions. However, should the parties embark upon a course of bureaucratization, they would not necessarily be democratically more responsive, since the bureaucratic mode of organization militates against democracy and mass participation. Indeed, this is the dilemma of the bureaucratization of American government.

NOTES

1. Walter Dean Burnham, "American Politics in the 1970s: Beyond Party?" in Louis Maisel and Paul M. Sacks, eds., *The Future of Political Parties* (Beverly Hills, Calif.: Sage Publications, 1975), p. 239.
2. Penn Kimball, *Bobby Kennedy and the New Politics* (Englewood Cliffs, N.J.: Prentice-Hall, 1968), pp. 1–2.
3. E. E. Schattschneider, *Party Government* (New York: Farrar and Rinehart, 1962), p. 1.
4. Avery Leiserson, "The Place of Parties in the Study of Politics," *American Political Science Review*, 51 (December 1957), 949.
5. Raymond E. Wolfinger, Martin Shapiro, and Fred I. Greenstein, *Dynamics of American Politics* (Englewood Cliffs, N.J.: Prentice-Hall, 1976), p. 249.

6. Committee on Political Parties of the American Political Science Association, *Toward a More Responsible Two-Party System* (New York: Holt, Rinehart and Winston, 1950), pp. 1, 2, 22.

7. Austin Ranney, *The Doctrine of Responsible Party Government* (Urbana, Ill.: University of Illinois Press, 1956), pp. 10–16.

8. William J. Keefe, *Parties, Politics and Public Policy in America*, 2nd ed., (Hinsdale, Ill.: Dryden, 1976), p. 163.

9. Charles E. Schutz, "Bureaucratic Party Organization Through Professional Political Staffing," *Midwest Journal of Political Science*, 8 (May 1964), 134.

10. Samuel Eldersveld, *Political Parties: A Behavioral Analysis* (Chicago: Rand McNally, 1964), p. 9.

11. Frank J. Sorauf, *Party Politics in America* (Boston: Little, Brown, 1968), p. 67.

12. Quoted in Schutz, "Bureaucratic Party Organization through Political Staffing," pp. 132–135.

13. Ibid.

14. Cornelius P. Cotter and Bernard C. Hennessy, *Politics Without Power: The National Party Committee* (New York: Atherton, 1964), p. 39.

15. Ibid., p. 67.

16. Quoted in Hugh A. Bone, *American Politics and the Party System* (New York: McGraw-Hill, 1971), p. 174.

17. Sorauf, *Party Politics in America*, pp. 126–127.

18. Donald E. Stokes, "Party Loyalty and Likelihood of Deviating Elections," *Journal of Politics*, 24 (November 1962), 682.

19. See, for example, Robert D. Hess and Judith V. Torney, *The Development of Political Attitudes in Children* (New York: Doubleday, 1968).

20. Paul R. Abramson, "Generational Change and the Decline of Party Identification in America: 1952–1974," *American Political Science Review*, 70 (June 1976), 469–478.

21. Robert Agranoff, "The New Styles of Campaigning: The Decline of Parties and the Rise of Candidate-Centered Technology," in Robert Agranoff, ed., *The New Style of Election Campaigns* (Boston: Holbrook, 1972), p. 4.

22. "Campaign Management Grows into National Industry," *Congressional Quarterly*, 26 (April 1968), 707.

23. Dan Nimmo, *The Political Persuaders* (Englewood Cliffs, N.J.: Prentice-Hall, 1970), pp. 35–37.

24. Ibid., p. 36.

25. Agranoff, "The New Styles of Campaigning," in Agranoff, ed., *The New Style of Election Campaigns*, p. 17.

26. Nimmo, *The Political Persuaders*, p. 39.

27. Ibid.

28. Ibid., p. 40.

29. "Campaign Management Grows into National Industry," p. 708.

30. Ibid., p. 709.

31. Walter DeVries, "Information Systems in Political Consulting." Paper delivered at the Seminar on Information Systems, Computers, and Campaigns, American Association of Political Consultants, New York, March 1971, p. 3.

32. "Campaign Management Grows into National Industry," p. 707.

33. Robert Agranoff, *The Management of Election Campaigns* (Boston: Holbrook, 1976), p. 107.

34. Robert Agranoff, "Information Systems at the Campaign," in Agranoff, ed., *The New Style of Election Campaigns*, p. 119. It is beyond the scope of this book to discuss information technology and its use in campaigns. See, for example, James N. Perry, *The New Politics: The Expanding Technology of Political Manipulation* (New York: Clarkson N. Potter, 1968); Robert L. Chartrand, "Information Technology and the Political Campaigner," in Agranoff, ed., *The New Style of Election Campaigns*, pp. 125–162.

35. Nimmo, *The Political Persuaders*, p. 70.

36. Eldersveld, *Political Parties*, pp. 350, 451.

37. Arthur H. Miller and Warren E. Miller, "Ideology in the 1972 Election: Myth or Reality—A Rejoinder," *American Political Science Review*, 70 (September 1976), 833.

38. Nimmo, *The Political Persuaders*, p. 141.

39. Robert MacNeil, *The People Machine* (New York: Harper & Row, 1968), p. 202.

40. Bardett A. Loomis, "Campaign Organizations in Competitive 1972 House Races." Ph.D. Dissertation, University of Wisconsin, 1974.

41. Xandra Kayden, *Campaign Organization* (Lexington, Mass.: Heath, 1978), p. 3.

42. Ibid., p. 4.

43. Agranoff, *The Management of Election Campaigns*, pp. 183–191.

44. Kayden, *Campaign Organization*, pp. 7–8.

45. James D. Barber, "The Presidency: What Americans Want," *The Center Magazine*, January/February 1971, p. 6.

46. William J. Crotty, *Political Reform and the American Experiment* (New York: Thomas Y. Crowell, 1977), p. 103.

47. *Congressional Quarterly Weekly Report*, 31 (Sept. 22, 1973), pp. 2515–2517.

48. David W. Adamany and George E. Agree, *Political Money* (Baltimore: Johns Hopkins University Press, 1975), p. 25.

49. Ibid.

50. Ibid., pp. 31–32.

51. Quoted in Herbert E. Alexander, *Financing the 1968 Election* (Lexington, Mass.: Heath, 1971), pp. 263–264.

52. For detailed documentation, see Crotty, *Political Reform and the American Experiment*, chap. 5; Adamany and Agree, *Political Money*, chap. 3.

53. Quoted in Herbert Alexander, *Political Financing* (Minneapolis: Burgess, 1972), p. 21.

54. For a detailed account of this case, see Carol S. Greenwald, *Group Power: Lobbying and Public Policy* (New York: Praeger, 1977), pp. 3–9.

55. The Federal Election Campaign Act Amendments of 1974, Public Law 93–433, 93rd Congress, 2nd Sess., 1974. See also *Buckley v. Valeo*, U.S. 96 S. Ct. 612 (1976).

8

Interest Groups

The Governance of Private Bureaucracies

As political parties weaken and the entire political system undergoes bureaucratization, interest groups become particularly significant mediators between citizens and government. One of the most pervasive themes in the study of American politics has been the importance of voluntary associations. As institutionalized channels for influencing public policy, interest groups represent a concentration of private power confronting public government. Individuals can form or join interest groups in an effort to advance their interests, and because these groups are voluntary organizations, they maintain the rights of self-government and self-regulation. But as in the case of public government, interest groups have adjusted to their complex environment by becoming increasingly bureaucratic. In the process, power has shifted to their professional executives and operating administrators. In fact, this transfer of power has been so pronounced that the term "private government" has been used to describe the internal governance of interest groups.

THE PROLIFERATION OF INTEREST GROUPS

America has often been called a society of joiners. The classic observation on the pervasiveness of voluntary associations in American society was made by Alexis de Tocqueville. Written in the 1830s, Tocqueville portrayed Americans as follows:

> Americans of all ages, all conditions, and all dispositions, constantly form associations. They have not only commercial and manufacturing companies, in which all take part, but associations of a thousand other kinds,—religious, moral, serious, futile, extensive or restrictive, enormous or diminutive. The

> Americans make associations to give entertainment, to found establishments for education, to build inns, to construct churches, to diffuse books, to send missionaries to the antipodes; and in this manner they found hospitals, prisons, and schools.[1]

In the early 1970s the United States had some 12,600 national nonprofit organizations devoted to everything from sports to religion to education to business to science. Table 8–1 lists these organizations in terms of their specialties. It can be observed that 23 percent are commercial organizations, and approximately 38 percent are concerned with health, education, science, and social welfare. Research shows that 62 percent of all adult Americans report belonging to at least one organization (not necessarily a national one), and 40 percent say they are active in at least one.[2] However, the rates of associational membership are not uniform among the various segments of the population. Men are somewhat more likely to be joiners than women, educated people than uneducated ones, whites

TABLE 8–1

National Nonprofit Organizations by Specialty, 1974

CATEGORY	NUMBER
Trade and business	2,916
Culture	1,196
Health and medicine	1,089
Education	868
Scientific, technical, engineering	817
Public affairs	791
Social welfare	752
Religions	728
Community exchanges and agriculture	608
Hobbies and vocations	607
Fraternal, foreign interest, nationality, ethnic	484
Athletics and sports	447
Government, public administration, military, legal	406
Greek-letter societies	332
Labor unions, associations, and federations	239
Veteran, patriotic	218
Chambers of commerce	108
Total	12,606

SOURCE: Margaret Fisk, ed., *Encyclopedia of Associations*, 9th ed. (Detroit: Gale Research Co., 1975), vol. I. Reprinted with permission.

than blacks, and people between the ages of thirty and forty-nine than those in any other age group.[3]

The proliferation of voluntary associations in American society raises an intriguing question about the reasons for them. One influential theory holds that they are an inevitable consequence of the differentiation, specialization, and complexity found in society. As a society becomes more complex, a greater diversity of values, attitudes, and interests emerges, and more groups are formed to represent them. As David Truman has expressed it,

> With an increase in specialization and with the continual frustration of established expectations consequent upon rapid changes in the related techniques, the proliferation of associations is inescapable. So closely do these developments follow, in fact, that the rate of association formation may serve as an index of the stability of a society, and their number may be used as an index of its complexity.[4]

Individuals organize in order to avoid being disadvantaged relative to other groups and institutions. The purpose of forming an interest group is to preserve or increase the economic, social, personal, or other well-being of a group of people. Events such as wars, economic crises, and business cycles are among the most obvious catalysts for the establishment of associations.

Robert Salisbury has stressed the role of group organizers in the creation of interest groups.[5] Basing his argument on exchange theory, he maintains that individuals enter interpersonal relationships because they derive some type of benefit, or "exchange," from the relationship. Organizers, or "entrepreneurs," make potential members aware of the benefits they may obtain by joining their organizations. Salisbury has incorporated the theory of organizational incentive systems in elaborating upon the benefits that organizers and members may receive from associations.[6] Three kinds of incentives can be secured by joining groups:

- Material Incentives Those related to tangible rewards that can readily be priced in monetary terms, including salaries, fringe benefits, reductions in taxes, and improvement in property values.
- Solidarity Incentives Rewards obtained from the socializing and friendships that grow out of group interaction.
- Purposive Incentives Rewards that an individual receives from the pursuit of indivisible goods. For example, a person may derive ideological satisfaction from the group's effort to achieve goals which do

not necessarily benefit the group's members in a direct or tangible way, such as the goal of environmental preservation.

Success in organizing a group depends on the quality of entrepreneurship. If the entrepreneur is rewarded (say, with a high salary, status, or personal satisfaction) and can provide sufficient material, solidarity, and purposive incentives, then the organization develops.

INTEREST GROUPS AND PUBLIC POLICY

As mediators between citizens and government, interest groups are particularly significant because the bureaucratization of government has closed off other channels for popular influence. Interest groups bring their own concerns directly into the public policymaking process. In fact, many government policies are tailored for particular groups rather than being inclusive in scope. The justification for this practice reflects the American public philosophy, often called "interest-group liberalism." Theodore Lowi, the originator of the term, says that it

> . . . may be called liberalism because it expects to use government in a positive and expansive role, it is motivated by the highest sentiments, and it possesses strong faith that what is good for government is good for society. It is "interest-group liberalism" because it sees as both necessary and good that the policy agenda and the public interest be defined in terms of the organized interests in society.[7]

Lowi's working model of interest-group liberalism assumes that

> (1) Organized interests are homogeneous and easy to define, sometimes monolithic. Any "duly elected" spokesman for any interest is taken as speaking in close approximation for each and every member. (2) Organized interests pretty much fill up and adequately represent most of the sectors of our lives, so that one organized group can be found effectively answering and checking some other organized group as it seeks to prosecute its claims against society. And (3) the role of government is one of ensuring access particularly to the most effectively organized, and of ratifying the agreements and adjustments worked out among the competing leaders and their claims.[8]

Interest-group liberalism, as a model for public policy, is derived from a more inclusive conceptualization of power relations and the role of the government in American society—namely, pluralism. The overall structure of society is viewed as a network of organized groups reflecting the diversity of social, political, and economic interests. Each group concentrates the powers and resources of its members for the purpose of achieving their particular objectives. However, no single organization or alliance of organizations can dominate on all issues. A complex society stimulates the formation of many different specialized groups with different and counterbalancing interests, resources, and bases of political influence. If in some cases a group is dominant, its dominance is limited to its special area of concern. This multiinfluence process, it is maintained, provides checks and balances among the numerous private interest groups outside government as well as among the institutions of government themselves.

Government institutions, according to the early proponents of pluralism, were created by a voluntary "social contract" among members of society. The contract was based on mutual consensus regarding certain fundamental rights and norms of public order which government is entrusted to protect. The other major role of government is to provide a context for expressing political conflict and reaching political compromise among contending interest groups within the larger constitutional consensus. Government is a "broker"; public officials mediate among competing interest groups. Political institutions are essentially reactive, in that their changing policies are viewed as reflecting the resolution of conflict among private groups. The legislature, for example, is seen as a "referee," ratifying the victories of the winning coalition of interests, and recording the terms of group victory or compromise in the form of statutes. Public bureaucracies implement the terms ratified by the legislature, and the judiciary is an instrument for working out a coherent pattern from the various strands of legal statutes and administrative decisions.[9]

Critics have objected to the proposition that public policy is merely the political "resultant of a parallelogram of organized interest group forces."[10] They argue that it ignores the expanded roles of government in public policymaking. Government does not passively reflect and record interest groups' interactions; it initiates most public policies.

Another major criticism leveled against the earlier interest-group theory is that not all groups have an equal chance to influence public policy. After all, the power of a group in the political process varies with its resources. Some interest groups exercise preponderant power in the policymaking process, whereas others are consistently in a disadvantageous position. The revised interest-group theory emphasizes the contemporary role of government in intervening on behalf of less powerful groups. Daniel Bell, for example, has suggested that government increasingly becomes an active instrument for converting political decisions arrived at through the process of interest-group politics into economic programs. At the same time, since government declares its support for the group rights of less advantaged interests, it also intervenes in the political process itself, in order to correct political disadvantages by establishing a balance among interest groups.[11]

Thus in current interest-group theory, government is viewed as a beneficent, positive force for allocating economic and social benefits to groups, on the condition that they can organize themselves in a politically effective manner. Furthermore, policymakers not only actively encourage the creation of interest groups, but are influenced in their political behavior by the interest groups with which they identify. "Congressmen are guided in their votes, Presidents in their programs, and administrators in their discretion, by whatever organized interests they have taken for themselves as the most legitimate; and that is the measure of the legitimacy of demands."[12]

With the expanding scope of public bureaucracies, interest groups have assumed an even greater role in the policy process. Interest-group support may be particularly useful to agencies in the appropriation process when budget makers look for evidence that an agency is performing valuable tasks. Interest groups supply agencies with useful information concerning technical, economic, and political matters. Often interest groups are instrumental in having an agency established, as was the case with the Civil Aeronautics Board. Groups desiring to be regulated may provide the drive for the creation of a regulatory agency.

In fact, a successful interest group may, for all intents and purposes, itself become the bureaucratic agency—the official agency for regulating a policy area. For example, professional groups, particularly at the state level, often become the official agency for regulating their profession. State medical societies have the power to regulate the medical profession within the state. State bar associations acquired similar power with respect to bar examinations. Although formal authority remains with an administrative agency, it is staffed and directed by members of the affected groups. Some regulatory agencies are staffed with individuals who have worked for, or who hope to work for, the regulated industry. Other agencies actively encourage the creation of interest groups. By proposing policies, public bureaucrats may create an organizational demand for their own services, as was the case with the Office of Economic Opportunity and its War on Poverty in the 1960s.

The central position of interest groups in the public policy process does not imply that all interest groups have the same amount of influence over public authorities. Groups' power depends on their resources and on their significance as perceived by policymakers. As noted earlier, public policymakers are guided in their behavior by the interest groups with which they identify, and this results in greater influence for some groups at the expense of others. Before discussing the bases of group power, it is useful to examine the various types of interest groups.

TYPES OF INTEREST GROUPS

An interest group is a collection of individuals who attempt to influence government. Members of an interest group do not necessarily have identical outlooks, but they do share a consensus that forms the basis of their policy preferences. Despite the vast numbers and diverse characters of interest groups, a distinction can be made between the two major types: economic and political.

Influencing the public policy process is not necessarily a primary purpose of economic interest groups; political action may be a by-product of their other activities. They were not formed specifically for political purposes but rather to provide services for their members:

> The common characteristic which distinguishes all of the large economic groups with significant lobbying organizations is that these groups are also organized for some other purpose. Large and powerful economic lobbies are in fact the by-products of the organizations that obtain their strength and support because they perform some function in addition to lobbying for collective goods.[13]

In contrast to economic interest groups, the primary objectives of political interest groups are political. These groups are not necessarily established, motivated, and sustained by providing their members with individual benefits. However, the distinction between economic and political interest groups is analytic: all groups are at times affected by government policies or have a desire to influence the government; any group may become politically active. Yet this distinction helps to explain variations in group resources and tactics of influence.

BUSINESS ASSOCIATIONS

The largest number of active interest groups represent the business community. With the expanding role of government regulation of the economy in general, many trade associations and business firms have developed a wide range of government involvement. Despite a measure of deregulation in the late 1970s, the air transport industry, for example, substantially remains "a creature of Washington. Everything—policy about rates, policy about airmail subsidies, policy about noise, policy about airport construction, policy about safety, policy about stewardess retirement . . . policy about international flights, policy about special treatment for preferred or prestigious passengers, policy about charter flights—depends upon government."[14]

There are some three thousand nationwide trade and business associations, ranging from the Bow Tie Manufacturers Association and National Pretzel Bakers Association to the National Association of Manufacturers and American Bankers Association. Business interests have several advantages in dealing with government. First, their associations are highly specialized, and their specialized information places them in a relatively advantageous position vis-à-vis more generalistic government officials. Second, business associations have preexisting organizations that were formed for a variety of reasons, such as providing information for their members, or dealing with trade unions. Once established, however, these organizations can readily serve the business community in attempting to influence public policy. Third, business associations generally have ample resources for making themselves heard in Washington. As discussed in the next section, tactics for influencing government, such as lobbying, public relations campaigns, and political action, are increasingly costly and not equally available to all groups. The business community can more easily mobilize resources, especially money, than other interest groups.

Specialized business associations focus on specific issues: representatives of textile manufacturers are active when it comes to tariffs on foreign textiles; the oil industry is deeply concerned with policies affecting oil imports or regulation of offshore drilling. The American Petroleum Institute, an association of 350 oil and gas companies and some 7,000 individual members, has a budget of over $16 million. It was successful, for instance, in its effort to enact a bill permitting the construction of the Alaskan pipeline. In addition to such specific interests, there are some concerns shared by all business groups. These are reflected in large "peak organizations," such as the NAM (National Association of Manufacturers) and the U.S. Chamber of Commerce.

U.S. Chamber of Commerce. Established in 1912, the U.S. Chamber of Commerce is a federated organization in which membership is either direct or by affiliation. A business or an individual may join the national Chamber directly as a "business member" or may be affiliated through membership in an "organization member" group which itself belongs to the national Chamber. Approximately 40,000 individuals and companies belong directly to the national Chamber. Some 920 "organization members" and 2,780 state and local chambers of commerce also have membership in the national Chamber.

To attract potential members and to legitimize the organization, the first officers of the national Chamber emphasized that it would play no role in partisan politics, would moderate business opposition to labor unions, and would resist being dominated by the needs of particular business interests.[15] In the early 1970s the national Chamber reaffirmed its generalist outlook by declaring that it seeks to defend "the American philosophy of enterprise favoring limited government and the motivation of production by incentives within the framework of the free competitive market economy."[16] In fact, the policymaking procedure within the national Chamber is designed to preserve consensus by avoiding issues that might divide the organization. As the Chamber's by-laws state, any member may propose a policy, but the national Chamber's board will reject without further consideration one that is not "national in character, timely in importance and general in application."[17]

The national Chamber employs some 400 people in its Washington headquarters and engages in a variety of activities, including lobbying and the publication of reports, magazines, and newsletters. As Figure 8–1 shows, these activities are carried out in specialized, hierarchically organized departments and divisions. The activities of the legislative action unit, for example, include coordinating lobbying activities of the national Chamber and directing the Chamber's congressional action program, legislative information program, and divisional congressional action program.

LABOR UNIONS

Traditionally American labor has not been highly organized. Less than 30 percent of all workers currently belong to a union. Unlike the situation in many other Western democracies, labor unions are not formally affiliated with political parties. Most of their resources and efforts are put into collective bargaining with employers for better wages and working conditions. However, the unions' economic goals depend to a large extent on government policies that affect the economy, their members, and collective bargaining. Consequently they have developed into a major interest group.

The American Federation of Labor (AFL), which dates from the late nineteenth century, was organized to represent skilled workers in craft unions. The AFL's original officers objected to the idea that unions should be politically involved and take sides between the parties in election campaigns or support individual candidates. In fact, the commitment to keep government out of union affairs was so strong that until the mid 1930s, the AFL opposed legislation to establish a federal minimum wage and the social security system.

The New Deal marked a new era for the labor movement. Many workers joined unions that were industry-wide rather than organized

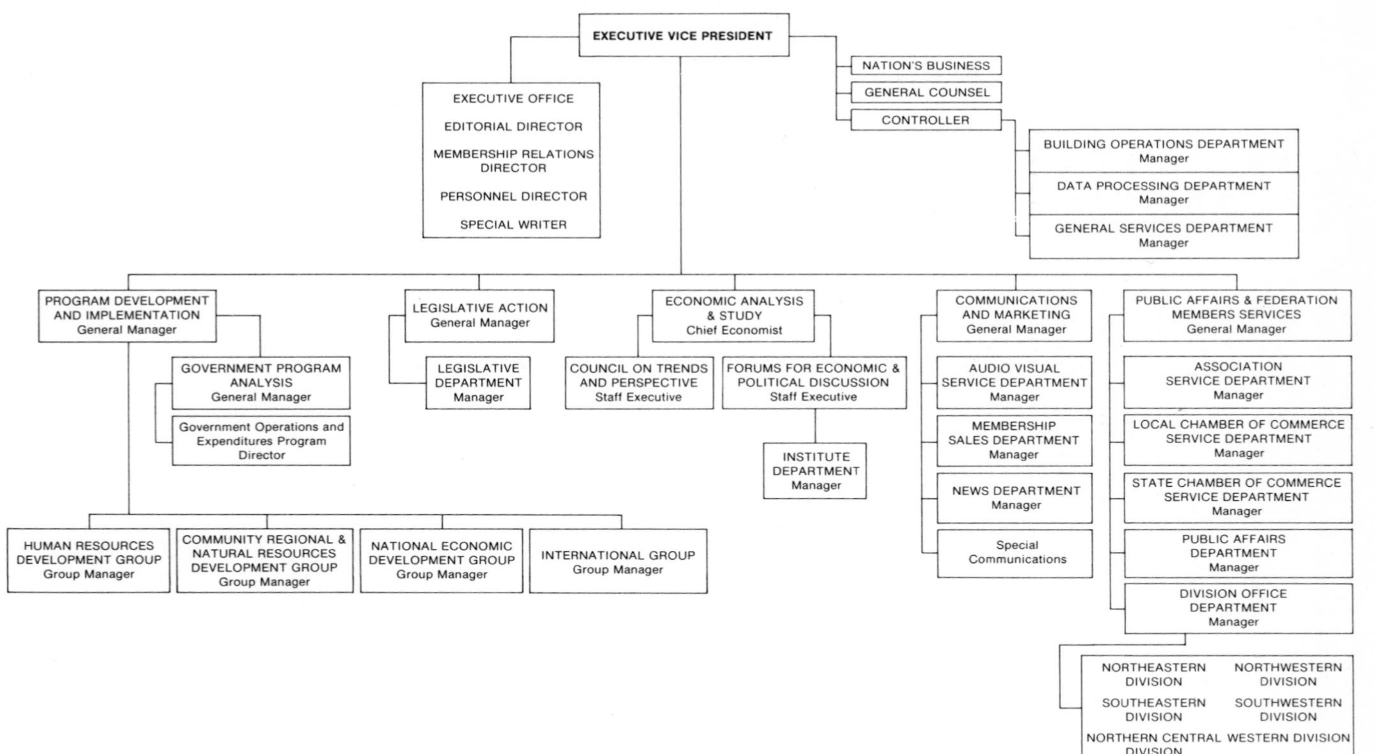

Figure 8–1 **Organizational Chart of the U.S. Chamber of Commerce**

around particular skills. All auto workers, for example, were grouped together regardless of the craft they practiced. This new principle of organization led to the establishment of the Congress of Industrial Organizations (CIO) in which, for the first time, unskilled and assembly line workers had effective unions to speak for them. In contrast to the AFL's principle of political noninvolvement, CIO leaders believed that labor should actively participate in the political process. The CIO's concept of political action became dominant when it merged with the AFL in 1955.

The AFL-CIO. The AFL-CIO is a peak confederated organization with a little over 14 million members. Each of the 109 constituent unions, called "international," maintains its own headquarters in Washington and its own lobbyists, campaign workers, and campaign funds. The AFL-CIO legislative department lobbies Congress actively not only on union-related matters, but increasingly on broad issues: tax reform, medical insurance, consumer issues, racial equality, and anything else that affects what it considers to be the well-being of workers, whether or not they belong to unions.

The AFL-CIO's principal political branch is the Committee on Political Education (COPE), which is actively involved in politics, political campaigns, and the training of campaign organizers. In 1972 organized labor contributed more money to congressional candidates than any other interest group, although in other years unions have contributed far less. In the series of special elections to fill vacancies in the House in 1974, a labor leader remarked: "The Democratic National Committee didn't give a thing—it was almost entirely labor effort. We don't need the DNC; they need us."[18]

PROFESSIONAL ASSOCIATIONS

Most major professional groups—lawyers, doctors, dentists, teachers, scientists, and so forth—have professional organizations that attempt to influence public policy. A profession can be viewed as an occupation which has assumed a relatively dominant position in the system of division of labor, so that it controls the substance of its own work. The hallmark of a profession is its autonomy; it claims to be the most authoritative evaluator of the nature of its work. As William Goode has suggested, professions exhibit two core characteristics—"a prolonged specialized training in a body of abstract knowledge, and a collectivity or service orientation." From these two core characteristics several other attributes are derived, five of which refer to autonomy:

1. The profession determines its own standards of education and training. . . .
2. Professional practice is often legally recognized by some form of licensure.

3. Licensing and admission boards are manned by members of the profession.
4. Most legislation concerned with the profession is shaped by that profession. . . .
5. The practitioner is relatively free of lay evaluation and control.[19]

The American Medical Association (AMA) has been involved in pressure politics so often and on such critical matters that it is a good example of the autonomous nature of professional interest groups.

American Medical Association. Of all the individuals and organizations concerned with health, the AMA has the greatest single influence on the nature of medical care in the United States. It is a national association composed of state and county societies. An individual cannot belong to the national AMA without holding membership in a county or local society. Indeed, a major source of the AMA's power over individual physicians is the fact that no other professional association provides the doctor with an alternative to membership in his or her local medical society. Membership, in turn, is critical to a doctor's career because it is required for many medical activities. For example, nonmembers may be ineligible for appointment to a hospital staff, or they may not be permitted to use hospital facilities for treating their patients. Generally they pay higher malpractice insurance premiums, and on occasion insurance is denied to them.

The AMA controls the quality and to a large extent the quantity of physicians available. All states require graduation from an acceptable medical school as a prerequisite for a medical license. But medical boards define "acceptable" schools as those accredited by a joint committee of the AMA and the Association of Medical Colleges. Although the states have the ultimate authority in matters of licensing, AMA representatives actually nominate the state officials.[20] Thus the medical profession is virtually granted autonomy by law, including the right to determine who can legitimately engage in the practice of medicine and what standards must be maintained.

PUBLIC INTEREST GROUPS

In the last decade or so, groups claiming to speak for "the people" or "the public" rather than for a particular interest or segment of the population have become increasingly prominent. At least seventy national public interest groups with Washington offices have been identified. Twenty-one of these groups are concerned with environmental issues, sixteen with peace-defense issues, thirteen with consumer affairs, and eleven with general political issues, including government reform. The remaining groups are involved in civil rights, religious, and miscellaneous issues.[21] Six public interest groups claim memberships of more than 200,000, four claim memberships between 100,000 and 200,000, fifteen between 25,000 and 100,000, fourteen between 1,000 and 25,000, and eight less than 1,000. Twenty-five organizations do not have mass memberships; they are supported by private charitable foundations.[22] Perhaps the best-known of all public interest groups is Common Cause.

Common Cause. A self-proclaimed citizens' lobby, Common Cause was founded in 1970 by John Gardner, former secretary of Health, Education, and Welfare. Six months after its establishment it had 100,000 members, and its membership reached more than 300,000 in early 1974. The initial membership solicitation for Common Cause was conducted through full-page advertisements in newspapers and by direct-mail appeals. The initial conception of Common Cause was reflected in its first public announcement:

> Common Cause is a national citizens' lobby. We will lobby in the public interest at all levels of government, but especially at the federal level. We will assist our members to speak and act in behalf of legislation designed to solve the nation's problems. We will press for reordering of national priorities. We will also press for the revitalization of the public process, to make our political and governmental institutions more responsive to the needs of the nation and the will of its citizens. We will uphold the public interest against all comers—special interests, self-seeking politicians, self-perpetuating bureaucrats, industry, professional groups.[23]

Common Cause focuses principally on lobbying in Congress. It concentrates on such issues as campaign financing, lobbyists' registration, reform of congressional procedures, and tax reform. The organization also tried to draw attention to certain issues during 1976 election campaigns by means of an elaborate citizens' network whose members asked candidates similar questions about government reform throughout the country. Members also compiled "issue profiles" of all presidential candidates and mailed them to the media as resource material.

GROUP RESOURCES

Group resources are the power base of an interest group. They include membership size, economic resources, and access to policymakers. The mobilization of resources and their effective utilization depend on organization. An interest-group organization "comes into existence when explicit procedures are established to coordinate the activities of a group in the interest of achieving specific objectives."[24] However, interest-group organizations have distinctive characteristics other than goal attainment. These include a division of labor, a normative order, a formal hierarchy, a power center, a communication system, and an incentive system which induces members to remain in the organization.

MEMBERSHIP SIZE

Interest groups with large memberships are likely to be more effective, especially if they can mobilize their members when attempting to influence public policy. For example, although most Americans favor some kind of gun control, the National Rifle Association (NRA) has succeeded in blocking strong gun-control legislation for years. The NRA's effectiveness is associated with its large membership: it has over one million members in 12,000 state and local gun clubs across the country. Its members are intensely concerned about the issue, and the organization keeps them informed about gun-control activities through its monthly magazine, *American Rifleman*, and through mailings of legislative bulletins. Members are given advance notice of hearings by state legislative committees on gun-control bills, and they often turn out in mass with forceful opposition.

As pointed out earlier, interest groups recruit and keep members through a system of economic, solidarity, and purposive incentives. Membership size is an important political resource when policymakers consider whether a group is representative of a specific segment of the population.

The history of organized labor provides a classic illustration of the significance of membership size. A labor union is an organization that seeks to enroll all or most of the members in an industry or a plant and to become their permanent exclusive representative. Union leaders rely on union security agreements to enroll and maintain members. These are contractual stipulations requiring that workers in a plant be union members and pay union dues if they wish to keep their jobs. Such a condition creates a union shop, and represents a form of coercion, even though a majority of workers willingly accept it. Unions have always sought such security agreements. "If they had to choose, union organizers would invariably prefer getting a union shop to getting better wages and hours."[25] The Wagner Act of 1935 made the private-sector union shop legal under federal law. Thus contracts providing for dismissal of employees who refuse to join the union can no longer be challenged in courts, except where they violate state law.

Membership in professional associations is often crucial to one's career because it is required or highly desirable for many professional activities. Professional associations also provide a variety of benefits and services for their members. The American Bar Association, for instance, offers the following advantages: lawyer placement services, retirement income plans, group life insurance programs, dependents' life insurance programs, group disability insurance programs, in-hospital insurance programs, specialized information on all sections of the law, legal publications and reports.

Generally, membership size in public interest groups varies with the public's awareness of issues. As consumer issues gained prominence in the late 1960s, the number of consumer groups as well as the size of their membership increased. Similarly, Zero Population Growth was established in 1969. With the intensifying public awareness of overpopulation problems, the group expanded to 30,000 by 1972. Then in early 1973, highly publicized government reports indicated that the birth rate had dropped to its lowest level ever. By mid 1973 membership in Zero Population Growth declined to 18,000.[26] For public interest groups to recruit and sustain membership, the public must be concerned about their issue. Membership benefits and services (for example, economic incentives) are not as important for political interest groups as they are for economic groups. The key is purposive incentives: "The intrinsic worth or dignity of the ends themselves are regarded by members as justifying effort."[27]

ECONOMIC RESOURCES

To recruit new members, to sustain membership size, to maintain viable organizations, and to advance their concerns in the policy process, interest groups need money. During its second year Common Cause spent $1.5 million (a third of its budget) in soliciting members. As mentioned earlier, the U.S. Chamber of Commerce has a permanent staff of 400 in its Washington headquarters. The National Education Association's Washington staff is about 670. Generally the number of full-time, paid staffers employed by an interest group reflects its financial resources, and economic interest groups have more resources than political interest groups.

THE LOBBYISTS

Financial resources are also needed for lobbying. This is a form of political action consisting of communications, made on behalf of interest groups, that are intended to influence public policy. Table 8–2 lists the organizations that spent most on lobbying in 1972 and 1973. However, these figures represent only a small fraction of the total spending. Although the Federal Regulation of Lobbying Act, passed in 1964, requires the registration and reporting of expenses, the law's vague language resulted in exemption of organizations whose main purpose is to engage in "grass-roots

TABLE 8–2

Top Lobbying Expenditures Reported in 1972 and 1973

ORGANIZATION	1973	1972
Common Cause	$934,835	$558,839
International Union, United Automobile, Aerospace Workers	460,992	no spending record
American Postal Workers Union (AFL-CIO)	393,399	208,767
American Federation of Labor–Congress of Industrial Organizations (AFL-CIO)	240,800	216,294
American Trucking Associations, Inc.	226,157	137,804
American Nurses Association, Inc.	218,354	109,642
United States Savings and Loan League	204,221	191,726
Gas Supply Committee	195,537	11,263
Disabled American Veterans	193,168	159,431
The Committee of Publicly Owned Companies	180,493	no spending record
American Farm Bureau Federation	170,472	180,678
National Education Association	162,755	no spending record
National Association of Letter Carriers	160,597	154,187
National Association of Home Builders of the United States	152,177	99,031
Recording Industry Association of America, Inc.	141,111	88,396
National Council of Farmer Cooperatives	140,560	184,346
National Insurance Association	139,395	82,395
The Farmers' Educational and Co-operative Union of America	138,403	113,156
Committee of Copyright Owners	135,095	no spending record
National Housing Conference, Inc.	125,726	77,906
American Petroleum Institute	121,276	38,656
American Medical Association	114,859	96,145
Citizens for Control of Federal Spending	113,659	no spending record
American Civil Liberties Union	102,595	73,131
National Association of Insurance Agents, Inc.	87,422	50,924

SOURCE: Congressional Quarterly Service, *The Washington Lobby*, 2nd ed. (Washington, D.C., 1974), p. 38.

lobbying" (that is, attempts to influence legislators through constituents). In effect, this amounts to the exemption of most organizations that lobby. The National Association of Manufacturers, for example, once spent about $2.5 million for grass-roots lobbying, which it did not have to report. Thus disclosures concerning lobbying expenditures immensely understate the amounts actually spent by interest groups.

Lobbyists transmit information and group demands to public policymakers. "The main part of a lobbyist's job in practice is to circumvent the legislation that already exists, to cut through red tape, to get priorities and preferences for clients who have no legal right to them."[28] Lobbyists are politically skilled tacticians who attempt to use their groups' resources to maximum advantage. Three general types of lobbying styles have been distinguished—contact man, lawyer-lobbyist, and administrator. The lobbyist who is a contact man sees the job in terms of whom he knows: "A lobbyist who has two or three good connections in high places in Washington can represent an unlimited number of clients, achieving more for them in five minutes than they could achieve in five months. In Washington, it is the quality, not the quantity of one's connections that counts."[29]

Lawyer-lobbyists have been characterized as the mavericks of the lobbying profession. The Washington lawyer "rarely litigates cases, he tries to appoint judges. He does not write to his congressman, he seeks to deliver a majority on the committee. . . . He is in a very real sense the interface between public and private interest. . . . His private practice steps on the brass rail of public policy every time he has an expense account lunch."[30] Most lobbyists, however are administrators, spending over half of their time at the office, acquiring information, following the development of legislation, evaluating it, describing it to their clients, and conveying the clients' reactions to policymakers.[31] For example, the seven Chamber of Commerce lobbyists spend most of their time testifying at hearings, gathering information, and following legislative developments.

Because of committee specialization in Congress and the increased importance of congressional staffs, lobbyists frequently attempt to influence congressional policymakers through staff members. As Table 8–3 shows, lobbyists dealing with noncontroversial issues are most likely to approach staffers, while other lobbyists tend to deal with members of Congress and staff about equally. Even when engaged with "campaign-defined controversial issues," about 20 percent of the lobbyists deal mostly with staff members.* As one lobbyist put it,

> I think probably on a time basis [we deal] more with the staff. But the times you are talking to the member, by then he has learned what you have given the staff. So on a time basis, you don't spend as much time with him, but you

* Noncontroversial issues do not place congressmen in the position of choosing between alternative policy group demands. In contrast, controversial issues force congressmen to choose among the demands of competing groups. Controversial issues are brought directly to congressmen either through the electoral process (e.g., by candidates for political office), or more typically, by interest groups that do not go through the electoral process. The former are *campaign-defined controversial,* the latter *group-defined controversial.* See John M. Bacheller, Bacheller, "Lobbyists and the Legislative Process: The Impact of Environmental Constraints," *American Political Science Review*, LXXI (March 1977), 252–254.

TABLE 8–3

Congressional Policymakers Contacted by Lobbyists (Percents)

TARGET OF CONTACT	NONCONTROVERSIAL	TYPE OF CONTROVERSY Group-Defined Controversial	Campaign-Defined Controversial	TOTAL
Mostly members of Congress	5.9	20.4	21.1	18.3
Members of Congress and staff equally	35.3	38.8	57.9	45.2
Mostly staff	58.8	40.8	21.1	36.5
Total	16.3	47.1	36.5	100
	(17)	(49)	(38)	(104)

SOURCE: John M. Bacheller, "Lobbyists and the Legislative Process: The Impact of Environmental Constraints," *American Political Science Review*, LXXI (March 1977), 260, table 6.

get as much done. For instance, he may have one or two questions that it has boiled down to that maybe you can supply the information about. When you start out with the staff man, it may be forty questions.[32]

GROUP ACCESS

All interest groups attempt to develop and maintain access to public decision makers. Access "becomes the facilitating intermediate objective"[33] of interest groups. Effective lobbyists have close ties with decision makers who are particularly important to their organizational concerns. In Congress lobbyists seek close relationships with committee and subcommittee chairmen, committee staffs, and a few influential members of relevant committees.

To cultivate access, interest groups use their varied resources, including campaign contributions. The American Medical Political Action Committee (AMPAC) was established to buy access to decision makers. Consequently, although most of its money goes to finance the campaigns of politicians who support its viewpoints, some goes to strategically located opponents in order to secure access if the latter win. In 1972 and 1974 AMPAC contributed a total of $1.5 million to 300 congressional candidates, and in 1976 it spent over $1 million in congressional races alone.[34]

Access is also acquired through mass communication and public relations techniques. As in the case of political parties, advertising and public relations personnel attempt to create a favorable public image of their interest groups. Some name prominent people to their boards of directors; the Red Cross, for example, makes the president of the United States its honorary chairman. Other interest groups use mass communication techniques to convince the general public that their interests coincide with the national welfare. For example, "good guy" advertising by oil companies misled the public on the extent of monopolistic practices until the drastic price rises of 1973, when many Americans believed that higher prices were linked to massive increases in oil profits.

GROUP ORGANIZATION

The interest group's mobilization and effective use of resources depend on its organization. In this sense, organization is perhaps the most valuable resource of an interest group. Interest-group organization is more than a matter of structuring and coordinating activities. It represents a way of relating power and activities to the pursuit of objectives.

Two basic organizational structures can be distinguished among the various interest groups: unitary and federated organizations. In the unitary form, members belong directly to the national organization. There may be state and local branches, but membership in the national organization gives the member admission to the locals: "A unitary organization is a single organization that may, and usually does, have subdivisions to carry on various functions or stages of functions. Membership is directly in the parent group, and derivative participation in the activities of subdivisions depends upon geographical location, occupation specialization, and so on."[35] The NAM, for example, is a unitary organization.

In contrast to the unitary form, a federated organization is one that "holds together other independent or related associations."[36] There is in effect a formal division of functions between the larger organization and its component groups. Membership in the larger group may be direct or indirect, that is, derived from membership in a constituent group. The U.S. Chamber of Commerce is a federated organization in which membership is either direct or by affiliation. As pointed out earlier, a business or an individual may belong directly to the Chamber as a "business member" or may be affiliated through membership in an "organization member" group which itself belongs to the Chamber. However, only organizational members, not "business members," are eligible to participate in the election of the board of directors, which in turn elects all the Chamber's officers.

Federated organizational structures have several important advantages. First, they can present a unified voice at the national level. Second, local activities conducted by the national organization can be used to the benefit of national and local associations. Third, the federated structure does not impinge on the autonomy of local branches. And fourth, the national organization can devote more effort to national issues and leave local issues to the local organizations. But when there are disagreements between the local and the national levels, the national organization cannot present a unified front and is weakened in its dealings with public policymakers. Furthermore, the very act of federation may establish rival centers of power which can immobilize the national organization. Local power centers may compete with the national leadership, resulting in uncoordinated efforts and wasted resources.[37] For example, although the national headquarters of the AFL-CIO federation declared a policy of neutrality in the 1972 presidential election, about a dozen of its unions supported Nixon and some forty supported McGovern.

Those who favor the unitary structure value the concentration of power in a single organization and the efficiency with which such an organization can operate. The major difficulty is that a unitary organization has to defend and promote its national policies at all levels. Furthermore, "If at the national level the group becomes completely identified with one national party (or with one national policy), not only is it handicapped when the opposition comes to power in Washington, but it may deny itself access to the other party in the states in which the latter is dominant."[38]

Whether a particular interest group is organized as a federation or as a unitary association is not necessarily a consequence of a calculated choice made by its present membership. "The form may be a single historical fact—the group began in that form and hasn't changed."[39] Moreover, regardless of the organizational form adopted, the viability of the organization depends upon the quality of its leadership. Leaders are more likely to have a stronger impact in voluntary organizations than in nonvoluntary ones.

PATTERNS OF GOVERNANCE

Most interest-group organizations are based on rational-legal administration. In general, larger, older, national organizations are more bureaucratic in structure and behavior than smaller, newly established, local associations. This reflects patterns of organizational adaptation to the environment within which interest groups operate. The more complex and the more bureaucratized the environment of an interest group (for example, government institutions and competing interest groups), the more likely that it will also become bureaucratized. Private interest groups reflect the same tendencies as public government. T. K. Quinn, who was a vice president of General Electric, observed, "Big business breeds bureaucracy and bureaucrats exactly as big government does."[40] The bureaucratization of interest groups is further accelerated by their attempts to maximize resources and to adopt the most economical incentive system possible.

Some interest groups—in particular, political interest groups—are formed "in a burst of member enthusiasm or purposive commitment, but enthusiasm tends to wane and commitments to falter."[41] In cases such as these the organization's leaders or entrepreneurs will seek ways of maintaining the organization in spite of declining enthusiasm. This effort usually involves the institutionalization and routinization of the group's activities:

> The association will start to issue a newsletter, will form committees to carry on routine tasks, and will seek regularized ways of meeting its budget. . . . To do all these things well or even at all, paid help is often required, and for this a larger budget is necessary. To raise a larger budget, more staff persons are required, and so on. What sets limits to the upward spiral of staff seeking dollars in order to hire more staff are the available resources and the degree of interest of the membership base.[42]

The role of leaders is crucial not only in maintaining the organization, but also in making it a viable apparatus in the public policymaking process. The leaders form the organization's policies and work to advance its objectives among public policymakers. Leaders can emerge in any group or organizational situation. But most important for interest groups is their leadership at the top. The critical activities of leadership fall into four general categories.[43] The first involves the definition of organizational objectives and roles. This is a dynamic process, obviously vital in a rapidly changing and uncertain environment. The second task is the "institutional embodiment of purpose," which involves integrating policies into the organizational structure and deciding upon the means and strategies to achieve objectives. The third activity is to defend the organization's integrity; leaders represent their organizations to the public, to the public policymakers, and to their own members as they try to persuade them to follow their decisions. Finally, leaders are engaged in managing internal organizational conflicts that may occur.

To cope with this wide range of activities, a form of "dual leadership" develops. On one hand, there are the elected officials, whose authority derives from the offices they occupy, and who fulfill expressive, affective functions having to do with maintaining the organization and good relations among its members, the public, and public policymakers. The responsibility for carrying out the remaining instrumental tasks rests in the hands of professional executives whose authority is based on expertise.*

* Some authors use the term "associational" or "professional" leaders. See Richard H. Hall, *Organizations: Structure and Process* (Englewood Cliffs, N.J.: Prentice-Hall, 1972), p. 262.

Professional executive directors are deferred to by group members not simply because of their official positions, but also because they are considered expert in the affairs of the organization. Indeed, the larger the organization and the more activities it performs, the more distinct is its dual leadership. Furthermore, the contributions of professional executives are perceived to be so crucial that power is concentrated in their hands. Elective officials, "formally the locus of authority in most voluntary associations, are more likely to wield that authority when their contributions are especially valuable (as when the organization is being created), when the organization is in crisis (especially financial crisis), or when a new executive must be chosen."[44] The transfer of power from the elected to the nonelected takes place in economic as well as political interest groups. Common Cause policy, for example, is created from start to finish by the professional staff, who routinely get approval from the elected board of directors. In other cases the elected officers are selected by the professional executive directors, and elections merely ratify the executives' choice. On the whole, although there are occasional exceptions, rule by professional executives is generally accepted by elected officials and the membership. The main reason for this has already been pointed out: the executive is believed to contribute most to the organization, and to the extent that this belief remains unchallenged, his or her authority is unquestioned. Another reason is that in most cases, members of voluntary interest groups do not see their membership as an opportunity for self-government but as a necessity for obtaining services and benefits in the organizational society.

Conclusion The Iron Law of Oligarchy

An organized interest group represents a concentration of private power, and a group that is effectively organized has, on the whole, a great advantage over unorganized groups. At the same time, the control of the organizational apparatus combined with passivity of the members contributes to the emergence of oligarchic patterns of governance and to the perpetuation of oligarchic rule. The general pattern of governance which characterizes interest groups was captured by Robert Michels in his "iron law of oligarchy": "It is organization which gives birth to the domination of the elected over the electors, of the mandataries over the mandators, of the delegates over the delegators. Who says organization says oligarchy."[45]

This and other observations concerning the nondemocratic nature of interest groups stand in sharp contrast to the official claims of group leaders that their organizations are democratic in procedure and substance.[46] Even interest groups ostensibly devoted to the extension of democracy are themselves undemocratically governed. The inevitable consequence of increased group bureaucracy is greater power at the top and less power among the ordinary members. Bureaucracy also gives incumbent leaders great power over the rank and file and over competing candidates for office. Their advantages include control over financial resources and internal communications, a claim to legitimacy, and a near monopoly on political skills.

The rationale for bureaucratization and concentration of power in the hands of nonelected group leaders is essentially that the group gains greater effectiveness in influencing public policy. Ironically, for many groups bureaucratization has not brought success in their influence attempts. Yet interest groups' bureaucratization and their oligarchic patterns of governance have accelerated the bureaucratization of the entire society. As Robert Presthus has pointed out, interest groups "increase the parameters of the bureaucratic situation, as they enlist every known organizational weapon to serve their ends of security, income, and influence—often for narrowly limited ends. In this sense, they have substantially increased the pace at which we are moving toward a society of increased rationality and control."[47] Furthermore, the management of interest groups creates problems not related to their original objectives. The routinized behavior of the professional executives is focused upon objectives of primarily internal significance, displacing the original objectives of the group. The maintenance of the organization's structure tends to become more significant than the advancement of its mission. Indeed, the bureaucratic myths, rites, and symbolism are remarkably successful in concealing the widening divergence between members' goals and the behavior of leaders.

NOTES

1. Alexis de Tocqueville, *Democracy in America*, trans. Henry Reeve (New York: Schocken, 1961), vol. II, p. 128.
2. Sidney Verba and Norman H. Nie, *Participation in America* (New York: Harper & Row, 1972), pp. 176–180.
3. Ibid., pp. 180–181.
4. David B. Truman, *The Governmental Process* (New York: Knopf, 1951).
5. Robert H. Salisbury, "An Exchange Theory of Interest Groups," *Midwest Journal of Political Science*, 13 (February 1969), 1–32.
6. Peter B. Clark and James Q. Wilson, "Incentive Systems: A Theory of Organizations," *Administrative Science Quarterly*, 6 (September 1961), 129–166.
7. Theodore J. Lowi, *The End of Liberalism* (New York: Norton, 1969), p. 71.
8. Ibid.
9. See Arthur F. Bentley, *The Process of Government* (Chicago: University of Chicago Press, 1908); E. Pendleton Herring, *The Politics of Democracy* (New York: Norton, 1940); Truman, *The Governmental Process*; and Earl Latham, *The Group Basis of Politics* (Ithaca, N.Y.: Cornell University Press, 1952).
10. Oliver Garceau, "Interest Group Theory in Political Research," *Annals of the American*

Academy of Political and Social Science, September 1958, 106. Cf. Joseph LaPalombara, "The Utility and Limitations of Interest Group Theory in Non-American Field Situations," *Journal of Politics*, 22 (February 1960), 29–49.

11. Daniel Bell, *The End of Ideology* (New York: Crowell-Collier, 1961), esp. pp. 47–74, 68–70.

12. Lowi, *The End of Liberalism*, p. 72.

13. Mancur Olson, Jr., *The Logic of Collective Action* (Cambridge, Mass.: Harvard University Press, 1965), p. 132.

14. Lewis A. Dexter, *How Organizations Are Represented in Washington* (Indianapolis: Bobbs-Merrill, 1969), p. 23.

15. Robert H. Wiebe, *Businessman and Reform: A Study of the Progressive Movement* (Cambridge, Mass.: Harvard University Press, 1962), pp. 37–40.

16. U.S. Chamber of Commerce, *Policy Declarations, 1970–1971*.

17. U.S. Chamber of Commerce, *By-Laws* (January 1968), art. 12, sec. 1.

18. *Congressional Quarterly Report*, June 8, 1974, pp. 1476–1478.

19. William J. Goode, "Encroachment, Charlatanism, and the Emerging Profession: Psychology, Medicine, and Sociology," *American Sociological Review*, 25 (1960), 903.

20. Eliot Freidson, *Profession of Medicine: A Study of the Sociology of Applied Knowledge* (New York: Harper & Row, 1970), pp. 23–33.

21. Jeffrey M. Berry, *Lobbying for the People* (Princeton, N.J.: Princeton University Press, 1977), pp. 12–14.

22. Ibid., p. 28.

23. John W. Gardner, *In Common Cause* (New York: Norton, 1972), p. 113.

24. Peter Blau, "Organizations," *International Encyclopedia of the Social Sciences* (New York: Macmillan–Free Press, 1968), vol. 11, pp. 297–298.

25. Quoted in James Q. Wilson, *Political Organizations* (New York: Basic Books, 1973), p. 120.

26. Berry, *Lobbying for the People*, pp. 32–33.

27. Clark and Wilson, "Incentive Systems: A Theory of Organizations," p. 146.

28. Robert Winter-Berger, *The Washington Pay-Off: A Lobbyist's Own Story of Corruption in Government* (Secaucus, N.J.: Lyle Stuart, 1972), pp. 16–17.

29. Ibid., p. 15.

30. Quoted in Carol S. Greenwald, *Group Power* (New York: Praeger, 1977), pp. 67–68.

31. See Lester Milbrath, *The Washington Lobbyists* (Chicago: Rand McNally, 1963).

32. Quoted in John Bacheller, "Lobbyists and the Legislative Process: The Impact of Environmental Constraints," *American Political Science Review*, LXXI (March 1977) 260.

33. Truman, *The Governmental Process*, p. 264.

34. Greenwald, *Group Power*, p. 156.

35. Truman, *The Governmental Process*, p. 116.

36. Delbert J. Duncan, ed., *Trade Association Management* (Chicago: National Institute for Commercial and Trade Organization Executives, 1948), p. 19.

37. See Donald R. Hall, *Cooperative Lobbying—The Power of Pressure* (Tucson: University of Arizona Press, 1969), chap. 4.

38. Truman, *The Governmental Process*, p. 296.

39. Hall, *Cooperative Lobbying—The Power of Pressure*, p. 140.

40. T. K. Quinn, *Giant Business: Threat to Democracy* (New York: Exposition, 1953), p. 106.

41. Wilson, *Political Organizations*, p. 225.

42. Ibid.

43. Phillip Selznik, *Leadership in Administration* (New York: Harper & Row, 1957).

44. Wilson, *Political Organizations*, p. 244.

45. Robert Michels, *Political Parties* (Glencoe, Ill.: Free Press, 1949), p. 401.

46. For a notable exception to the "iron law of oligarchy," see Seymour Martin Lipset, Martin Trow, and James S. Coleman, *Union Democracy: The Internal Politics of the International Typographical Union* (New York: Free Press, 1956).

47. Robert Presthus, *The Organizational Society*, rev. ed. (New York: St. Martin's, 1978), p. 69.

9

The Evolving Bureaucratic Citizen

The bureaucratization of American politics, which has been accompanied by the concentration of power in the hands of bureaucrats and staff members, is changing the relation between citizen and government. In the process it is severely challenging the fundamental principle that a democratic government is "of the people, by the people, for the people."

Clearly, the one facet of this maxim which is specific to democracy is "by the people." However, the vision of a direct participatory democracy in which *all the people* resolve public issues through rational open debate and majority vote, as exemplified by the New England town meeting, has not materialized. The quest for efficiency, effectiveness, and expediency in managing the continuing affairs of American government led to the institutionalization of and reliance upon a representative government—governance by individuals ultimately elected by the people and accountable to them. For all its desirability, however, a representative government is one stage away from a participatory democracy. A second stage of removal occurs when elected representatives delegate powers to other officials, appointed but subject to dismissal by the representatives. A third stage away from participatory democracy is seen when the locus of power shifts from elected representatives and politically appointed officials to entrenched professional bureaucrats. Indeed, the rationale for this power shift is similar to the one advanced for the institutionalization of representative government: professional bureaucrats can cope most effectively with the complexities and uncertainties inherent in our economic, social, and political environments.

In a participatory democracy the individual is envisioned as *homo politicus*. He or she is politically informed and "deliberately allocates a very sizable share of his resources to the process of gaining and maintaining control over the policies of government. Control over policies usually requires control over officials."[1] In contrast, a representative government fosters the emergence of *homo civicus*, to whom political activity is rather remote from the main focus of life. He or she is aware of the ballot as a resource for influencing public officials: "Although the prevailing public doctrine of American society places a high value on this resource, and *homo civicus* may himself give lip service to that doctrine, in fact he may doubt its value and rarely if ever employ it, or he may vote merely out of habit and sense of duty. Or he may see the ballot as a useful device for influencing politicians."[2] The bureaucratic polity enhances the rise of *homo bureaucratus,* who is apolitical and sees neither the ballot nor electoral and party politics as a means of influencing government. The emergence of the bureaucratic citizen is discussed in the next section.

BUREAUCRATIC SOCIALIZATION

Bureaucratic socialization is the process through which individuals learn values, norms, and behavior enabling them to deal effectively with bureaucracies, as either clients or members. Bureaucratic socialization starts in childhood and continues throughout life. Individuals move in and out of various social settings, learning the requirements of each situation and the conditions of interacting successfully. Bureaucratic socialization is likely to require a person to relinquish certain predispositions and behavior in order to obtain what he or she desires from bureaucracies.

Socialization into the bureaucratic order begins early in life. An exploratory study of the value orientations of families in which the father was employed in a bureaucratic position revealed that their child-rearing practices help mold the personalities of their children to suit the structural and behavioral characteristics of bureaucracy.[3] Indeed, prominent among the child's values that are congruent with bureaucracy are those concerning authority, authority figures, hierarchy, rules, and interpersonal rights and obligations. By the time young people graduate from high school, they have already been exposed to bureaucracy for several years: "The process of obtaining passes, excuses, and permission slips to be granted entrance or exit serves as a useful apprenticeship for dealing with the bureaucracies later in life."[4]

The young child (in the second to the fifth grade) perceives authority figures and institutions of government as powerful, competent, and benevolent. He or she trusts them to give protection and help. In the United States the child's initial awareness of government authority involves the president, "whom he sees in highly positive terms, indicating his basic trust in the benevolence of government."[5] Generally young Americans display faith in authority and authority figures. This is especially noteworthy because conceptions of authority and authority figures seem "to spring up in a singularly haphazard manner. . . . There is little formal adult effort to shape the political information and attitudes of grade school children. No mandatory provision for training in the subject matter once called civics exists until eighth grade."[6] The most important source of the child's conceptions of authority is the informal learning which is incidental to normal activities in the family. Children overhear adult conversations; they sense their parents' attitudes toward authority and authority figures. Moreover, "it is likely that adults—even politically cynical adults—more or less unconsciously sugarcoat the political explanations they pass on to children."[7]

The child's idealization of authority figures has also been interpreted in terms of psychoanalytic theory. Authority figures are unconsciously perceived as the analogues of parents and other individuals in hierarchical roles with whom the child often interacts. "The public figure becomes invested with powerful private feelings; response to him assures some of the qualities of response to family members and others in the face-to-face environment."[8] As the child matures, a more realistic conception of authority develops, and a shift from idealization occurs during adolescence. However, the transition from childhood idealism to adult realism does not erase all aspects of early learning. "Learning which takes place early in life should have especially great influence on lasting personality characteristics."[9] Acceptance of, or devotion to, authority are pervasive phenomena. Given the centrality of the value of authority in bureaucracy, an individual's reaction to it—specifically, his or her deference to authority and authority figures—is a basic measure of effective bureaucratic socialization.

The police officer is another authority figure of importance to the child. Middle-class children believe that the police officer is "nurturant and that his job is to help persons in trouble and to prevent crime, rather than to exercise the more punitive functions of catching and punishing criminals."[10] Similarly, young Americans have a high respect for law and law enforcement authorities. The elementary school child sees laws as just, absolute, and unchanging. He or she believes that punishment is an inevitable consequence of wrongdoing: "Norms about the justice of law and necessity for conformity are established firmly at an early age."[11] Teachers reinforce compliance norms by emphasizing their applicability within the context of school and classroom regulations. Summing up findings relating to the child's acceptance of authority and induction into compliant behavior, Hess and Torney conclude:

> The origins of orientations toward the compliance system are fourfold: first, the fund of positive feeling for government, particularly the President, which is extended to include laws made by governmental authorities; second, the core of respect for power wielded by authority figures, particularly the policeman; third, experience in subordinate, compliant roles, acquired by the child at home and school; fourth, the normative belief that all systems of rules are fair. These elements are central to a young child's induction into the compliance system.[12]

Some social scientists suggest that the principal values upon which bureaucracy relies are ingrained in American culture. Wilcox, for example, examined the extent to which children can identify hierarchy and hierarchical relationships as symbolized in organization charts.[13] He found that the fourth-grader showed a remarkable ability to interpret organization charts and to describe the relationships they represent. Older children did even better. In fact, by the time they reached high school, students were able to perform as well as college students and city managers on the test. The administrative experience of city managers, and the formal instruction in organization theory given college students, apparently did not confer any advantage in performance on the test. Consequently, Wilcox concluded: "The principles of organization do constitute a cultural trait of high school students. . . . the most important period of acculturation in relation to the trait is prior to age eleven and possibly age nine."[14] Notwithstanding problems of research design in Wilcox's study, it can be tentatively concluded that, early in life, children internalize the forms of behavior appropriate to interaction with bureaucratic organizations.

Bureaucratic socialization may force individuals to relinquish values and behavior that are incongruent with organizational life. This has been clearly demonstrated with people who were raised in subcultures where the concepts of authority, impersonality, and compliance are not dominant. A survey of contemporary Appalachian culture, for instance, suggests the pervasiveness of a "person-oriented behavior accompanied by an ideology of leveling, both parts of a system recognizing no patterned authority. For the personalism of the mountaineer's suppression of authority, the bureaucracy posits a hierarchical structure based on a nearly total acceptance of authority."[15] But when placed in a bureaucratic setting, these individuals soon learn and accept the bureaucratic way of life: "Representatives of the nonorganizational society are socialized at least with respect to this central bureaucratic value [authority] as they participate in organization activity. With respect to deference to authority, the organizational culture can, as an agent of resocialization, overcome even the influence of the local area's civic culture."[16] Elsewhere it has been found that when interacting with individuals from nonorganizational societies or subcultures, public bureaucrats act in the additional roles of teachers and leaders: "The bureaucrat takes the time and effort to teach a client something about his (the bureaucrat's) expectations concerning how the client role is to be played. In other words, the bureaucrat teaches the client how to be a client so that he (the bureaucrat) can go on being a bureaucrat."[17] The client in turn has to learn bureaucratic norms if he or she is to cope with, or benefit from, bureaucracy. Thus bureaucratic socialization processes operate at two levels—as cultural transmission and as individual learning—producing the bureaucratic self.

THE BUREAUCRATIC SELF

Americans acquire a complex of information, beliefs, and feelings which help them comprehend, evaluate, and relate to the bureaucratic world around them. They develop a *bureaucratic self*. This term refers to a person's entire complex of orientations regarding the bureaucratic world. George H. Mead wrote of the more inclusive social self:

> The self is something which has a development; it is not initially there, at birth, but arises in the process of social experience and activity, that is, develops in the given individual as a result of his relations to that process as a whole and to other individuals within that process.[18]

Although the set of bureaucratic orientations that make up the bureaucratic self is large and diverse, several dimensions can be distinguished. These involve varying amounts of information about bureaucracy and the bureaucratization of politics. They consist of positive, neutral, or negative views and a great range of expectations about what a bureaucracy will provide in services, protection, or assurances. In other words, an individual bureaucratic self is likely to include awareness of the impact of bureaucracy, feelings about the bureaucracy and evaluations of its performance, and a self-image of the person's own effectiveness in coping with bureaucracy.[19]

AWARENESS AND INFORMATION

The bureaucratization of political institutions means that much of what citizens see as "government" is actually bureaucracy. Indeed, public bureaucrats provide services, implement regulations, and are more salient to the average American than elected officials are. But to what extent do Americans perceive government as having an effect on them as individuals, and to what extent do they actually interact with public bureaucrats?

Table 9–1 reports the American public's perception of the impact of different levels of government on their lives. A large majority of Americans believe that the federal government has a greater influence on them than local government does. These findings are especially interesting when compared with a similar investigation more than a decade ago. They show that the average American believes the federal government has taken on far greater importance. In 1960 only 41 percent of the population felt that the federal government had a great impact on their daily lives, but by 1973 the figure had risen to 63 percent.

TABLE 9–1

Perceived Degree of Impact of Federal and Local Government, 1960 and 1973 (Percents)

DEGREE OF IMPACT*	LOCAL GOVERNMENT 1960	LOCAL GOVERNMENT 1973	FEDERAL GOVERNMENT 1960	FEDERAL GOVERNMENT 1973
Great deal	35	38	41	63
Only somewhat	53	33	44	21
Hardly at all	10	26	11	13
Not sure	2	3	4	3
	100%	100%	100%	100%
Total	(970)	(16,166)	(970)	(16,051)

SOURCES: The 1960 figures are reported in Gabriel Almond and Sidney Verba, *The Civic Culture* (Boston: Little, Brown, 1965), pp. 46, 47. The 1973 data are reported in U.S. Congress, Committee on Government Operations, Subcommittee on Intergovernmental Relations, *Confidence and Concern: Citizens View American Government* (Washington, D.C.: U.S. Government Printing Office, 1973), part 2, p. 61.

* The actual text of the question in the 1960 survey: "Thinking about the national (local) government, about how much effect do you think its activities have on your day-to-day life?" In the 1973 survey: "How much do you feel the following (local government, federal government) affects your life personally?"

Although most Americans are aware of the expanding role of the federal bureaucracy, there are important variations depending on their backgrounds. As reported in Table 9–2, educated persons and those with higher incomes are more aware of the federal government's importance in their lives. Whites tend to perceive the effect of the government as stronger than blacks do. There are no significant differences among Democrats, Republicans, and independents—a result which reinforces the conclusion of Chapter 7 that party identification has become a less meaningful political symbol among Americans. The degree of information and awareness in the bureaucratic self tends to vary only with the person's position in the social structure as defined by education, income, and race.

Overwhelmingly, Americans see the impact of the federal government as wielded through bureaucratic channels and programs. Thus taxation ranks high on people's lists of ways in which the government influences them. Also prominent on these lists are benefits such as social security, pensions, Medicare, and education, and policies and regulations concerning the cost of living and inflation, including wage and price controls.[20] Generally, the scope of government activities that the public sees as influential involves service, support, regulation, and control. The extent to which Americans in their day-to-day lives are in fact dependent on public bureaucracies is suggested by Table 9–3, which shows the

TABLE 9–2

Degree of the Federal Government's Impact by Education, Income, Race, and Party Identification (Percents)

BACKGROUND	DEGREE OF IMPACT				TOTAL*	
	Great Deal	Only Somewhat	Hardly At All	Not Sure		
Education						
Primary school	50	21	21	8	100%	(2,409)
High school	63	20	13	3	100%	(7,871)
College	69	21	8	1	100%	(5,685)
Income						
Under $5,000	55	20	19	6	100%	(3,119)
$5,000–9,999	60	21	15	4	100%	(4,522)
$10,000–14,999	67	22	10	1	100%	(3,981)
$15,000 and over	71	20	8	1	100%	(3,854)
Race						
White	65	21	12	3	100%	(13,775)
Black	55	18	20	7	100%	(1,573)
Party Identification						
Republican	64	23	9	4	100%	(3,494)
Democrat	64	20	13	3	100%	(7,116)
Independent	65	21	12	2	100%	(4,309)

SOURCE: U.S. Congress, *Confidence and Concern,* part 2, pp. 61–62.
*Because of rounding, not all figures add to 100 percent.

TABLE 9–3

Americans' Contacts with Service Agencies

NUMBER OF CONTACTS	PERCENT
None	42.2
One	29.0
Two	17.7
Three or more	10.8
No answer	.3
	100.0%
Total	(1,431)

SOURCE: Daniel Katz et al., *Bureaucratic Encounters* (Ann Arbor, Mich.: Institute for Social Research, 1975), table 2.1, p. 20.

number of reported encounters between the public and the various federal agencies that provide services. Almost 60 percent of the respondents to this national survey reported that they used at least one government service agency. About half did so for only one type of problem. Some 11 percent were in frequent contact with these agencies; they turned to them for three or more kinds of problems. Almost all respondents had at least one encounter with control or regulatory agencies, either to file an income tax return or to get a driver's license.[21] Furthermore, the use of bureaucratic services is found throughout the population and does not vary with social structure:

> Being poor and unemployed predicts very weakly the total utilization of government services. The poor may seek public assistance more than the affluent, and the unemployed may turn more to unemployment agencies than the employed, but the use of public offices for many services is widely distributed throughout the population. Governmental services . . . are the way of life for the whole nation.[22]

Not only is bureaucracy a way of life for Americans, but the bureaucratic citizen embraces it. Approximately 60 percent of the American population reject the proposition that "the best government is the government that governs least," and only 32 percent agree with it.[23] This fact, however, does not imply that the bureaucratic citizen is fully satisfied or uncritical of governmental operations. On the contrary; the next section will show that as bureaucratization increases, so does the gap between the public and its government.

EVALUATION OF BUREAUCRATIC GOVERNMENT

Americans interact with and approve of "big government" in the abstract, but how do they evaluate government performance specifically? To assess their general feelings about government, the following question was asked in a national survey: "As far as you personally are concerned, do you feel that federal government has improved the quality of life in the past few years, made it worse, or not changed it much either way?"[24] The responses are reported in Table 9–4, which compares them with responses given to a similar question in 1960. They show that although Americans believe government now plays a larger part in their lives, they do not think it has improved the quality of life. Most people (71 percent) believe that the federal government has either not affected the quality of life much, or changed it for the worse. This finding indicates that the evaluative component of the bureaucratic self is changing, because in 1960 more than 70 percent of the population felt that the federal government was improving conditions. It seems likely that Americans' growing

TABLE 9–4

Character of Impact of Federal Government on the Quality of Life (Percents)

DIRECTION OF IMPACT	1960	1973
Improved	76	23
Made it worse	3	37
Not changed it much*	19	34
Not sure	2	6
	100%	100%
Total	(821)	(16,162)

SOURCES: The 1960 figures are reported in Gabriel A. Almond and Sidney Verba, *The Civic Culture* (Boston: Little, Brown, 1965), p. 48. The 1970 data come from U.S. Congress, *Confidence and Concern*, part 2, p. 147.

* The response categories in the 1960 survey are not entirely identical with the language of the 1973 survey. The nearest category in 1960 to "Not changed it much" is "Sometimes improves conditions, sometimes does not."

dependency on government partly explains their current dissatisfaction with its performance. But the increased awareness of dependency did not foster the emergence of an uncritical bureaucratic citizen. In fact, the bureaucratic citizen believes that the bureaucratization of public life and the concentration of power in the hands of nonelected authorities are the major causes of government's poor performance.

Denunciation of "bureaucracy" has been commonplace in American political rhetoric. Elected officials are among the loudest and most intense critics of public bureaucracies. Some claim that bureaucrats make it difficult for legislators to be responsive to their constituencies. Others simply use the bureaucracy as a scapegoat for their own impotence. It is not surprising, then, that many citizens have come to see the bureaucracy as being responsible for the failures of government. As Table 9–5 indicates, overwhelming majorities of the citizenry (73 percent) and of elected officials (80 percent) believe that the federal government has become too bureaucratic.

The bureaucratization of government has shifted power to the hands of nonelected officials. This shift of power is more generally perceived than one might have suspected. As shown in Table 9–6, 65 percent of the public and 57 percent of its elected officials agree with the statement: "The trouble with government is that elected officials have lost control over the bureaucrats, who really run the country." Significantly, this belief is widespread among citizens from all walks of life. It is found

TABLE 9–5

Citizens' and Elected Officials'* Perception of the Bureaucratization of Federal Government (Percents)

FEDERAL GOVERNMENT HAS BECOME TOO BUREAUCRATIC	CITIZENS	ELECTED OFFICALS
Agree	73	80
Disagree	16	12
Not Sure	11	7
	100%	100%
Total	(16,068)	(269)

SOURCE: U.S. Congress, *Confidence and Concern,* part 2, p. 114, and part 3, p. 60.

* This was a sample of state and local officials drawn from 15 states.

among city, suburban, and rural residents; among the highly educated and those with no more than primary school education; among the relatively well-to-do and the poor; among whites and blacks; and among Democrats, Republicans, and independents.[25] Indeed, the decline of elected officials' control over government is a central aspect of the bureaucratization of public life, and both the bureaucratic citizen and the elected official are fully aware of it.

The belief that bureaucracy dominates politics, and that power has shifted to bureaucrats, is the central element responsible for the transformation of the self from *homo civicus* to *homo bureaucratus*. To *homo civicus*, politics is rather remote from the main focus of life. Nevertheless,

TABLE 9–6

Loss of Control by Elected Officials (Percents)

THE TROUBLE WITH GOVERNMENT IS THAT ELECTED OFFICIALS HAVE LOST CONTROL OVER THE BUREAUCRATS, WHO REALLY RUN THE COUNTRY	PUBLIC	ELECTED OFFICIALS
Agree	65	57
Disagree	17	29
Not Sure	17	14
	100%	100%
Total	(16,142)	(270)

SOURCE: U.S. Congress, *Confidence and Concern,* part 2, p. 115, and part 3, p. 61.

out of habit, loyalty, or a sense of duty, *homo civicus* maintains a limited interest and involvement in it and on occasion uses the ballot either to attempt to influence political authorities or to confer legitimacy upon them. *Homo bureaucratus,* on the other hand, being aware that bureaucrats, not elected officials, play the key role in managing the polity, considers partisan and electoral politics to be virtually inconsequential.

THE EFFICACY OF HOMO BUREAUCRATUS

The bureaucratization of public life transforms the nature of citizenship and the relationship between citizens and the political community. Bureaucratic citizens believe that the bureaucracy has a great impact on their lives; they do not think that the bureaucracy has improved the quality of life; and a vast majority believe that elected officials have lost control over the bureaucrats. Major questions for the bureaucratic society are whether citizens can influence a bureaucratic government and to what extent they attempt to exercise such influence.

Bureaucratic efficacy refers to the extent to which citizens believe themselves to be effective when dealing with bureaucracies and bureaucrats. For example, does an individual feel that he or she can influence the outcome of decisions made within a governmental bureaucracy? Bureaucratic efficacy is a subjective matter; it concerns a person's sense of probability that his or her attempts at influencing the bureaucracy will be successful. It concerns neither actual attempts nor the influence itself. Yet such a subjective feeling is indicative of the nature of citizens' influence. Where citizens feel helpless, bureaucratic dominance is likely to be more intense and unchallenged.

As Table 9–7 reports, in 1973 a majority of Americans (58 percent) felt

TABLE 9–7

Bureaucratic Efficacy, 1960 and 1973 (Percents)

BUREAUCRATIC EFFICACY	1960	1973
High	77	58
Low	23	34
Uncertain	—	8
Total	100% (960)	100% (16,079)

SOURCE: The 1960 findings—Gabriel A. Almond and Sidney Verba, *The Civic Culture* (Boston: Little, Brown, 1965), p. 142. The 1973 results—U.S. Congress, *Confidence and Concern*, part 2, p. 275.

that there was something they could do about an unjust public regulation. Back in 1960, however, 77 percent felt they could do something about it. Furthermore, bureaucratic efficacy is distributed unevenly among the population: city dwellers feel considerably less efficacious than suburban, small town, and rural residents; people with more formal education feel more efficacious than those with less; the well-to-do feel more efficacious than lower-income Americans; whites feel considerably more efficacious than blacks; Republicans feel slightly more efficacious than Democrats or independents (Table 9–8). In other words, whereas patterns of awareness do not vary with social structure, bureaucratic efficacy does. Presumably, people who are higher on the social scale feel better equipped to interact with the bureaucracy either as clients or as members of it.

The fact that a citizen feels bureaucratically efficacious does not

TABLE 9–8

Bureaucratic Efficacy by Residential Area, Education, Income, Race, and Party Identification (Percents)

BACKGROUND	BUREAUCRATIC EFFICACY			TOTAL	
	High	Low	Uncertain		
Area					
Cities	50	39	11	100%	(5,185)
Suburbs	62	31	7	100%	(4,310)
Towns	66	29	5	100%	(2,367)
Rural	59	34	7	100%	(4,217)
Education					
Primary school	35	51	14	100%	(2,410)
High school	54	37	9	100%	(7,890)
College	72	24	4	100%	(5,706)
Income					
Under $5,000	46	42	12	100%	(3,095)
$5,000–9,999	56	35	9	100%	(4,550)
$10,000–14,999	59	35	6	100%	(3,989)
$15,000 and over	69	27	4	100%	(3,876)
Race					
White	60	33	7	100%	(13,797)
Black	40	41	19	100%	(1,579)
Party Identification					
Republican	63	30	7	100%	(3,525)
Democrat	56	35	9	100%	(7,143)
Independent	59	34	7	100%	(4,286)

SOURCE: U.S. Congress, *Confidence and Concern*, part 2, pp. 275–276.

TABLE 9–9
Citizens' Initiated Contacts with Government Bureaucracies (Percents)

HAVE YOU EVER GONE TO YOUR LOCAL/STATE/FEDERAL GOVERNMENT TO GET THEM TO DO SOMETHING?	LEVEL OF GOVERNMENT Local	State	Federal
Yes	24	13	11
No	75	87	89
Not sure	1	—	—
	100%	100%	100%
Total	(16,073)	(16,098)	(16,111)

SOURCE: U.S. Congress, *Confidence and Concern*, part 2, pp. 297, 307, 317.

mean that he or she will actually attempt to change bureaucratic regulations. In fact, as shown in Table 9–9, only a tiny minority of Americans initiated interaction with the relevant federal agencies (11 percent), state agencies (13 percent), and local bureaucracies (24 percent). The vast majority of Americans have never attempted to influence bureaucratic outcomes.

Although some discrepancy between subjective bureaucratic efficacy and actual attempts to influence bureaucratic decisions is to be expected, the fact that the average American does not attempt to influence public bureaucracies reinforces bureaucratic dominance and expands the gap between citizens and government. In the words of Emmette Redford,

> The first characteristic of the great body of men subject to the administrative state is that they are dormant regarding most of the decisions being made with regard to them. Their participation cannot in any manner equal their subjection. Subjection comes from too many directions for man's span of attention, much less his active participation, to extend to all that affects him. Any effort of the subject to participate in all that affects him would engulf him in confusion dissipate his activity, and destroy the unity of his personality.[26]

In summary, the self of *homo bureaucratus* is molded by bureaucratic socialization occurring throughout life. The bureaucratic citizen acquires the basic principles of bureaucratic organization and behavior at a fairly early age, and develops more specific information, feelings, and reactions to bureaucratic politics later. Typically, *homo bureaucratus* believes that government has a great influence on his or her life, and accepts the expanded role of government. But much of what bureaucratic citizens see as government is in fact public bureaucracy, and they regard its impact on them as negative. They believe that elected officials have lost control over the bureaucrats. Although bureaucratic citizens may be bureaucratically efficacious, most of them do not actually try to influence bureaucratic policy-making. *Homo bureaucratus* sees his role as a subject of the bureaucratic government, not a participant in it.

Conclusion The Crisis of Legitimacy

What Americans believe about politics and bureaucracy is generally related to what is actually happening in the political system. The dominant position of bureaucracy, accompanied by the expansion of bureaucrats' power, obviously militates against either a participatory or a representative government. At the same time, these trends lead to the emergence of *homo bureaucratus,* who not only avoids attempting to influence bureaucratic decisions, regulations, and behavior, but also withdraws from political life. Political nonparticipation is the bureaucratic citizen's response to the bureaucratization of the polity.

Political participation, however, is central to the quality of American political life. If democracy is interpreted as "rule by the people," then questions of how much participation and who participates are crucial. Democracy deteriorates when few people participate in the political process. Although it could be argued that such an interpretation of "rule by the people" is too restrictive because it does not refer to important principles and procedures (such as regular elections, free speech, majority rule, and guarantees of minority rights), the idea of political participation does reach "the heart of the matter, since all other institutions associated with democracy can be related to the general questions of who participates or is able to participate in political life."[27] This is particularly true in the United States, where political participation is the essence of the democratic political formula. Discussing the progress of democracy in nineteenth-century America, Tocqueville pointed to an "invariable rule in the history of society": Once the first step had been taken to reduce the qualification for the vote, it would be impossible to halt the movement at any point short of universal suffrage. Indeed, much of American political history can be interpreted as a movement to reduce formal barriers to electoral participation. In the 1960s and the early 1970s, the term "participation" became an integral part of political rhetoric. Public policies, as exemplified by the model cities and community action programs, included the objective of "maximum feasible participation" for those concerned.

The significance of political participation to American democracy stems from its three major and interrelated functions. First, participation is a means of expressing support for government and thus conferring legitimacy upon political institutions and authorities. Legitimacy concerns the extent to which government structures, their personnel, and their activities are accepted as correct and proper by the citizenry. A legitimate democratic government is one that formulates and carries out its activities in accordance with the needs, values, or wishes of the citizenry. The second function of political participation is more instrumental. It is aimed at influencing the selection of government personnel and/or influencing their decisions. Through political participation, the goals of society are set "in a way that is assumed to maximize the allocation of benefits in a society to match the needs and desires of the populace. Participation . . . is a technique for setting goals, choosing priorities, and deciding what resources to commit to goal attainment."[28] Political participation is also a means of communication. Effective communication makes the government potentially more responsive to the citizenry, who in turn may confer greater legitimacy upon it.

Despite the acknowledged significance of political participation, the removal of legal restrictions to voting, the prevention of illegal denials of the franchise, and elected officials' policy commitments to increase political participation, Americans currently participate less in political affairs than they did in earlier periods. Perhaps the strongest measure of political nonparticipation is voter turnout, because voting most directly and least ambiguously serves the three functions of political participation. As V. O. Key pointed out:

> Elections are basic means by which the people of a democracy bend their government to their wishes. In both their symbolism and their reality free elections distinguish democratic regimes. They occupy a prominent place in the political faith of democratic orders. . . . Obviously one cannot maintain that public opinion is projected through elections with a crystalline clarity to animate governments to actions in accord with patterns it prescribes in precise detail. If such were the reality, governments would be hamstrung. Nevertheless, by elections the people make great decisions, which may have a heavy substantive policy content.[29]

In recent decades the proportion of voting-age citizens who actually vote in presidential elections has never been as high as 65 percent. In off-year congressional elections, the average turnout is 43 percent, and no off-year election has brought as much as half of the population to the polls. Table 9–10 shows the turnout in presidential and congressional elections since 1952. Significantly, turnout in other Western democracies is considerably higher.

TABLE 9–10

Participation in Presidential and House Elections, 1952–1976

YEAR	PERCENTAGE OF THE VOTING-AGE POPULATION Vote for President	Vote for House
1952	61.6	57.6
1954		41.7
1956	59.3	55.9
1958		43.0
1960	62.8	58.5
1962		45.4
1964	61.9	57.8
1966		45.4
1968	60.9	55.1
1970		43.5
1972	55.5	50.9
1974		36.1
1976	54.5	49.5

SOURCE: *Historical Abstracts of the United States: 1977* (Santa Barbara, Calif.: American Bibliographical Center), p. 508.

The generally low turnout in American elections has been interpreted as the outcome of both situational factors and the personal characteristics of citizens. It is contended that the higher voter turnouts in European democracies reflect the fact that these countries have automatic national permanent registration, whereas Americans who want to vote must register in advance of the election. Therefore they face an extra hurdle which discourages many from voting.[30] Another situational factor is the kind of election. For example, presidential contests attract more voters than congressional elections, as shown in Table 9–10. Nonsituational factors found to increase the likelihood of voting include interest in politics and campaigns, age, education, and party identification: (1) People who say that they are interested in a campaign are more likely to vote; (2) As age increases, so does turnout, reaching its peak in the years from forty-five to sixty-four; (3) The more formal education one has, the more likely one is to vote; and (4) Party identification has the effect of bringing people to the polls.[31]

Notwithstanding the situational and personal factors involved in variations in electoral participation, the more fundamental transformation of the polity—that is, the bureaucratization of political life and the concentration of power in the hands of nonelected authorities—has not so far been advanced as a major explanation of electoral nonparticipation and voter abstention. The traditional institutional separation between politics and bureaucracy has been tacitly carried on in studies of political behavior. Bureaucracy, according to this tradition, is a system of organization—not governance. And bureaucrats are value-free policy implementers—not wielders of political power. Accordingly, the information, feelings, and evaluations that compose the citizen's bureaucratic self have not been viewed as significant factors in influencing his or her political behavior. But as discussed throughout this book, politics and bureaucracy are thoroughly intertwined. Bureaucracy has become a system of governance, and the locus of power has shifted to the hands of bureaucrats. The bureaucratization of political life, often propounded as a solution to the problem of the greater complexity facing private and government institutions, has become the problem of political life and democratic government.

Homo bureaucratus is well aware of the bureaucratization of the polity and the elected officials' loss of control over the bureaucrats. Even the elected officials (Table 9–6) admit having lost control to bureaucrats. Not surprisingly in such a situation, electoral participation has become futile as an instrumental activity. The ballot is not perceived as an instrument that can force the elected officials to keep government under their control and make it more responsive. Principled abstention is also the bureaucratic citizens' way of withholding popular legitimacy from government institutions and authorities.[32] Caught between their growing dependency on public and private bureaucracies on the one hand, and their lack of ability to control them either directly of through their elected representatives on the other, the bureaucratic citizens' reaction is bureaucratic in character: they do not vote, thus pointing out that the basis of political authority is bureaucratic power rather than popular consent.

Notes

1. Robert A. Dahl, *Who Governs?* (New Haven, Conn.: Yale University Press, 1961), p. 225.
2. Ibid., p. 224.
3. Daniel R. Miller and Guy E. Swanson, "Child Training in Entrepreneurial and Bureaucratic Families," in Elihu Katz and Brenda Danet, eds., *Bureaucracy and the Public* (New York: Basic Books, 1973), pp. 108–121.
4. Daniel Katz et al., *Bureaucratic Encounters* (Ann Arbor, Mich.: Institute for Social Research, 1975), p. 193.
5. Robert D. Hess and Judith V. Torney, *The Development of Political Attitudes in Children* (Garden City, N.Y.: Anchor Books, 1968), p. 243. Events such as Watergate affect the per-

ceptions of a small number of children. See Marjorie Randan Hershey and David B. Hill, "Watergate and Preadults' Attitudes Toward the President," *American Journal of Political Science,* 21 (November 1975), 703–726.

6. Fred I. Greenstein, *Children and Politics* (New Haven, Conn.: Yale University Press, 1965), p. 43.

7. Ibid., p. 45.

8. Ibid., p. 46.

9. Irvin L. Child, "Socialization," in Gardner Lindzey, ed., *Handbook of Social Psychology* (Reading, Mass.: Addison-Wesley, 1954), p. 678.

10. Hess and Torney, *The Development of Political Attitudes in Children*, p. 244.

11. Ibid.

12. Ibid., p. 68.

13. Herbert G. Wilcox, "The Cultural Trait of Hierarchy in Middle Class Children," *Public Administration Review,* 28 (May/June 1968), 222–235.

14. Ibid., p. 231.

15. Quoted in Robert B. Denhardt, "Bureaucratic Socialization and Organizational Accommodation," *Administrative Science Quarterly,* 13 (December 1968), 442.

16. Ibid., p. 446.

17. Elihu Katz and S. N. Eisenstadt, "Bureaucracy and Its Clientele—A Case Study," in Amitai Etzioni, ed., *Readings in Modern Organizations* (Englewood Cliffs, N.J.: Prentice-Hall, 1969), p. 236.

18. George Herbert Mead, *Mind, Self, and Society* (Chicago: University of Chicago Press, 1934), p. 135.

19. For the development of a classification scheme for political orientations based on the various aspects of the polity toward which orientations are directed, see Gabriel Almond and Sidney Verba, *The Civic Culture* (Boston: Little, Brown, 1965). For an inclusive typology of orientations toward a public bureaucracy, see David Nachmias and David H. Rosenbloom, *Bureaucratic Culture: Citizens and Administrators in Israel* (New York: St. Martin's, 1978).

20. U.S. Congress, Committee on Government Operations, Subcommittee on Intergovernmental Relations, *Confidence and Concern: Citizens View American Government* (Washington, D.C.: U.S. Government Printing Office, 1973), part 1, p. 110.

21. Daniel Katz et al., *Bureaucratic Encounters*, p. 201.

22. Ibid., p. 38.

23. U.S. Congress, *Confidence and Concern,* part 2, p. 116.

24. Ibid., p. 147.

25. Ibid., pp. 115, 120.

26. Emmette S. Redford, *Democracy in the Administrative State* (New York: Oxford University Press, 1969), p. 66.

27. Sidney Verba and Norman H. Nie, *Participation in America* (New York: Harper & Row, 1972), p. 1.

28. Ibid., p. 4.

29. V. O. Key, Jr., *Public Opinion and American Democracy* (New York: Knopf, 1964), pp. 458–459.

30. See Philip E. Converse, "Change in the American Electorate," in Angus Campbell and Philip E. Converse, eds., *The Human Meaning of Social Change* (New York: Russell Sage Foundation, 1972), pp. 284–292.

31. For a detailed analysis of these findings, see Verba and Nie, *Participation in America.*

32. Theodore J. Lowi, "A 'Critical' Election Misfires," *The Nation,* Dec. 18, 1972.

Bibliography

BOOKS

Adamany, David W., and George E. Agree. *Political Money.* Baltimore: Johns Hopkins University Press, 1975.

Agranoff, Robert. *The Management of Election Campaigns.* Boston: Holbrook, 1976.

Albrow, Martin. *Bureaucracy.* New York: Praeger, 1970.

Barber, James D. *The Presidential Character.* Englewood Cliffs, N.J.: Prentice-Hall, 1972.

Barker, Ernest. *The Development of Public Services in Western Europe.* Hamden, Conn.: Archon Books, 1966.

Berkley, George. *The Craft of Public Administration.* Boston: Allyn and Bacon, 1975.

Bernstein, Marver. *Regulating Business by Independent Commission.* Princeton, N.J.: Princeton University Press, 1955.

Berry, Jeffrey M. *Lobbying for the People.* Princeton, N.J.: Princeton University Press, 1977.

Blau, Peter, and Marshall Meyer. *Bureaucracy in Modern Society.* New York: Random House, 1971.

Braybrooke, David, and Charles E. Lindblom. *A Strategy of Decision.* New York: Random House, 1971.

Burnham, James. *The Managerial Revolution.* Bloomington, Ind.: Indiana University Press, 1960.

Chapman, Brian. *The Profession of Government.* London: Unwin University Books, 1959.

Clausen, Aage R. *How Congressmen Decide.* New York: St. Martin's, 1973.

Corson, J., and R. Paul. *Men Near the Top.* Baltimore: Johns Hopkins University Press, 1966.

Corwin, Edward S. *The President: Office and Powers, 1787–1957.* 4th rev. ed. New York: New York University Press, 1957.

Cotter, Cornelius P., and Bernard C. Hennessy. *Politics without Power: The National Party Committee.* New York: Atherton, 1964.

Cronin, Thomas E. *The State of the Presidency.* Boston: Little, Brown, 1975.

Crotty, William J. *Political Reform and the American Experiment.* New York: Crowell, 1977.

Dahl, Robert. *Democracy in the United States.* 2nd ed. Chicago: Rand McNally, 1972.

Dahl, Robert. *Modern Political Analysis.* Englewood Cliffs, N.J.: Prentice-Hall, 1963.

Dahl, Robert. *Who Governs?* New Haven, Conn.: Yale University Press, 1961.

Davidson, Roger. *The Role of the Congressman.* New York: Pegasus, 1969.

Dexter, Lewis A. *How Organizations Are Represented in Washington.* Indianapolis: Bobbs-Merrill, 1969.

Downs, Anthony. *Inside Bureaucracy.* Boston: Little, Brown, 1967.

Dye, Thomas, and L. Harmon Zeigler. *The Irony of Democracy.* 3rd ed. North Scituate, Mass.: Duxbury Press, 1975.

Eisenstein, James. *Counsel for the United States.* Baltimore: Johns Hopkins University Press, 1978.

Eldersveld, Samuel. *Political Parties: A Behavioral Analysis.* Chicago: Rand McNally, 1964.

Fiorina, Morris P. *Congress: Keystone of the Washington Establishment.* New Haven, Conn.: Yale University Press, 1977.

Galbraith, John Kenneth. *The New Industrial State.* New York: Signet, 1968.

Gawthrop, Louis. *Bureaucratic Behavior in the Executive Branch.* New York: The Free Press, 1969.

Goldman, Sheldon, and Thomas Jahnige. *The Federal Courts as a Political System.* New York: Harper & Row, 1971.

Goodnow, Frank. *Politics and Administration.* New York: Macmillan, 1900.

Greenwald, Carol S. *Group Power: Lobbying and Public Policy.* New York: Praeger, 1977.

Hall, Donald R. *Cooperative Lobbying—The Power of Pressure.* Tucson: University of Arizona Press, 1969.

Heady, Ferrel. *Public Administration: A Comparative Perspective.* Englewood Cliffs, N.J.: Prentice-Hall, 1966.

Hess, Robert D., and Judith V. Torney. *The Development of Political Attitudes in Children.* New York: Doubleday, 1968.

Hess, Stephen. *Organizing the Presidency.* Washington, D.C.: Brookings, 1976.

Horowitz, Donald L. *The Courts and Social Policy.* Washington, D.C.: Brookings, 1977.

Hummel, Ralph P. *The Bureaucratic Experience.* New York: St. Martin's, 1977.

Jacoby, Henry. *The Bureaucratization of the World.* Berkeley: University of California Press, 1973.

Katz, Daniel, et al. *Bureaucratic Encounters.* Ann Arbor, Mich.: Institute for Social Research, 1975.

Kaufman, Herbert. *Red Tape.* Washington, D.C.: Brookings, 1977.

Kaufman, Herbert. *Are Government Organizations Immortal?* Washington, D.C.: Brookings, 1976.

Kayden, Xandra. *Campaign Organization.* Lexington, Mass.: Heath, 1978.

Keefe, William, and Morris Ogul. *The American Legislative Process.* 4th ed. Englewood Cliffs, N.J.: Prentice-Hall, 1977.

Keefe, William J. *Parties, Politics and Public Policy in America.* Hinsdale, Ill.: Dryden, 1976.

Kingdon, J. W. *Congressmen's Voting Decisions.* New York: Harper & Row, 1973.

Klein, Fannie J. *Federal and State Court Systems—A Guide.* Cambridge, Mass.: Ballinger, 1977.

Krislov, Samuel. *Representative Bureaucracy.* Englewood Cliffs, N.J.: Prentice-Hall, 1974.

Laski, Harold J. *The Limitations of the Expert.* London: Fabian Society, 1931.

Lipset, Seymour Martin, Martin Trow, and James S. Coleman. *Union Democracy: The Internal Politics of the International Typographical Union.* New York: Free Press, 1956.

Lowi, Theodore J. *The End of Liberalism.* New York: Norton, 1969.

McConnell, Grant. *Private Power and American Democracy.* New York: Knopf, 1966.

MacNeil, Robert. *The People Machine.* New York: Harper & Row, 1968.

Mankiewicz, Frank. *U.S. v. Richard M. Nixon.* New York: Ballantine, 1975.

Mann, Dean E. *The Assistant Secretaries.* Washington, D.C.: Brookings, 1965.

Mayhew, D. *Congress: The Electoral Connection.* New Haven, Conn.: Yale University Press, 1974.

Michels, Robert. *Political Parties.* Glencoe, Ill.: Free Press, 1949.

Mosher, Frederick. *Democracy and the Public Service.* New York: Oxford University Press, 1968.

Murphy, Walter F., and C. Herman Pritchett. *Courts, Judges, and Politics.* New York: Random House, 1961.

Nachmias, David. *Public Policy Evaluation.* New York: St. Martin's, 1979.

Nachmias, David, and David Rosenbloom. *Bureaucratic Culture.* New York: St. Martin's, 1978.

Nimmo, Dan. *The Political Persuaders.* Englewood Cliffs, N.J.: Prentice-Hall, 1970.

Olson, Mancur, Jr. *The Logic of Collective Action.* Cambridge, Mass.: Harvard University Press, 1965.

Orfield, Gary. *Congressional Power.* New York: Harcourt Brace Jovanovich, 1975.

Pitkin, Hannah. *The Concept of Representation.* Berkeley: University of California Press, 1967.

Presthus, Robert. *The Organizational Society.* New York: St. Martin's, 1978.

Pritchett, C. Herman. *The American Constitution.* 3rd ed. New York: McGraw-Hill, 1977.

Pynn, Ronald E., ed. *Watergate and the American Political Process.* New York: Praeger, 1975.

Ranney, Austin. *The Doctrine of Responsible Party Government.* Urbana: University of Illinois Press, 1956.

Redford, Emmette S. *Democracy in the Administrative State.* New York: Oxford University Press, 1969.

Rieselbach, Leroy. *Congressional Reform in the Seventies.* Morristown, N.J.: General Learning Press, 1977.

Rosenbloom, D. *Federal Equal Employment Opportunity.* New York: Praeger, 1977.

Rosenbloom, D. *Federal Service and the Constitution.* Ithaca, N.Y.: Cornell University Press, 1971.

Ross, Robert S. *American National Government.* Chicago: Markham, 1972.

Rourke, Francis E. *Bureaucracy, Politics, and Public Policy.* 2nd ed. Boston: Little, Brown, 1969.

Schattschneider, E. E. *Party Government.* New York: Farrar and Rinehart, 1962.

Schlesinger, Arthur, Jr. *The Imperial Presidency.* Boston: Houghton Mifflin, 1973.

Schubert, Glendon. *Judicial Policy Making.* Chicago: Scott, Foresman, 1965.

Seidman, Harold. *Politics, Position, and Power.* 2nd ed. New York: Oxford University Press, 1975.

Sharkansky, Ira. *Public Administration.* Chicago: Rand McNally, 1975.

Sherrill, Robert. *Why They Call It Politics.* 2nd ed. New York: Harcourt Brace Jovanovich, 1974.

Solberg, Winton U., ed. *The Federal Convention and the Formation of the Union of the American States.* Indianapolis: Bobbs-Merrill, 1958.

Sorauf, Frank J. *Party Politics in America.* Boston: Little, Brown, 1968.

Sorenson, Theodore. *Decision-Making in the White House.* New York: Columbia University Press, 1963.
Stanley, David T., Dean E. Mann, and Jameson W. Doig. *Men Who Govern.* Washington, D.C.: Brookings, 1967.
Tausky, Curt. *Work Organizations.* Itasca, Ill.: Peacock, 1978.
Thompson, Victor. *Modern Organizations.* New York: Knopf, 1961.
Tocqueville, Alexis de. *Democracy in America.* Translated by Henry Reeve. New York: Schocken, 1961.
Truman, David B. *The Governmental Process.* New York: Knopf, 1951.
Van Riper, Paul P. *History of the United States Civil Service.* Evanston, Ill.: Row, Peterson, 1958.
Veblen, Thorstein. *The Engineers and the Price System.* New York: Viking, 1921.
Verba, Sidney, and Norman H. Nie. *Participation in America.* New York: Harper & Row, 1972.
Volger, David J. *The Third House.* Evanston, Ill.: Northwestern University Press, 1971.
Wade, L., and R. Curry, eds. *A Logic of Public Policy.* Belmont, Calif.: Wadsworth, 1970.
Wayne, Stephen J. *The Legislative Presidency.* New York: Harper & Row, 1978.
Weber, Max. *From Max Weber: Essays in Sociology*. Translated and edited by H. H. Gerth and C .W. Mills. New York: Oxford University Press, 1958.
Wilensky, Harold L. *Organizational Intelligence.* New York: Basic Books, 1967.
Wilson, James Q. *Political Organizations.* New York: Basic Books, 1967.

ARTICLES

Allison, Graham T. "Conceptual Models and the Cuban Missile Crisis." *American Political Science Review,* 63 (September 1969), 689–718.
Argyris, Chris. "The Individual and Organization: Some Problems of Mutual Adjustment." *Administrative Science Quarterly*, 2 (June 1957), 1–24.
Barber, James D. "The Presidency: What Americans Want." *The Center Magazine,* January/February 1971, p. 6.
Bartlett, J., and D. Jones. "Managing a Cabinet Agency." *Public Administration Review,* 34 (January/February 1974), 62–70.
Bazelon, D. "The Impact of the Courts on Public Administration." *Indiana Law Review,* 52 (1976), 101–110.
Black, Charles. "The National Court of Appeals: An Unwise Proposal." *Yale Law Journal,* 83 (1974), 883.
Bonafede, Dom. "White House Staffing: The Nixon-Ford Era." In *The Presidency Reappraised,* edited by Thomas E. Cronin and Rexford G. Tugwell. New York: Praeger, 1977.
Burnham, Walter Dean. "American Politics in the 1970s: Beyond Party?" In *The Future of Political Parties,* edited by Louis Maisel and Paul M. Sacks. Beverly Hills, Calif.: Sage Publications, 1975.
Carey, William D. "Presidential Staffing in the Sixties and Seventies." *Public Administration Review,* 29 (September/October 1969), 450–458.
Chayes, A. "The Role of the Judge in Public Law Litigation." *Harvard Law Review,* 89 (1976): 1281.

Denhardt, Robert B. "Bureaucratic Socialization and Organizational Accommodation." *Administrative Science Quarterly,* 13 (December 1968), 442.

Drew, Elizabeth. "HEW Grapples with PPBS." *The Public Interest,* 8 (Summer 1967), 9–27.

Katz, Elihu, and S. N. Eisenstadt. "Bureaucracy and Its Clientele—A Case Study." In *Readings in Modern Organizations,* edited by Amitai Etzioni. Englewood Cliffs, N.J.: Prentice-Hall, 1969.

Emerson, Richard M. "Power Dependence Relations." *American Sociolgical Review,* 27 (February 1962), 32.

Erickson, R. "The Electoral Impact on Congressional Roll Call Voting." *American Political Science Review,* 65 (December 1971), 1018–1032.

Fox, Harrison, and Susan Hammond. "The Growth of Congressional Staff." In *Congress against the President,* edited by Harvey Mansfield. New York: Academy of Political Science, 1975.

French, John R. P., and Bertram Raven. "The Bases of Social Power." In *Group Dynamics,* edited by Dorwin Cartwright and Alvin Zander. New York: Harper & Row, 1968, pp. 259–269.

Gallas, Edward. "The Court as a Social Force." *Public Administration Review,* 31 (March/April 1971), 143–149.

Greenstein, Fred I. "The Benevolent Leader Revisited." *American Political Science Review,* 69 (December 1975), 1371–1398.

Hershey, M. Randan, and David B. Hill. "Watergate and Preadults' Attitudes toward the President." *American Journal of Political Science,* 21 (November 1975), 703–726.

Leiserson, Avery. "The Place of Parties in the Study of Politics." *American Political Science Review,* 51 (December 1957), 949.

Lindblom, Charles. "The Science of Muddling Through." *Public Administration Review,* 19 (Spring 1959), 79–88.

Long, Norton. "Power and Administration." *Public Administration Review,* 9 (Autumn 1949), 257–264.

McGregor, Eugene B., Jr. "Politics and the Career Mobility of Bureaucrats." *American Political Science Review,* 68 (March 1974), 18–26.

Malbin, Michael. "Congressional Committee Staffs: Who's in Charge Here?" *The Public Interest,* 47 (Spring 1977), 16–40.

Maslow, Abraham J. "A Theory of Human Motivation." *Psychological Review,* 50 (July 1943), 370–396.

Meier, K., and L. Nigro. "Representative Bureaucracy and Political Preferences." *Public Administration Review,* 36 (July/Agust 1976), 458–469.

Miller, Arthur H., and Warren E. Miller. "Ideology in the 1972 Election: Myth or Reality—A Rejoinder." *American Political Science Review,* 70 (September 1976), 833.

Miller, Warren, and Donald Stokes. "Constituency Influence in Congress." *American Political Science Review,* 57 (March 1963), 45–56.

Moynihan, Daniel P. "Imperial Government." *Commentary,* 65 (June 1978), 25–32.

Nachmias, David, and David Rosenbloom. "Bureaucracy and Ethnicity." *American Journal of Sociology,* 83 (January 1978), 967–974.

Nelson, Garrison. "Assessing the Congressional Committee System." *Annals of the American Academy of Political and Social Science,* 411 (January 1974), 120–132.

Ornstein, Norman, Robert Peabody, and David W. Rohde. "The Changing Senate: From the 1950s to the 1970s." In *Congress Reconsidered,* edited by Lawrence C. Dodd and Bruce I. Oppenheimer. New York: Praeger, 1977.

Pyhrr, P. "The Zero-base Approach to Government Budgeting." *Public Administration Review,* 37 (January 1977), 1–8.

Reissman, Leonard. "A Study of Role Conceptions in Bureaucracy." *Social Forces,* 27 (March 1949), 305–310.

Rosenbloom, David, and J. Featherstonhaugh. "Passive and Active Representation in the Federal Service." *Social Science Quarterly,* 57 (March 1977), 873–882.

Rosenbloom, David "Accountability in the Administrative State." In *Accountability in Urban Society,* edited by S. Greer et al. Beverly Hills, Calif.: Sage Publications, 1979. *Urban Affairs Annual,* vol. 15.

Salisbury, Robert H. "An Exchange Theory of Interest Groups." *Midwest Journal of Political Science,* 13 (February 1969), 1–32.

Schutz, Charles E. "Bureaucratic Party Organization through Professional Political Staffing." *Midwest Journal of Political Science,* 8 (May 1964), 134.

Scully, Michael. "Reflections of a Senate Aide." *The Public Interest,* 47 (Spring 1977), 41–48.

Shick, Alan. "A Death in the Bureaucracy." *Public Administration Review,* 33 (March/April 1973), 146–156.

Stokes, Donald E. "Party Loyalty and Likelihood of Deviating Elections." *Journal of Politics,* 24 (November 1962), 682.

Weber, Max. "The Three Types of Legitimate Rule." In *A Sociological Reader on Complex Organizations,* edited by Amitai Etzioni. New York: Holt, Rinehart and Winston, 1969.

Weissberg, Robert. "Collective versus Dyadic Representation in Congress." *American Political Science Review,* 72 (June 1978), 535–574.

Wilcox, Herbert G. "The Cultural Trait of Hierarchy in Middle Class Children." *Public Administration Review,* 28 (May/June 1968), 222–235.

Wynia, Bob. "Federal Bureaucrats' Attitudes toward a Democratic Ideology." *Public Administration Review,* 34 (March/April 1974), 156–162.

Index